2009 JINAN DAXUE HUAQIAO DAXUE LIANGXIAO LIANZHAO
QUANGUO LIANZHAO KAOSHITI JIEJI

2009

暨南大学华侨大学两校联招 全国联招

考试题解集

主编 何修文 张训涛

暨南大学出版社
JINAN UNIVERSITY PRESS
中国·广州

图书在版编目（CIP）数据

2009暨南大学华侨大学两校联招、全国联招考试题解集/何修文，张训涛主编．—广州：暨南大学出版社，2010.3（2010.10重印）
ISBN 978-7-81135-303-7

Ⅰ.①2009… Ⅱ.①何… ②张… Ⅲ.①课程—高中—解题—升学参考资料
Ⅳ.①G632.479

中国版本图书馆CIP数据核字（2010）第031667号

出版发行：暨南大学出版社

地　址：中国广州暨南大学
电　话：总编室（8620）85221601
营销部（8620）85225284　85228291　85228292（邮购）
传　真：（8620）85221583（办公室）　85223774（营销部）
邮　编：510630
网　址：http://www.jnupress.com　http://press.jnu.edu.cn

排　版：暨南大学出版社照排中心
印　刷：广州市怡升印刷有限公司

开　本：787mm×1092mm　1/16
印　张：12.625
字　数：287千
版　次：2010年3月第1版
印　次：2010年10月第2次
印　数：3001—5000册

定　价：32.00元

（暨大版图书如有印装质量问题，请与出版社总编室联系调换）

目录
CONTENTS

■2009 年中华人民共和国普通高等学校联合招收华侨、港澳地区、台湾省学生入学考试题目答案

■2009 年两校联招、全国联招试题比较分析

2009 年暨南大学、华侨大学招收港、澳、台、华侨、华人及其他外籍学生入学考试题目

语　文

答卷时间：150 分钟

一、基础知识（共 30 分）

（一）单项选择题（在下列备选答案中选择一个正确答案，并将这个答案的代码写在答题卷上相应的表格框内。每题 2 分，共 14 分）

1. 下面各组词语的字形完全正确的一组是（　）

A. 沟通　渡假　梳装　辍学　抉择

B. 喝彩　倘若　攻讦　参与　好象

C. 宣泄　竣工　家俱　轶事　部署

D. 委屈　曼延　禅让　彪悍　讴歌

2. 下面句子中加框成语使用完全正确的一项是（　）

A. 参加保险，虽不能使人化险为夷，但却能在灾祸不期而至时，使投保者得到一笔赔偿，尽量减轻损失。

B. 海拉尔的夜景更迷人，街道宽阔整齐，灯火阑珊，颇具草原明珠的气息。

C. 由于班上同学良莠不齐，王老师上课时非常讲究方法，照顾到了每位同学，同学们都很喜欢上他的课。

D. 暴雨很快就到了，为了抢救邮件，职工们倾巢而出，将堆放在门口马路边的邮件袋拽回不足 20 平方米的营业厅。

3. 下列句子表达完全正确的一项是（　）

A. 不知是曾几何时，报刊上出现了越来越多的缅怀往事的文章，慨叹现代生活中人与人之间关系的冷漠。

B. 一种为家庭提供烹饪劳务的计时服务近日来在华南地区格外走俏，为失业工人再就业提供了一条门路。

C. 如果美术工作者看不到儿童自身发展的主动性，过早地让他们接受专业绘画知识，那么就会变成束缚儿童发展的枷锁。

D. 来自广州地区的 10 多所高校的教师、学生及科技工作者参加了这次技术交流会。

4. 依次填入下列横线处的词语，恰当的一组是（　）

①阿 Q 这个艺术形象，______了鲁迅对国民灵魂弱点的认识深度。

②次贷危机发生后，为防止经济衰退，美国中央银行______利率，并向主要银行注资，以确保金融系统的安全稳定。

③近年来，世界上一些国家和地区诸如英国、香港的绿色组织______人们参与“绿色圣诞行动”，不寄或少寄贺卡，而代之以其他的问候方式。

A. 体现　削减　呼吁　　B. 表现　减少　呼吁

C. 表现　削减　倡议　　D. 体现　减少　倡议

5. 对巴斯卡所说“人是一根能思想的苇草”的比较全面的理解是（　）

A. 人的生命就像苇草一样脆弱，一口气、一滴水就足以致他死命了。

B. 人和苇草不一样的地方是其有思想，但有思想的苇草也终逃不过苇草的命运。

C. 虽然人有思想，但在万物、在永恒的宇宙面前，人也不过是一根苇草罢了。

D. 人和苇草一样脆弱，但人能认识到这一点，苇草却不能。这正是人和苇草本质上的不同。

6. 把后面的句子分别填入下面［1］、［2］句中画横线处，最恰当的一组是（　）

［1］西陵峡比较宽阔，但是江流至此变得特别凶恶，处处是急流，处处是险滩。______。

［2］远眺群山环抱，______近看小河流水，茶园葱绿，松竹并茂。

①船一下像流星随着怒涛冲去，一下又绕着险滩迂回浮进。

②船一下绕着险滩迂回浮进，一下又像流星随着怒涛冲去。

③白云缭绕，层林叠翠。

④层林叠翠，白云缭绕。

A. ①③　　B. ②③　　C. ①④　　D. ②④

7. “大明湖畔，趵突泉边，故居在垂杨深处；漱玉集中，金石录里，文采有后主遗风”，这副对联说的是哪位古代文人（　）

A. 韩愈　　B. 苏轼　　C. 李清照　　D. 辛弃疾

（二）多项选择题（在下列备选答案中选出两个或两个以上的正确答案，并将这些答案的代码写在答题卷上相应的表格框内；多选少选均不给分。每题 2 分，共 6 分）

8. “白发三千丈，缘愁似个长。不知明镜里，何处得秋霜。”一诗所用的修辞手法有（　）

A. 比喻　　B. 比拟　　C. 借代　　D. 夸张　　E. 双关

9. 下列各句中加框虚词使用正确的有（　）

A. 大材小用固然不好，但总比大材不用要好吧。

B. 尽管他卖了房子，还是无法筹措到足够资金，公司只能宣告破产。

C. 他热爱篮球事业，即使是奔四十的人了，仍驰骋在CBA的赛场上。

D. 他通过参加社会实践活动，关于社会有了更深入的了解，他的人生目标也就更明确了。

E. 他的普通话里夹杂着浓重的南方口音，况且因为激动，越说越快，我连一半也没有听懂。

10. 下列作品属于律诗的有（　）

A. 王昌龄《出塞》　B. 王维《山居秋暝》　C. 李白《将进酒》

D. 杜甫《登高》　E. 李商隐《锦瑟》

（三）填空题（请在答题卷上相应的横线上填空，每空1分，共5分）

11. 身既死兮神以灵，__________。（屈原《国殇》）

12. 寻寻觅觅，冷冷清清，__________。（李清照《声声慢》）

13. __________，非宁静无以致远。（诸葛亮《诫子书》）

14. 李煜在《虞美人》（春花秋月何时了）中说"故国不堪回首月明中"，这里的"故国"是指__________。

15. "上、下、刃、末、本"等字的造字方法属于汉字造字法中的__________。

（四）判断题（判断下列各题所表述的意思是否正确。如果正确，请在答题卷上相应的表格框内打"√"，否则打"×"。每题1分，共5分）

16. 《陈情表》、《出师表》中的"表"都是古代臣子向皇帝上书言事的一种文体。

17. 王维、王昌龄、孟浩然都是唐代著名的山水田园诗人，以描写山水田园、闲适生活见长。苏轼称王维的诗画是"诗中有画，画中有诗"。

18. 《三国演义》、《水浒传》和《红楼梦》都是由文人独立创作的长篇章回体小说。

19. 法国著名思想家蒙田在《热爱生命》中说"生之本质在于死"，表达了人应有一种超越死亡的达观精神，既乐生又不惧死。整篇文章告诉人们要珍惜生活，并采用适当的方法享受生活。

20. 甲骨文是指殷商时代刻写在龟甲或兽骨上的文字，金文是指古代铸或刻在青铜器上的文字，隶书则是秦代和汉代的官吏专门用于书写公文的文字。

二、阅读理解（共50分）

（一）文言文阅读（每题3分，共30分）

晏子方食，景公使使者至，分食食之。使者不饱，晏子亦不饱。使者反，言之公。公曰："嘻！晏子之家，若是其贫也。寡人不知，是寡人之过也。"使人致千金与市租，请以奉宾客。晏子辞，三致之，终再拜而辞曰："婴之家不贫。以君之赐，泽覆三族，延及交游，以振百姓，君之赐也厚矣！婴之家不贫也。婴闻之，夫厚取之君，而施之民，是臣代君君民也，忠臣不为也；厚取之君，而不施于民，是为筐箧之藏也，仁人不为也；进取于君，退得罪于士，身死而财迁于它人，是为宰藏也，智者不为也。夫十总之布，一豆之食[1]，足于中免也。”景公谓晏子曰：“昔吾先君桓公，以书社[2]五百封管仲，不辞而受。子辞之，何也？”晏子曰：“婴闻之，圣人千虑，必有一失；愚人千虑，必有一得。意者管仲之失，而婴之得者耶？故再拜而不敢受命。”

［1］豆：量词。四升为一豆。十总之布：粗布。古代丝或布八十缕为总。

［2］书社：写有社里居民姓名的社。古代每二十五户为里，每里居民及其土地为一社。五百社，居民达一万二千五百户。

21. 翻译下列句子：

以君之赐，泽覆三族，延及交游，以振百姓，君之赐也厚矣！

22. 翻译下列句子：

意者管仲之失，而婴之得者耶？故再拜而不敢受命。

23. 下列对本文中加方框的字的注释，错误的是（　）

A. 使者反，言之公。　　　反：后来写作“返”，返回。

B. 寡人不知，是寡人之过也。　　知：后来写作“智”，明智。

C. 延及交游，以振百姓。　　振：通“赈”，赈济，救济。

D. 一豆之食，足于中免也。　　免：通“晚”。中免，指中晚年。

24. 下列句子中加方框的代词“之”字，用以指人，可译作“他”的是（　）

A. 景公使使者至，分食食之。

B. 使者反，言之公。

C. 夫厚取之君，而施之民。

D. 子辞之，何也？

25. 下列对本文文意的理解及分析，错误的是（　）

A. 从本文看，景公应该是鲁国国君。

B. 晏婴认为把国君赏赐的财物分给老百姓是不好的行为。

C. 晏婴对管仲的做法不以为然。

D. 从本文看，晏婴是个清廉的官员。

《五代史·冯道传》曰：“礼义廉耻，国之四维，四维不张，国乃灭亡。”善乎，管生之能言也！礼义，治人之大法；廉耻，立人之大节；盖不廉则无所不取，不耻则无所不为。人而如此，则祸败乱亡，亦无所不至；况为大臣而无所不取，无所不为，则天下其有不乱，国家其有不亡者乎？然而四者之中，耻尤为要。故夫子之论士，曰：“行己有耻。”孟子曰：“人不可以无耻。无耻之耻，无耻矣。”又曰：“耻之于人大矣，为机变之巧者，无所用耻焉。”所以然者，人之不廉，而至于悖礼犯义，其原皆生于无耻也。故士大夫之无耻，是谓国耻。

吾观三代以下，世衰道微，弃礼义，捐廉耻，非一朝一夕之故。然而松柏后凋于岁寒，鸡鸣不已于风雨，彼昏之日，固未尝无独醒之人也！顷读《颜氏家训》有云："齐朝一士夫尝谓吾曰：'我有一儿，年已十七，颇晓书疏，教其鲜卑语，及弹琵琶，稍欲通解，以此伏事公卿，无不宠爱。'吾时俯而不答。异哉，此人之教子也！若由此业自致卿相，亦不愿汝曹为之。"嗟乎！之推不得已而仕于乱世，犹为此言，尚有《小宛》诗人之意，彼阉然媚于世者，能无愧哉！

罗仲素[1]曰："教化者朝廷之先务，廉耻者士人之美节；风俗者天下之大事。"朝廷有教化，则士人有廉耻；士人有廉耻，则天下有风俗。

古人治军之道，未有不本于廉耻者。《吴子》曰："凡治国治军，必教之以礼，励之以义，使有耻也。夫人有耻，在大足以战，在小足以守矣。"《尉缭子》言："国必有慈孝廉耻之俗，则可以死易生。"而太公对武王："将有三胜，一曰礼将，二曰力将，三曰止欲将。故礼者，所以班朝治军而兔罝之武夫，皆本于文王后妃之化；岂有淫刍荛，窃牛马，而为暴于百姓者哉！"《后汉书》：张奂为安定属国都尉，"羌豪帅感奂恩德，上马二十匹，先零酋长又遗金鐻八枚，奂并受之，而召主簿于诸羌前，以酒酹地曰：'使马如羊，不以入厩；使金如粟，不以入怀。'悉以金马还之。羌性贪而贵吏清，前有八都尉率好财货，为所患苦，及奂正身洁己，威化大行"。呜呼！自古以来，边事之败，有不始于贪求者哉？吾于辽东之事有感。

杜子美诗"安得廉颇将，三军同晏眠"，一本作"廉耻将"。诗人之意，未必及此，然吾观《唐书》，言王佖为武灵节度使，先是，土蕃欲成乌兰桥，每于河壖先贮材木，皆为节帅遣人潜载之，委于河流，终莫能成。蕃人知佖贪而无谋，先厚遗之，然后并役成桥，仍筑月城守之。自是朔方御寇不暇，至今为患，由佖之黩货也。故贪夫为帅而边城晚开。得此意者，郢书燕说，或可以治国乎！

[1] 罗仲素：古代学者，程朱理学的奠基者。

26. 对下列语句中加方框的词语的解释，正确的是（ ）

A. 第二段：弃礼义，捐廉耻。　　捐：捐献。

B. 第二段：鸡鸣不已于风雨。　　已：止，停止。

C. 第五段：委于河流，终莫能成。　　委：保管。

D. 第五段：至今为患，由佖之黩货也。　　货：货物。

27. 下列各组句子中，加方框的虚词意义与用法完全相同的一组是（ ）

A. 其：①国家其有不亡者乎（见第一段）

②教其鲜卑语，及弹琵琶（见第二段）

B. 于：①然而松柏后凋于岁寒（见第二段）

②之推不得已而仕于乱世（见第二段）

C. 以：①凡治国治军，必教之以礼（见第四段）

②悉以金马还之（见第四段）

D. 而：①蕃人知佖贪而无谋（见第五段）

②故贪夫为帅而边城晚开（见第五段）

28. 文中所举的各个例子中，作者将其作为正面典型的人物是（　）

A. 齐朝士大夫　　B. 先零酋长　　C. 张奂　　D. 王佖

29. 下列对文章内容的概括，错误的一项是（　）

A. 从第一段看，作者认为耻之所以比廉还重要，是因为不廉是无耻导致的。

B. 从第二段看，作者视颜之推为独醒之人，颇为推崇。

C. 从第五段看，作者确认杜子美的诗句中“廉颇将”三个字出现了错误，应该是“廉耻将”。

D. 全文分别从士人、军人两个角度谈知耻对于治国的重要性。

30. 根据内容推断，本文应写作于下列哪一个朝代（　）

A. 汉朝　　B. 魏晋　　C. 唐朝　　D. 清朝

（二）现代文阅读（每小题2分，共20分）

所谓“艺术魅力”的提法，并不是一个精确的科学术语，而是一个模糊性概念。模糊性概念是美国应用数学家查德在一九六五年首先提出的。这个概念的产生是由于所描述的系统大而复杂，变量及参数众多所造成的。它是个多变量综合的结果，不是单一变量的特性；是系统整体的表现，不是局部和个体的特点。总之，模糊性是事物现象不确定性在整体上的总和，它是一种复杂的、不确定的概念，相对于精确的科学概念。科学概念的特征是二值逻辑思维，即是非分明或真假分明。而模糊概念的特征则是多值逻辑思维，它反映事物的系统性、多因性和动态性。事物的存在往往都带有模糊性的特点。我们通常讲科学是精密的、确定的，这只是对研究对象的不确定性的某种程度的简化或抽象的处理，而实际过程则往往是复杂的、不确定的，因而是模糊的。因此，人们在描述事物的复杂运动过程时，就要借助于模糊概念。现代思维科学中有所谓模糊思维，现代数学中有所谓模糊数学，都是为了处理这种模糊现象的。在日常生活中，人们也经常不自觉地运用模糊思维，别林斯基说过一段话就是一例：“当人恋上一个人的时候，不是把他当作观念，而是把他当作活的个性，爱他的整体，特别是爱这个人身上的没有法子确定它、叫出它名称来的东西。”模糊思维在文艺欣赏以至文艺批评中有着特殊的意义。我们在探讨艺术魅力的现象时，也要运用模糊思维的方法。

总之，我们要把艺术魅力作为一个模糊概念来对待，这样，我们的研究就可以省掉很多不必要的纠缠。比如，我们就不要花时间去为它规定具有确定的概念外延的定义，而把它看成是艺术的迷惑力（例如使人产生幻觉、错觉等）、吸引力、诱导力、感染力、感动力等征服人心的力量的总称。只要艺术品具有这样一些美感效应，我们都笼而统之地称之为艺术魅力。另外，我们把艺术魅力看成是模糊概念，就会注意到它的系统性、多因性、动态性的特点。

所谓系统性，就是说：艺术魅力是文艺作品的美感动力系统，它产生于美的整体性，是多种社会功能的影响力，而不是作品的某一局部所产生的单一功能的作用力。每一部作品的魅力都是一个系统，要揭示一部作品的魅力的秘密，就要具体考察它的系统结构。而每一部优秀作品的魅力的系统结构都是有区别的，不能用对这一作品的分析来代替对另一作品的分析。所谓多因性，即构成作品魅力的美学因素是多种多样的，而不是单一的。比如，艺术的魅力离不开描写的真实性，但单纯地追求逼真就未必具有魅力；艺术的魅力也离不开独创性，但单纯地追求新奇，也很难获得艺术的魅力。所谓动态性，指的是艺术魅力表现为审美主客体在审美环境（“场”）的作用下辩证运动的过程，它是动态发展着的。比如，同一部作品在不同的欣赏环境、不同的欣赏者身上会有不同的美感效应。有的作品一时被哄抬到天上，刹那间却又无人问津；有的作品长期被冷落之后突然产生经久不衰的魅力。欣赏者对作品往往有偏爱，每个人对不同作品的感受力都是不一样的。即使同一个欣赏者欣赏同一个作品，由于时间、地点、心境的不同，也会产生不同的感受。这些现象都是艺术魅力动态性的体现。

31. 如果给本文加一个标题，下面比较合适的是（　）（2分）

A. 模糊概念及其意义　　B. 模糊思维及其作用

C. 模糊思维及其对美学研究的意义　　D. 艺术魅力的特性

32. 某士兵在观看戏剧表演时，不自觉地进入了剧情之中，以至于开枪打死了扮演坏蛋的演员，这主要是下列哪一方面的艺术魅力的体现（　）（2分）

A. 吸引力　　B. 迷惑力　　C. 感染力　　D. 感动力

33. 根据本文第三段阐述的道理，下列各种文艺现象，分别是艺术魅力的什么特征的体现？请把答案的代码分别填入答题卡上相应的表格框内（A. 系统性　B. 多因性　C. 动态性）（每题2分，共8分）

（1）鲁迅评论《红楼梦》说：“单是命意，就因读者的眼光而有种种：经学家看见《易》，道学家看见淫，才子看见缠绵，革命家看见排满，流言家看见宫闱秘事……”

（2）李白诗歌高度的想象力、奔放的激情、夸张的笔调、清新的语言，构成了其诗歌飘逸奔放的基本格调。

（3）有些较差的影片，经常抄袭其他成功影片的桥段，却无法达到后者原有的感染观众（如使之感动流泪）的艺术效果，反而引来观众的嘲笑。

（4）某些画家一生穷困潦倒，乏人问津；死后其画作却价值连城。

34. 判断下列各题所表述的意思是否正确。如果正确，请在答题卡上相应表格框中打“√”，否则打“×”。（每题2分，共8分）

（1）相对于“模糊概念”的灵活，科学概念显得死板而过时。

（2）出现“模糊概念”，是因为生活中有太多充满不确定因素的事物。要研究这些复杂的事物，就需要使用模糊思维、模糊概念。

(3) 俗话说："男人不坏，女人不爱"，这正是现实生活中应用了模糊思维的例子。

(4) 在分析艺术魅力的概念时运用模糊思维，至少有两个好处：既便于让人非常精密地界定"艺术魅力"这一基本概念，又引导人注意到其独有特点。

三、语言文字表达（共 70 分）

35. 在汶川地震一周年之际，某大学同学准备举办一个纪念晚会，同时也筹集捐款支持灾区重建。学生会布置会场时需要一副对联，宣传部长小张想出了一个上联：天地无情，能撼广厦成废墟。请你为这个上联对出一个下联。(3 分)

36. 某中学高一年级的学生李某不幸身患重病，因家贫不能得到应有治疗。校学生会为此决定在全校举行募捐活动。请你为募捐活动的海报拟一条口号。要求能有震撼力、号召力。(8 ~ 20 个字)(3 分)

37. 续写（4 分）

著名诗人莫非，应邀到北京师范大学中文系作家班举行讲座。讲到自己的诗时，准备朗诵一段，但诗稿放在一个学员的桌子上，于是他走下讲台去拿。由于是阶梯式教室，回讲台时，从下到上要上两层阶梯。上第二层时，前脚抬得太低，踏在台阶边上，滑了下去，一个趔趄，整个身子大幅度晃了几晃，差点倒下，有几个学员笑了起来……

诗人稳住身子，转向学员，指着第二层台阶，从容地说了一段话。一边说着，一边装作用力的样子走上讲台，继续他的讲座。

（请在答题卡相应题号的横线上补写诗人说的话。要求适应当时的场景与话题，体现诗人与学员共勉的意图，不超过 40 个字。）

38. 从下面两个题目中任选一个，按要求写一篇作文。(60 分)

题目一：屠格涅夫说："不会宽容别人的人，是不配受到别人的宽容的。"莎士比亚说："宽容就像天上的细雨滋润着天地。它赐福于宽容的人，也赐福于被宽容的人。"雨果说："最高贵的复仇方式是宽容。宽容就像清凉的甘露，浇灌了干涸的心灵；宽容就像温暖的壁炉，温暖了冰冷麻木的心；宽容就像不熄的火把，点燃了冰山下将要熄灭的火种；宽容就像一支魔笛，把沉睡在黑暗中的人叫醒。"孟子说："爱人者，人恒爱之；敬人者，人恒敬之。"

依据材料，以"宽容"或"宽恕"为题，写一篇作文。除诗歌外，文体不限。文言字数不少于 400 字，白话文字数不少于 700 字。

题目二：目前，网络（internet）已成为人们生活中不可或缺的一种通信手段。一位网友说："网络是一把双刃剑，美丽却拥有着毒性。"

请以网络为话题，自拟题目，写一篇作文。除诗歌外，文体不限。文言文字数不少于 400 字，白话文字数不少于 700 字。

数　学

答卷时间：120分钟

一、选择题：本大题共15小题，每小题4分，共60分，每小题所列四个选项中只有一个是正确的，把你的选择按题号填入答题纸.

1. 不等式 $2x>3-x$ 的解集是（　）

A. $x>3$　　B. $x<3$　　C. $x>1$　　D. $x<1$

2. 已知集合 $A=\{0, 1, 2\}$，$B=\{0, 2, 4\}$，则集合 $A\cap B$ 等于（　）

A. $\{0, 2\}$　　B. $\{0, 1\}$　　C. $\{1, 2\}$　　D. $\{0\}$

3. 复数 $\left(\frac{1}{2}+\frac{\sqrt{3}}{2}i\right)^3$ 的值为（　）

A. $-i$　　B. i　　C. -1　　D. 1

4. 要得到 $y=3\sin(2x+\frac{\pi}{4})$ 的图像只需将 $y=3\sin 2x$ 的图像（　）

A. 向左平移$\frac{\pi}{4}$个单位　　B. 向右平移$\frac{\pi}{4}$个单位

C. 向左平移$\frac{\pi}{8}$个单位　　D. 向右平移$\frac{\pi}{8}$个单位

5. 若 $f(\cos x)=\cos 2x$，则 $f(\cos 15°)$ 等于（　）

A. $-\frac{\sqrt{3}}{2}$　　B. $\frac{\sqrt{3}}{2}$　　C. $\frac{1}{2}$　　D. $-\frac{1}{2}$

6. 角度30°的弧度数为（　）

A. $\frac{\pi}{3}$　　B. $-\frac{\pi}{3}$　　C. $\frac{\pi}{6}$　　D. $-\frac{\pi}{6}$

7. 在 $\left(x^{11}+\frac{1}{x}\right)^{10}$ 的展开式中，系数之和为（　）

A. 2^8　　B. 2^9　　C. 2^{10}　　D. 2^{11}

8. 掷一枚骰子，掷得奇数点的概率是（　）

A. $\frac{1}{6}$　　B. $\frac{1}{2}$　　C. $\frac{1}{3}$　　D. $\frac{1}{4}$

9. 过点（0，2）的直线的斜率为 -2，则直线的方程为（　）

A. $y=2x+2$　　B. $y=2x-2$

C. $y=-2x+2$　　D. $y=-2x-2$

10. 函数 $f(x)=\sqrt[3]{x}$ 的反函数 $f^{-1}(x)$ 为（　）

A. x^3 （$x \in \mathbf{R}$）　　B. x^3 （$x>0$）

C. x^3 （$x<0$）　　D. x^2 （$x \geqslant 0$）

11. 已知数列$\{a_n\}$是等差数列，且 $a_1+a_2+a_3=18$，则 a_2 为（　）

A. 5　　B. 6　　C. 7　　D. 8

12. 圆 $x^2+y^2-2x-4y=0$ 的圆心到直线 $x-y+2=0$ 的距离为（　）

A. $\sqrt{2}$　　B. 2　　C. 3　　D. $\frac{\sqrt{2}}{2}$

13. 在$\triangle ABC$ 中，内角 A、B、C 对边的长度分别为 a、b、c，且 $a^2+b^2<c^2$，则这个三角形一定是（　）

A. 锐角三角形　　B. 钝角三角形

C. 直角三角形　　D. 等边三角形

14. 一条直线和两条异面直线中的一条平行，则它和另一条的位置关系是（　）

A. 平行　　B. 相交　　C. 异面　　D. 相交或异面

15. 将 3 个不同的小球放入 4 个盒子中，则不同放法的种数是（　）

A. 81　　B. 64　　C. 12　　D. 14

二、填空题：本大题共 5 小题，每小题 4 分，共 20 分，把答案按题号填入答题纸.

16. 在函数 $y=\sqrt{x+1}$中，自变量 x 的取值范围是________.

17. 某学校在开展的“节约每一滴水”的活动中，从七年级的 180 名同学中任选出 10 名同学汇报了各自家庭一个月的节水情况，将有关资料整理如下（见下表）：

节水量（吨）	0.5	1	1.5	2
同学数（人）	2	3	4	1

请你估计这 180 名同学的家庭一个月节约用水的总量大约是________.

18. 非零向量 $\vec{a}$、$\vec{b}$ 满足 $|\vec{a}|=|\vec{b}|=|\vec{a}+\vec{b}|$，则 $\vec{a}$ 和 $\vec{b}$ 的夹角为________.

19. 函数 $y=\sin 2x$ 的最小正周期为________.

20. $\sqrt{2}(\sqrt{2}+\sqrt{8})=$________.

三、解答题：本大题满分 70 分. 在第 21、22、23、24、25 题中任选三题作答，若解答超过三题，按所答前三题计分. 第 26、27 题为选考历史或地理的考生必做，第 28、29 题为选考物理、化学或生物的考生必做. 把解答过程写入答题纸，解答时应写出文字说明、证明过程或演算步骤.

21.（本小题满分 14 分）

已知 $\tan\alpha=3$，求 $\sin\alpha\cos\alpha$.

22. （本小题满分 14 分）

如右图所示，A、B、C、D 为空间四点．在 $\triangle ABC$ 中，$AB=2$，$AC=BC=\sqrt{2}$，$\triangle ADB$ 为等边三角形，平面 $ADB\perp$ 平面 ABC，求 CD.

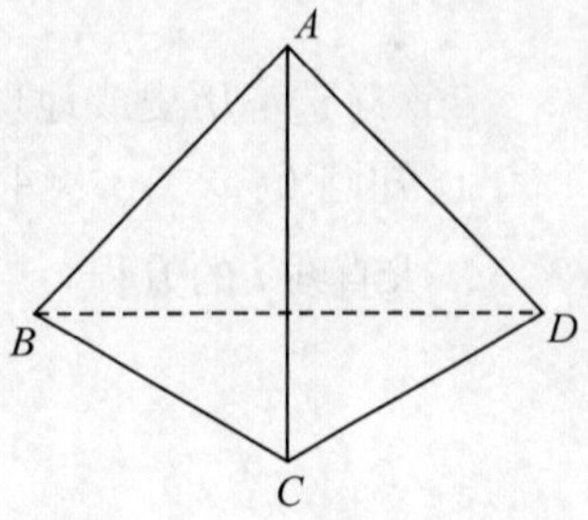

23. （本小题满分 14 分）

在 $\triangle ABC$ 中，内角 A、B、C 对边的长度分别为 a、b、c. 已知 $c=2$，$C=\dfrac{\pi}{3}$，$\triangle ABC$ 的面积为 $\sqrt{3}$，求 a、b.

24. （本小题满分 14 分）

已知数列 $\{a_n\}$ 的前 n 项和为 S_n，且 $S_n=\dfrac{1}{2}na_{n+1}$，n 为正整数，其中 $a_1=1$，求数列 $\{a_n\}$ 的通项公式．

25. （本小题满分 14 分）

已知函数$f(x)=x^3+ax^2+3x+b$，且$g(x)=f(x)-2$是奇函数，求a、b.

26. （选考历史或地理的考生必做）（本小题满分 14 分）

已知圆C：$x^2+y^2=4$，直线l过点$P(1,2)$，且与圆交于A、B两点，若$|AB|=2\sqrt{3}$，求直线l的方程.

27. （选考历史或地理的考生必做）（本小题满分 14 分）

2008 年，“三聚氰胺”事件给中国的牛奶制造业带来了巨大的冲击，为了保障人们的饮食安全，国家质检部门把查处的问题奶集中进行无害化处理．某单位承担了本地区问题奶的处理任务，在国家科技部门的支援下，该单位经过科技攻关，采用了新工艺，把问题奶转化为一种可利用的化工产品，每吨可获利 2 万元．已知该单位每月可处理 7～12 吨，其处理成本y（万元）与月处理量x（吨）之间的函数关系可近似地表示为：

$$y=\frac{1}{4}x^2-3x+16.$$

该单位能否获得利润？如果能，求出最大利润．

28.（选考物理、化学或生物的考生必做）（本小题满分14分）

过圆 $x^2+(y-2)^2=4$ 外一点 $A(2,-2)$ 引圆的两条切线，切点为 T_1、T_2，求直线 T_1T_2 的方程．

29.（选考物理、化学或生物的考生必做）（本小题满分14分）

某小公司生产陶瓷，根据历史的情况可知，生产陶瓷每天的固定成本为500元，每生产一件产品，成本增加28元．已知该产品的日销售量 $f(x)$ 与产量 x 之间的关系为：

$$f(x)=\begin{cases}\frac{1}{5}x, & 0\leqslant x\leqslant 400\\ 80, & x>400\end{cases}$$

每件产品的售价 $g(x)$ 与产量 x 之间的关系为：

$$g(x)=\begin{cases}-\frac{1}{2}x+240, & 0\leqslant x\leqslant 400\\ 40, & x>400\end{cases}$$

（Ⅰ）写出该陶瓷厂的日销售利润 $Q(x)$ 与产量 x 之间的关系式；

（Ⅱ）若要使得日销售利润最大，每天该生产多少件产品，并求出最大利润．

英　语

答卷时间：120 分钟

Paper One（第一卷）

Part Ⅰ　Listening Comprehension（30 **points**）

Section A（1 ×5）

Directions: *In this section you will hear five sentences, which will be spoken only once. In each sentence there is a number. Listen carefully and decide the correct number you have heard. Then, mark your answer by blackening the corresponding letter on the Answer Sheet.*

1. A. 7632, 27th Avenue　B. 6723, 26th Avenue　C. 6743, 25th Avenue　D. 7623, 23rd Avenue
2. A. 2:14　B. 2:16　C. 3:15　D. 2:15
3. A. 5:30 – May 26th　B. 6:30 – May 27th　C. 6:50 – March 27th　D. 6:15 – March 27th
4. A. 546 – 7　B. 536 – 6　C. 547 – 6　D. 645 – 7
5. A. 7:36　B. 9:37　C. 8:36　D. 8:53

Section B（1 ×5）

Directions: *In this section you will hear 5 questions. The questions will be spoken only once. When you hear a question, read the four possible answers in your test paper and choose the most suitable one. Then, mark your answer by blackening the corresponding letter on the Answer Sheet.*

Example:

You will hear: Does he know that there will be a lecture on American poetry this afternoon?

You will read: A. Yes, there will.
B. Yes, he does.
C. No, it isn't.
D. No, he will not.

The most suitable answer is B. So you should blacken the letter B on your Answer Sheet.

6. A. Yes, I will wait a while.　B. No, I didn't.　C. Yes, it is a while.　D. No, I haven't been able to.

7. A. Yes, it is fine. B. $345.
C. Yes, he often breaks the rules. D. He came to a fine place.

8. A. Yes, she desires.
B. Yes, everything she does is satisfactory.
C. No, she isn't transferred.
D. Yes, I hope so.

9. A. No, they didn't want to pay.
B. They are studying in Harvard University.
C. They plan to work part time.
D. Both of them major in physics.

10. A. Yes, in the waiting-room. B. Mr. Johnson did.
C. No, this is mine. D. Sorry, I don't know.

Section C (2×5)

Directions: *In this section you will hear 5 short conversations between two speakers. At the end of each conversation, a third voice will ask a question about what was said. The conversation and the question will be spoken only once. After you hear a conversation and the question about it read the four possible answers in your test paper and choose the best one to the question you have heard. Then, mark your answer by blackening the corresponding letter of your choice on the Answer Sheet.*

11. A. He is giving the woman directions.
B. He is expressing his doubt about the place.
C. He is offering a warning.
D. He is trying to help.

12. A. She is a job seeker. B. She is a secretary.
C. She works in a newspaper. D. She calls to make an ad.

13. A. Something that happened these days.
B. Something disgusting.
C. The wet weather.
D. The thing which couldn't last.

14. A. Two friends met each other by chance.
B. They last met each other in June.
C. The woman was glad to know a friend.
D. They remembered seeing each other in June.

15. A. To a supermarket. B. To a hotel.
C. To a baker. D. To a bank.

Section D (2×5)

Directions: *In this section you will hear a short talk. The talk will be spoken twice. After* *the talk you will be asked questions. When you hear a question, read the four possible answers in your test paper and choose the best answer to the question you have heard. Then, mark your answer by blackening the corresponding letter on the Answer Sheet.*

16. A. About a week ago. B. About a year ago.
    C. Two days before. D. Half a year ago.
17. A. Because he had just cashed a check.
    B. Because he didn't want to carry too much money.
    C. Because he wanted to stay in the hotel for another 2 nights.
    D. Both A and B.
18. A. Yes, he was.
    B. No, but he gave him another proof for the money.
    C. No, he didn't.
    D. Yes, he gave him a receipt for the money.
19. A. To return to the hotel with him.
    B. To put the clerk to a court.
    C. To leave another hundred-dollar bill with the clerk.
    D. Both A and C.
20. A. The author successfully put the lawyer's plan in action.
    B. The author got the money back from the clerk.
    C. The author had to pay the lawyer a hundred dollars for advice.
    D. All of the above.

Part Ⅱ Reading Comprehension (**40 points**)

Directions: *There are 4 passages in this part. Each passage is followed by some questions or unfinished statements. For each of them there are 4 choices marked A, B, C and D. You should decide on the best choice and mark your answer by blackening the corresponding letter on the Answer Sheet.*

Questions 21 to 25 are based on the following passage:

I was 16, an age that most people see as too young for overseas travel, but I had a great desire to explore and learn about other cultures and ways of life. When I learned about an organization called International Cultural Adventures, I called and talked with the program director, David Pruskin, about my interest in Nepal and their 6-week Nepal Cultural Immersion Experience program. I told him I would talk to my parents and see if I could go on this program.

To make my parents believe that I could go so far away from my home alone. I did all sorts of things. I raised my good grades in school, and did research on the country to show that it really wasn't dangerous.

Several weeks later, my dream came true. Once in Nepal, I found the Nepalese people unbelievably friendly and open to sharing their culture with visitors. There was hardly a day when someone didn't invite me into their house or shop to drink "chiyaa", a common milky tea.

For a part of the program, I taught English to elementary school kids. I had no idea how I was going to be a success. I told them things about Nepal. It was good for all of us.

Another teacher and I went to climb Annapurna Mountains. In Nepal during the summer the mountains are sometimes covered by clouds; the views were amazing, though. The villages we walked through were some of the most beautiful places I've ever seen.

After the experience in Nepal, I was more confident about doing things independently.

21. The author wanted to go to Nepal because he wanted to ______.

A. appreciate the beauty of the country

B. become a teacher in Nepal

C. experience and learn foreign cultures

D. learn how to do things independently

22. According to the first two paragraphs, it wasn't easy for the author to join in the program because ______.

A. the organization thought that he was too young

B. the organization thought that he didn't get excellent scores in class

C. his parents were afraid that he would fall behind in study

D. his parents thought that Nepal was unsafe and that he couldn't do things independently

23. We know from the passage that the author ______.

A. came to Nepal in autumn

B. doubted the kindness of the natives in Nepal

C. believed in his ability of teaching

D. got on well with the local people in Nepal

24. The author did many things in Nepal EXCEPT ______.

A. doing research on Nepal with the natives

B. drinking the milky tea with the natives

C. teaching English in elementary schools

D. going sightseeing with his teammates

25. How does the author most probably feel about his travel in Nepal?

A. Rather busy. B. A bit regretful.

C. Very enjoyable. D. Fairly boring.

Questions 26 to 30 are based on the following passage:

Workers aren't bridging the generation gap because 20-something employees rarely chat to those in their 50es and 60es, according to a new survey. The poll of 3,494 adults by employment services group Randstad USA showed that 51 percent of baby boomers (婴儿潮出生的人) and 66 percent of older workers seldom have interaction with their younger workmates.

Employment experts fear the lack of communication could create a shortage of US skilled labor because retiring baby boomers aren't passing on their knowledge and experience. "In older workers' view, younger workers are not competent and not having a work ethic (道德规范)," said Eric Buntin, managing director of marketing and operations for Randstad USA. "Younger workers view the older as not thinking outside the box." He said the different generations of employees do not have the same expectations of work and values of employment, which is a difficult gap to bridge.

"The key is that organizations find a way structurally for generations to interact but it can't be a coffee or lunch," Buntin said, "It has to be bringing them together in meaningful ways so that they're engaged in projects together."

The survey examined four generations: Generation Y, born between 1980 and 1988; Generation X, born between 1965 and 1979; baby boomers born between 1946 and 1964 and matures born before 1945. The survey also showed that three of the four generations said they have little interaction with the most experienced workers—matures.

26. The underlined sentence in the second paragraph means "______".

A. The young are unwilling to learn from the old

B. The young should follow the example of the old

C. The old think the young are too lazy

D. The young think the old are too conservative

27. Workers of different ages don't chat enough because ______.

A. older workers think younger workers are not competent

B. the young don't respect the old

C. they don't know each other very well

D. they have different expectations and values

28. From the passage it can be inferred that ______.

A. it's easy to deal with the gap among the different generations of employees

B. drinking coffee or eating lunch together may lead to generations interacting

C. making friends with older workers is the best way to interact

D. so far no proper ways have been found to bridge the generation gap

29. Baby boomers in the passage refer to people who were born ______.

A. between 1946 and 1964 　　B. between 1980 and 1988

C. between 1965 and 1979　　　　D. before 1945

30. The topic of the passage is ______.

A. the advantage of the young employees

B. the generation gap among office workers

C. the disadvantage of the old employees

D. the way of communication between the young and the old

Questions 31 to 35 are based on the following passage:

Book clubs are a great way for adults to get together, have some fellowship, and have intellectual（智力的）conversation. Sure, book clubs may seem more popular to women than men, but I know plenty of fantastic men who love their "book clubs" just as much as I do! So why are we not getting our kids to take part in these types of activities more?

Reading is the biggest push in education today. If our kids do not or cannot read, the future of this country will be in jeopardy. Educators are working overtime, round the clock, trying to teach kids to read. Think of a strategy（策略）to make a child interested in reading? The school systems are doing it. But all students should be enrolled（加入）in some sort of reading class based on their reading needs.

And we can do plenty about this at home! If you are busy and do not have the chance to stay at home with your child, then read to them every night before bedtime. Let them touch the books, hold the books, eat the books if they want to! Any interaction（互动）a child has with a book is good and should be made to be a positive thing. Find a couple of friends with children in your age group and get them together once a month, just like the adults, and seat them in a circle with a pile of books. Do not expect them to discuss which characters they like or hate, instead, have them "play" together with the books.

As they get older, have them read to each other. If we make reading fun and part of what they do with their friends, we still have a chance to teach our future leaders how to be good readers!

31. The first paragraph intends to tell us that ______.

A. we'd better encourage our kids to join the book clubs

B. many parents get together with their children in book clubs

C. women love book clubs as much as men

D. children shouldn't take part in too many activities

32. The underlined phrase "in jeopardy" (in paragraph 2) can best be replaced by "______".

A. in common　　　B. in trouble　　　C. in peace　　　D. in place

33. According to the third paragraph, the author thinks it is good for children to ______.

A. discuss what kinds of books they like best

B. become familiar with each other through reading books

C. become more positive to make friends

D. enjoy doing anything just with a book

34. It can be inferred from the passage that in order to really make children interested in reading, ______.

A. parents and teachers should relate reading to every aspect of life

B. stronger or additional interventions are needed

C. parents should bear the most responsibilities

D. enrolling in reading class is the only solution

35. What's the main idea of this passage?

A. Book clubs are important to us in our daily life.

B. We should try to make our children good readers.

C. It is necessary for us to communicate with our children.

D. Children usually have a good time together.

Questions 36 to 40 are based on the following passage:

Everglades National Park is the most endangered national park in America. The purpose of making a national park is to protect the plants and animals that live there. But things that happen outside the park also affect the life within it.

Everglades National Park is part of a much larger area known as the Everglades. At one time, water flowed freely in the Everglades. During the rainy season, water would fill the Kissimmee River. Then it flowed into Lake Okeechobee. Once the lake became full, water spilled over onto the flatland. From there a shallow sheet of water moved slowly down the Florida Peninsula. Then it emptied into Florida Bay. This shallow sheet of water was the Everglades River. It was only a few inches deep in some spots. But it was up to 50 miles wide and over 100 miles long.

The Everglades is home to many plants and animals found nowhere else in the world. Today, some of these plants and animals are in danger of disappearing forever.

The main reason is that Everglades is no longer a free-flowing river. Canals have been built to drain (排干) most of the shallow river. People have also built a dam to hold back water from Lake Okeechobee. Most of the water from the Everglades is trapped in man-made lakes. Cutting off the flow of water into Everglades National Park has done more harm than good. Now it threatens the wildlife in the park.

Water pollution is another reason some plants and animals are disappearing. Years ago, large areas of the Everglades were drained and turned into farmland. Today the fertilizers used on crops are polluting the water. The "river of grass" is slowly disappearing. Many kinds of plants are disappearing. Animals that depend on these plants for food no longer have anything to eat.

The problems facing Everglades National Park are very serious. But there is still hope. Work is already under way to save the Everglades. The federal government, the state of Florida, and several other groups are all working together to try to undo the damage.

36. What is the best title for the passage?

A. Following the River B. Rare Plants and Animals

C. A Park in Danger D. Canals, Dam and Lakes

37. What is the main source of problem in the Everglades?

A. The rainy season is too short.

B. There are too many plants and animals.

C. Water is no longer allowed to flow freely.

D. Water spills out of Lake Okeechobee.

38. The underlined part "river of grass" refers to "______".

A. The Kissimmee River B. the Everglades

C. Lake Okeechobee D. Florida Bay

39. Which of the following is NOT true according to the passage?

A. If the non-park areas are not protected, Everglades National Park will lose an important and unique ecosystem.

B. Everglades National Park was preserved not for its scenic wonders but because of the magnificence of its biological resources.

C. Threats to the integrity of the Everglades ecosystem became a reality with the arrival of people.

D. The land in the Everglades is very flat and the wetlands are quite deep.

40. What's the author's attitude towards Everglades National Park?

A. Pleased and optimistic. B. Anxious and desperate.

C. Curious and confused. D. Worried but hopeful.

Part Ⅲ Vocabulary (20 **points**)

Section A (10 **points**)

Directions: *There are 10 incomplete sentences in this part. For each sentence there are four choices marked A, B, C and D. Choose the ONE answer that best completes the sentence. Then mark your answer by blackening the corresponding letter on the Answer Sheet.*

41. After enjoying their wonderful performances, the teacher showed his ______ by nodding his head constantly.

A. satisfaction B. imagination C. realization D. preparation

42. You must be very careful when you ______ the difficult problem.

A. come about B. happen to C. deal with D. depend on

43. Table tennis is such an interesting game that people all over the world ______ it.

A. fight B. play C. compete D. wonder

44. More trees should be ______ to make our school a beautiful place to study in.

A. placed B. programmed C. planted D. proposed

45. It was so noisy in the classroom that I couldn't ______ my essay.

A. be faced with B. take place

C. turn up D. focus on

46. It is not ______ to expect all students to pass the final exam. In my opinion, some of them will fail.

A. realistic B. modern C. traditional D. cultural

47. In most developed countries the government provides free education ______ children.

A. with B. for C. on D. of

48. Colleges usually teach skills which ______ students to follow a career after graduation.

A. empower B. enable C. expect D. endanger

49. Now that he has ______ that he stole the bicycle, you should forgive him.

A. excused B. suffered C. admitted D. offered

50. It won't be easy, but I'll get across the river ______.

A. meanwhile B. somehow C. possible D. immediate

Section B (10 **points**)

Directions: *There are 10 sentences in this part. For each sentence there are four choices marked A, B, C and D. Choose the ONE word or phrase that is closest in meaning to the underlined part. Then mark your answer by blackening the corresponding letter on the Answer Sheet.*

51. A special expert team has already been set up to do research into the wild life in the area.

A. established B. kept C. found D. followed

52. If you have trouble falling asleep, some people suggest breathing slowly and deeply.

A. fear B. difficulty C. afraid D. safety

53. It is widely believed that it is impossible to live completely free of stress.

A. power B. crisis C. carelessness D. pressure

54. It is good for elderly people to be involved in community services.

A. come across B. take part in

C. set about D. put aside

55. In order to gain a bigger share in the international market, many companies are try-

ing to make their products more competitive.

A. offer　　B. beat　　C. succeed　　D. obtain

56. Don't worry about him. I believe the child will get over his shock sooner or later.

A. suggest　　B. propose　　C. suppose　　D. oppose

57. Over the past ten years people have become aware of the significance of healthy eating habits.

A. memory　　B. importance　　C. limit　　D. spirit

58. Arguing about the details took up much of their valuable time.

A. consumed　　B. organized　　C. increased　　D. suited

59. They will draw a lesson from the recent milk scandal and seize the opportunity to improve food safety.

A. energy　　B. effect　　C. chance　　D. resource

60. She was upset because her mother blamed her for not sharing any housework.

A. shouted　　B. argued　　C. discussed　　D. criticized

Part Ⅳ　Grammatical Structure (10 points)

Directions: *There are 10 incomplete sentences in this part. For each sentence there are four choices marked A, B, C and D. Choose the ONE that best completes the sentence. Then mark your answer by blackening the corresponding letter on the Answer Sheet.*

61. You didn't go to Prof. Smith's lecture yesterday, ______?

A. was it　　B. wasn't it

C. did you　　D. didn't you

62. I will get a headache next morning if I sleep with the window ______ at night.

A. shut　　B. shutting　　C. to shut　　D. shouts

63. I would suggest that the training course ______ every afternoon next week.

A. be arranged　　B. was arranged

C. arranged　　D. is arranged

64. Only by working hard ______ succeed in doing everything.

A. we can　　B. can we　　C. are we　　D. we are

65. The more known the brand name, ______ people want to copy it.

A. more　　B. many　　C. the more　　D. the many

66. It was not until Tom had arrived home ______ he remembered his appointment with the doctor.

A. when　　B. where　　C. which　　D. that

67. The air in this city is ______ severely polluted that it is not a suitable place to live in.

A. too　　B. rather　　C. so　　D. much

68. Alicia was absent from English class this morning so she _______ be sick because she is fond of this course.

A. can B. will C. must D. shall

69. Put on more clothes when you go out, Kevin, _______ you will catch a cold.

A. and B. that C. which D. or

70. When Mr. Black went back to get the car, he found that someone _______ it.

A. has stolen B. stole C. would steal D. had stolen

Part V Cloze (20 **points**)

Directions: *There are 20 blanks in the following passage. For each blank there are 4 choices marked A, B, C and D. You should choose the ONE that best fits into the passage. Then mark your answer by blackening the corresponding letter on the Answer Sheet with a single line through the center.*

The word "sport" first meant something that people did in their free time. Later it often meant __71__ wild animals and birds. __72__ a hundred years ago the word was first used for __73__ games. This is the __74__ meaning of the word today. People spend a lot of their spare time __75__ football, basketball, tennis and many __76__ sports. Such people play __77__ they want to. A few people are __78__ for the sport they play. These people are __79__ professional sportsmen. They may be sportsmen for only a few years, but __80__ that time the best ones can earn a lot of money.

For example, a professional footballer in England earns more than £ 3,000 a year. The stars earn a lot __81__. International golf and tennis champions can make more than £ 50,000 in a year. Of course, only a few sportsmen can earn as __82__ money as that. It is only possible __83__ sports for individuals, like golf, tennis and motor-racing. Perhaps the most __84__ thing about sportsmen and money is this: the stars can earn more money from advertising __85__ from sport. An advertisement for sports equipment does not simply say "Buy our thing". It says "Buy the same shirt and shoes __86__ ..." Famous sportsmen can __87__ advertise things like watches and food. They __88__ the companies to use their names __89__ a photograph of them and they are paid for this. Sport is __90__ just something for people's spare time.

71. A. to hunt B. hunting C. hunted D. hunt

72. A. At B. For C. About D. In

73. A. formed B. organized C. checked D. played

74. A. usual B. seldom C. often D. always

75. A. to play B. at play C. playing D. played

76. A. others B. another C. other D. the other

77. A. since B. because C. as D. while

78. A. paying B. pay C. paid D. to pay

79. A. named	B. naming	C. calling	D. called
80. A. on	B. for	C. in	D. during
81. A. many	B. much	C. few	D. more
82. A. much	B. more	C. enough	D. adequate
83. A. for	B. in	C. to	D. at
84. A. surprised	B. surprising	C. surprise	D. surprisingly
85. A. as	B. and	C. about	D. than
86. A. of	B. in	C. like	D. as
87. A. even	B. hardly	C. seldom	D. normally
88. A. admit	B. promise	C. allow	D. give
89. A. but	B. just	C. yet	D. or
90. A. no longer	B. not longer	C. no any longer	D. not for long

Paper Two（第二卷）

Part Ⅵ　Proof Reading（10 points）

Directions: *Read each line carefully to find out the mistakes.*

1. If there is no mistake in the line, mark √ on the right hand side.

2. If there is a redundant（多余的）word in the line, first write it off with a slanting line（＼）, and then write the word on the right hand side with the slanting line.

3. If there is a word missing in the line, put a missing word sign（∧）there and write the missing word on the right hand side.

4. If there is a wrong word in the line, draw a line under it and write the correct one on the right hand side.

Example:

When I have free time I go ∧ a long walk. Some　(1) for
people read the\ books or watch television while others have　(2) the\
sports. Charles and Linda Mason do all of these things as　(3) √
well as climbed buildings.　(4) climb

When I first came to the United States, I made friend with a neighbor　91. ____
who used to live a block from my street. We used to visit each other, do　92. ____
some activities, and go out sometimes. This friend teach me a lot about　93. ____
American culture. One day this friend invited me to party. It wasn't a　94. ____
real party, some kind of informal get-together. Since it was summer, he　95. ____
had a cookout where most of his American friends knows me, but there　96. ____
were others I had never met for before. It was a most embarrassing party　97. ____
for me after I noticed everyone was wearing jeans and simple T-shirts for the　98. ____

day, while I arrived formal dress with my shoes and hair all fixed for a fancy 99. ____
party. I felt my face burning hot with the embarrassment. I wished I had never 100. ____
come to the party.

Part Ⅶ Composition (20 points) (任选一题)

Directions: *Write on ONE of the following topics on the Composition Sheet. A 200 – 250 word limit is required.* （作文请写在作文纸上）

Ⅰ. *Write a composition of no less than 200 words in three paragraphs. You are given the first sentence of each paragraph and are required to develop the idea in completing the paragraph. Your part of the composition should be no less than 200 words, not including the words given.*

Enough Sleep, Better Performance

1. Sleep is very important to everybody because ______________________________.
2. However, many people suffer from inadequate sleep. There are many reasons for it.
   ____
3. There are some tips to ensure that we have a good sleep. ____________________

Ⅱ. *Look at the following pictures and write a composition of no less than 200 words based on these pictures.*

Your family will make a trip to a beautiful place this summer. Choose four different means of transport and compare their advantages and disadvantages. In the last paragraph, choose the most suitable one for your family.

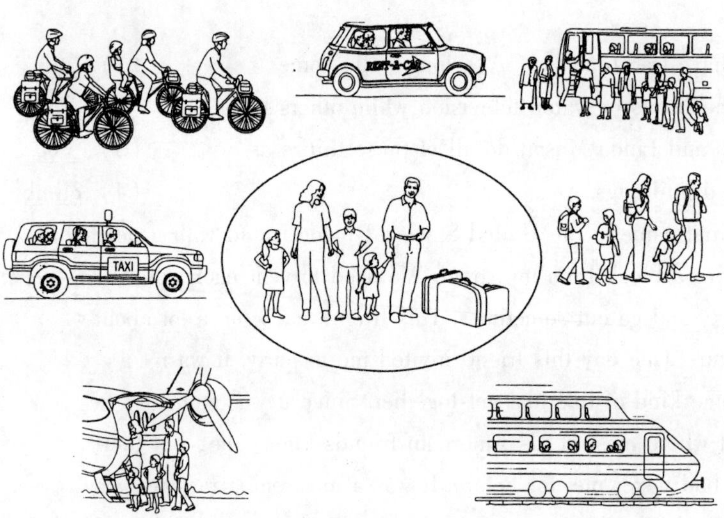

Composition Sheet（作文纸）

历 史

答卷时间：120 分钟

一、单项选择题（请将所选答案的代号填在答题纸上。每小题 2 分，共 40 分）

1. 我国境内现在已知的最早远古居民是（ ）

A. 北京人　　B. 马坝人　　C. 元谋人　　D. 蓝田人

2. 公元前十一世纪中，周武王伐纣，建立周朝，定都在镐京。镐京位于今天的（ ）

A. 洛阳　　B. 西安　　C. 安阳　　D. 开封

3. 西汉时期张骞出使西域，促进了中西经济文化的交流。下列不属于从西域传入中土的物种是（ ）

A. 骆驼　　B. 葡萄　　C. 玉米　　D. 胡萝卜

4. 维吾尔族的祖先在唐代被称作（ ）

A. 靺鞨　　B. 吐蕃　　C. 南诏　　D. 回纥

5. 下列不属于宋朝时期著名抗金将领的是（ ）

A. 岳飞　　B. 宗泽　　C. 文天祥　　D. 韩世忠

6. 1689 年，清政府与沙俄在平等的基础上签订的中俄第一个边界条约为（ ）

A.《辛丑条约》　　B.《伊犁条约》

C.《尼布楚条约》　　D.《马关条约》

7. 鸦片战争期间，英国通过强迫清政府签订一份条约，割占了九龙司。该条约是（ ）

A.《南京条约》　　B.《天津条约》　　C.《北京条约》　　D.《瑷珲条约》

8. 鸦片战争的战败使中国一批开明知识分子睁眼看世界，主张学习西方。其中魏源在他编写的一部书中明确提出了“师夷长技以制夷”的主张。该书是（ ）

A.《皇朝经世文编》　　B.《海国图志》

C.《四洲志》　　D.《瀛环志略》

9. 洋务运动期间，李鸿章创办的当时国内最大的兵工厂是（ ）

A. 福州船政局　　B. 江南制造总局

C. 湖北枪炮厂　　D. 金陵机器局

10. 1915 年，袁世凯恢复帝制、当上皇帝后，是谁率先在云南发动反袁护国运动，并引发全国各地的响应（ ）

A. 黄兴　　B. 邹容　　C. 蔡锷　　D. 唐才常

11. 1921 年，中国共产党第一次全国代表大会在上海召开。下列人物中，没有出

席此次大会的是（　）

A. 李达　　B. 张国焘　　C. 毛泽东　　D. 陈独秀

12. 下列哪场战役不属于抗战期间国民党正面战场的战役之一（　）

A. 徐州会战　　B. 太原会战　　C. 长沙会战　　D. 百团大战

13. 抗战胜利后，毛泽东赴重庆与国民党进行和平谈判。1945 年 10 月 10 日，国共双方签订《双十协定》，即（　）

A. 《停战协定》　　B. 《政府与中共代表会谈纪要》

C. 《和平建国纲领》　　D. 《宪法草案》

14. 地理大发现和新航路的开辟引起了“价格革命”。以下关于这种“价格革命”的说法不正确的是（　）

A. 金银供应增加，物价上涨　　B. 金银供应增加，物价下降

C. 促进了资本主义的发展　　D. 扩大了世界各地的经济往来

15. 以下哪一项不属于发生在 17、18 世纪的历史巨变（　）

A. 英国机器生产开始取代工厂手工业

B. 欧洲思想领域出现了改造旧社会的政治构想

C. 资本主义世界发生了经济危机

D. 法国大革命震撼了欧洲大陆

16. 美国 1787 年宪法规定最高法院大法官应由（　）

A. 国会提名，总统任命　　B. 总统任命，国会批准

C. 总统提名，众议院任命　　D. 总统任命，参议院同意

17. 日本明治维新（　）

A. 使日本确立了民主共和政体　　B. 是在大名和武士的领导下进行的

C. 目的在于维护封建君主的统治　　D. 顺应了当时世界发展的潮流

18. 1918 年德国历史学家斯宾格勒目睹当时世界的状况，出版了《西方的没落》这本名著。根据你的理解，这里的西方指的是（　）

A. 美洲　　B. 欧洲　　C. 德国　　D. 英国

19. 第二次世界大战全面爆发的标志是（　）

A. 卢沟桥事变　　B. 苏德战争爆发

C. 英、法对德宣战　　D. 日军偷袭珍珠港

20. 以美国为首的北约首次不经联合国授权而采取的军事行动是（　）

A. 越南战争　　B. 科索沃战争　　C. 海湾战争　　D. 两伊战争

二、材料解析题（请将答案写在答题纸上，共 3 小题，40 分，其中第 21 小题 12 分，第 22 和 23 小题各 14 分）

21. 阅读下面的材料，解答问题（12 分）

材料 1：

选举之法，大略有四：曰学校，曰科目，曰荐举，曰铨选。学校以教育之，科目

以登进之，荐举以旁招之，铨选以布列之，天下人才尽于是矣。明制，科目为盛，卿相皆由此出，学校则储才以应科目者也。其径由学校通籍者，亦科目之亚也，外此则杂流矣。然进士、举贡、杂流三途并用，虽有畸重，无偏废也。

——选自《明史》

材料2：

今虽内设国子监，恐不足以尽延天下之俊秀，其令天下郡县，并建学校，以作养士类。其府学，设教授一员，秩从九品，训导四员，生员四十人；州学设学正一员，训导三员，生员三十人；县学设教谕一员，训导二员，生员二十人。师生月廪食米人六斗，有司给以鱼肉，学官月俸有差。学者专治一经，以礼、乐、射、御、书、数设科分教，务求实才，顽不率者黜之。

——选自《明太祖实录》

根据所学历史知识和材料内容，请回答：

（1）根据材料1，明代选官途径有哪三种？（3分）其中哪种最为兴盛，此种官吏选拔制度始于哪个朝代？（2分）

（2）根据材料2，明朝官办学校制度分为哪四级？（4分）明政府设立学校制度的目的是什么？（3分）

22. 阅读下面材料，解答问题（14分）

材料：

甲午一役后，中国人士不欲为亡国之民者，群起以呼啸叫号，发鼓击钲，声撼大地。或主张变法自强之议，或吹煽开智之说，或立危词以警国民，或故自尊大以鼓舞国民之志。未几而播海内外，风靡回应，皆惧为亡国之民，皆耻为丧家之狗。未几有戊戌变法自强之举，此振兴之自上者也。逾年有长江一带之骚动，此奋起自下者也。同时有北方诸省之乱，此受外族之侵凌，忍之无可忍，乃轰然而爆发者也。

——蔡锷：《军国民篇》，载《蔡锷集》

此段材料综述了甲午战争后至20世纪初救亡图存浪潮中，中国国内思想文化及社会政治运动的概况，结合所学历史知识和材料内容，请回答：

（1）材料中“戊戌变法自强之举”、“长江一带之骚动”、“北方诸省之乱”分别指当时发生的什么事件？（8分）

（2）“或主张变法自强之议，或吹煽开智之说，或立危词以警国民，或故自尊大以鼓舞国民之志”指的是当时流行的几种理论学说，请具体指出其中三种学说的名称。（6分）

23. 阅读下面材料，解答问题（14分）

材料1：1946年3月5日丘吉尔在美国的“铁幕”演说

“我认为我们不能如此酣睡，因为时局已然逆转，一些共产主义或新法西斯主义的国家已经暂时操控了那些可怜的附属国……从波罗的海的什切青到亚得里亚海的特列斯特，一块铁幕已经降下，并贯穿大陆。在这条线之后，坐落着中欧和东欧古老国家的首都，华沙、柏林、布拉格、维也纳、布达佩斯、贝尔格莱德、布加勒斯特，所有这些名城及其周围的民众都在苏维埃的范围之内，都以某种形式不仅接受苏维埃的影响，而且接受来自莫斯科的日益严密的控制。”

——选译自托玛斯·帕特森《冷战的起源》

材料2：尼基塔·赫鲁晓夫1961年关于资本主义“铁幕”的演说

“我们的社会对于那些从外国来到我们这里的人是敞开的，对诚实贸易、科学技术和文化交流以及真实的信息是敞开的。如果我们说存在着一个铁幕，那它应该存在于资本主义世界。尽管资本主义世界自吹为“自由世界”，却不时地向苏联人关闭它的大门，有时是对厨师，有时是对我们的国际象棋棋手。……我们坚信，最终所有人都会做出正确的选择，选择真正自由的社会主义制度，放弃所谓的资本主义“自由世界”。

——摘引自杰里·本内特和赫伯特·齐格勒所著《新全球史》

请回答以下问题：

（1）材料1和材料2中提到的“铁幕”分别指的是什么？（4分）二者有何不同？（2分）

（2）两篇演说发表时间相差15年，其时代环境有何不同？（4分）

（3）这两则材料具有什么样的共同点？这种共同点体现了冷战的何种特点？（4分）

三、简答题（本大题共3小题，任选2小题作答。每小题20分，共40分。请注明所答小题号）

24. 简述隋朝修建大运河的过程及意义。

25. 戊戌维新运动的历史意义及失败的原因是什么？

26. 19 世纪中期英国在世界工业中居于压倒性的优势地位，但它为何在 19 世纪末 20 世纪初丧失了这种地位?

四、论述题（本大题共 2 小题，任选 1 小题作答。两小题均为 30 分。本题不预设固定答案，考生可以表达个人见解。考生答题应观点明确，并能正确引用史实加以论证。请注明所答小题号）

27. 今年是五四运动九十周年。五四运动以及随后陈独秀、胡适等人倡导的新文化运动，展开了对传统文化的激烈批判。有人认为，这是中国现代化的必经过程，因此其影响是积极的、建设性的。但是也有人认为，这种批判是全盘反传统，并导致了中国文化血脉的中断，给此后几十年中国社会的发展带来了很大的负面影响和破坏性作用。你的观点是什么？请予论述。

28. 从独立战争到第二次世界大战结束，美国用不到两百年的时间便成长为一个世界霸国。有人认为以宪法为基础的宪政制度是其崛起的主要原因，而有人则将美国的崛起归因于其独特的地理位置和资源禀赋。你认为哪种观点更有说服力？请予论述。

地　理

答卷时间：120 分钟

一、填空题（填对一空格得1分，全题共20分）

1. 亚、非两洲以______运河为界；南、北美洲以______运河为界。

2. 根据气候类型的分布规律，一般在南北纬30°～40°的大陆西岸为______气候，在南北纬40°～60°的大陆西岸为______气候。

3. 亚洲和非洲都不具有的气候类型是______气候，而这种气候类型在______洲最为典型。

4. 欧洲运输最繁忙的河流是______河，它的出海口有世界重要港口______。

5. 美国最大的城市和商港是______，最大的汽车制造工业中心是______，中部最大的城市、机械钢铁工业中心是______，最大的华侨聚居地是______。

6. 从气候的干湿状况看，中国的秦岭—淮河一线是______地区与______地区的分界线。

7. 我国的外流河受地势______的制约，以向东流入______洋为主。

8. 我国第二阶梯海拔在1000米到2000米之间，其主要地形是______和______。

9. 地震按其成因可分两类：一是______地震，二是______地震。

二、单项选择题（下列各小题均有四个答案，其中只有一个是正确的，请把正确答案的序号填在答题纸上，选对一题得3分，全题60分）

1. 中国旱涝灾害形成的最重要原因是（　）

A. 雨热同期

B. 各地气温状况不同

C. 降水量地区分布不均

D. 降水量季节分配不均，年际变化大

2. 中国夏季气温最低的是（　）

A. 青藏高原　　B. 大兴安岭山区

C. 吐鲁番盆地　　D. 内蒙古高原

3. 中国划分温度带的根据是（　）

A. 纬度的高低　　B. 无霜期的长短

C. ≥10℃的积温的多少　　D. 一月平均气温的多少

4. 黄河的泥沙主要是来自（　）

A. 上游河段　　B. 中游河段

C. 下游河段　　D. 中、下游河段

5. 在南半球，运动着的物体在地球自转偏向力的作用下（　）

A. 向左偏转　　B. 向右偏转　　C. 向前偏转　　D. 向后偏转

6. 在同一纬度地区，形成海洋性和大陆性气候差异的主要原因是（　）

A. 大气环流　　B. 海陆热容量

C. 地面受热不均　　D. 季风环流的影响

7. 甲地的地理坐标是40°N，120°E；乙地的地理坐标是10°S，150°W。甲地在乙地的（　）

A. 西北方向　　B. 东南方向　　C. 东北方向　　D. 西南方向

8. 从赤道向两极走，纬线长度（　）

A. 越来越长　　B. 没有变化

C. 长短没规律　　D. 越来越短

9. 地球上昼夜长短变化最小的地方是（　）

A. 北回归线　　B. 两极　　C. 赤道　　D. 南回归线

10. 地图上的比例尺表示（　）

A. 地图的面积大小　　B. 地图的宽度

C. 地图上距离缩小的程度　　D. 地图的高度

11. 本初子午线是（　）

A. 东经度和西经度的起始线　　B. 东半球和西半球的分界线

C. 最短的纬线　　D. 最长的纬线

12. 在同一时区内，各地的（　）

A. 地方时都相同　　B. 没有两地的地方时是相同的

C. 区时都相同　　D. 区时都不同

13. 6月下旬，甲、乙、丙、丁四地白昼长度分别是11小时、14小时、17小时和21小时，它们中谁在南半球（　）

A. 甲　　B. 乙　　C. 丙　　D. 丁

14. 形成“V”谷的主要原因是（　）

A. 下蚀　　B. 溯源侵蚀　　C. 冰蚀　　D. 侧蚀

15. 美国“硅谷”的主导产业是（　）

A. 微电子工业　　B. 汽车工业

C. 造船工业　　D. 化学工业

16. 世界上水稻种植业集中在（　）

A. 温带湿润地区　　B. 热带和亚热带季风区

C. 中纬度大陆西岸　　D. 主要的发达国家

17. 由内力作用引发的地质灾害是（　）

A. 塌方　　B. 地震　　C. 泥石流　　D. 滑坡

18. 三种水循环中都包括的环节是（　）

A. 下渗和蒸腾　　B. 地表径流
C. 蒸发和降水　　D. 地下径流

19. 中国下列地区中水资源最紧张的是（　）
A. 广州　　B. 大连　　C. 新疆　　D. 重庆

20. 自然带呈明显带状分布，且南北对称的是（　）
A. 亚欧大陆　　B. 澳大利亚　　C. 非洲大陆　　D. 北美大陆

三、判断改正题（答案用符号填在答题纸上，正确符号为√，不正确符号为×；需改正的，请在保留有下划线的词或句子的基础上写出正确句子。每小题2分，共10分）

1. 加利福尼亚州是美国离亚洲最近的一个州。（　）
正确的句子：

2. 世界上流量最大、流域面积最广的河流是亚马孙河。（　）
正确的句子：

3. 对中国季风区影响最显著的季风是西南季风。（　）
正确的句子：

4. 我国内流河的主要水源是雨水。（　）
正确的句子：

5. 我国东部地区的雨季，由北向南出现的时间愈来愈晚。（　）
正确的句子：

四、读图填空或连线题（每填对一空或画对一条线得2分，全题40分）

1. 读中国主要山脉的分布图，填出标有数字符号的山脉名称：

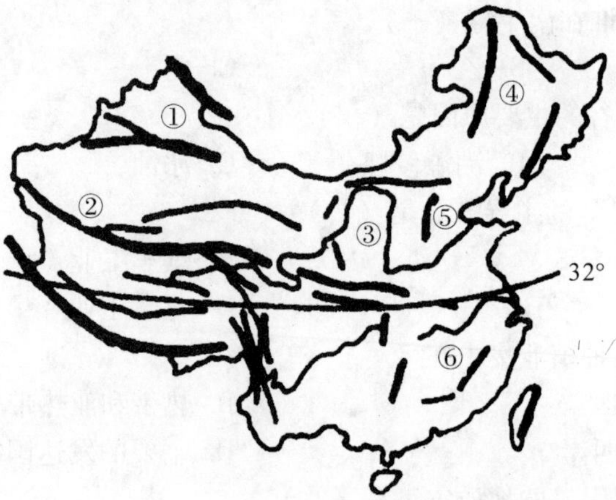

①＿＿＿＿＿＿＿＿，②＿＿＿＿＿＿＿＿，③＿＿＿＿＿＿＿＿，

④________，⑤________，⑥________。

2. 把欧洲河流、湖泊的特征与形成条件连接起来：

①河湖水量充沛，河网密布　　　　A. 受冰川作用

②无长河　　　　B. 降水多、平原多

③斯堪的纳维亚半岛和阿尔卑斯山两侧多湖泊　　　　C. 有运河连接

④形成方便的内河运输网　　　　D. 大陆轮廓曲折且受山岭限制河流

3. 读“某地近地面大气垂直方向25℃等值线分布图”，做下列填空：

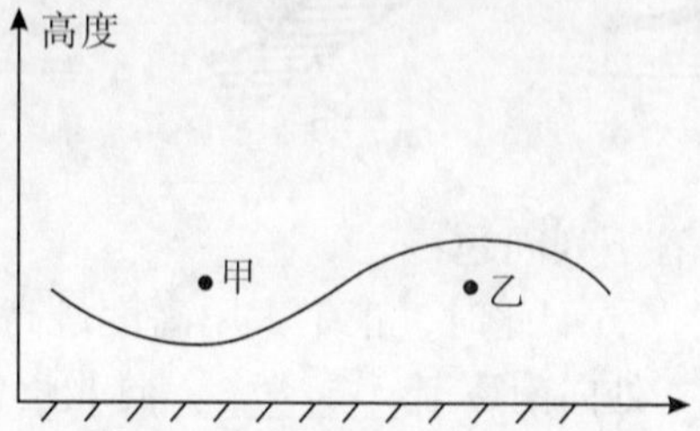

甲地气温________25℃，乙地气温________25℃；________地气流下沉，________地气流上升。

4. 读下列某地等高线地形图并作下列填空：

图中________处是山脊，________处是陡崖，________处是鞍部，________处是山峰；甲、乙两点的相对高度是________，图中两个村庄的直线距离是________公里（取小数点后一位数）。

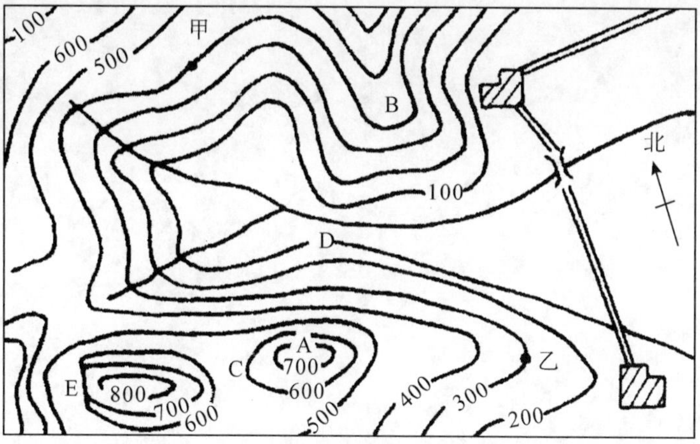

1∶50000

五、读图分析题（每小题10分，全题20分）

1. 读下面三种典型的地形图片，并回答下列问题：

1）A地形的名称是______，它主要形成于______，其基本成因是______。

2）B 地形的名称是______，它主要出现在______。

3）C 景观的名称是______，它形成于______，是因______作用而形成的。

A

B

C

2. 读下面示意图并回答下列问题：

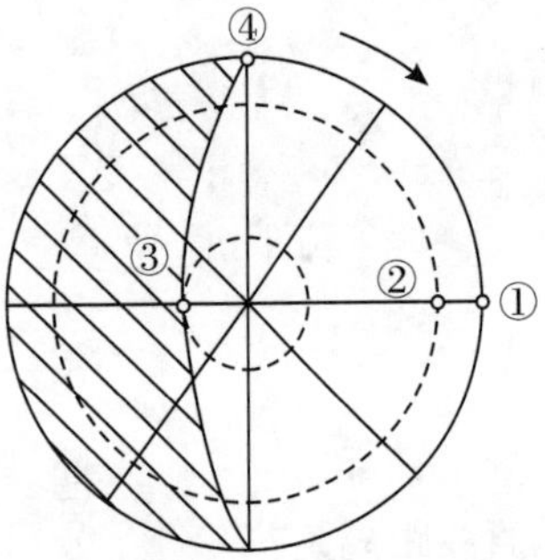

此时，正午太阳高度最高点在________处，并于此处向南逐渐________，向北逐渐________。③点的正午太阳高度角为________度，昼长________小时。

物　理

答卷时间：120分钟

一、选择题（60分）

以下各小题中只有一个答案是正确的，把你认为正确的答案分别填入答题卡对应的表格中．每小题选对的给4分，多选、错选或不选的不给分．

1. 一个物体在五个共点力的作用下保持静止状态，则错误的说法是（　）

A. 这五个力的合力（total force）为零

B. 其中任何一个力必和其他四个力的合力的大小相等，方向相反

C. 若撤除其中的一个力，物体仍可保持静止状态

D. 若撤除其中的一个力，物体将沿此力方向的反方向做加速运动

2. 可以断定物体做匀变速直线运动（rectilinear motion with a constant acceleration）的是（　）

A. 物体在某两段相等的时间内速度的变化相等

B. 物体在某两段相等的时间内速度的变化不相等

C. 物体在任意两段相等的时间内速度的变化相等

D. 物体在任意两段相等的时间内速度的变化不相等

3. 若单摆（simple pendulum）的摆长不变，摆球的质量增加为原来的4倍，摆球经过平衡位置时的速度减小为原来的1/2，则单摆振动的（　）

A. 频率（frequency）不变，振幅（amplitude）不变

B. 频率不变，振幅改变

C. 频率改变，振幅改变

D. 频率改变，振幅不变

4. 下列关于物体的惯性（inertia）的说法，错误的是（　）

A. 任何具有质量的物体都有惯性，惯性是物体的固有属性

B. 外力能改变物体的运动状态，因此外力能改变物体的惯性

C. 一汽车装载的货物越多，它的惯性就越大

D. 物体的运动状态越难改变，它的惯性就越大

5. 在透镜左侧有一光源 AB，在透镜右侧的光屏 S 上得到光源清晰的像．现移去光屏，从光源 A 点发出的光线 AP（如图1所示），经过透镜后的折射光线（　）

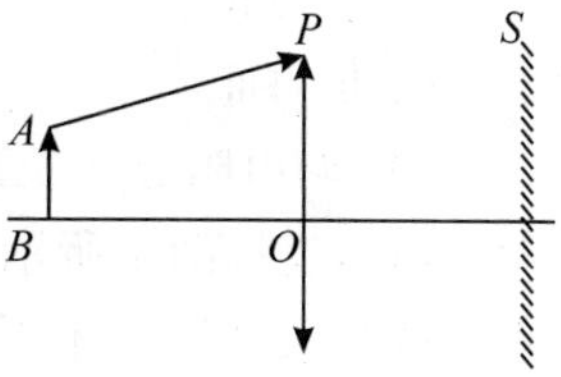

图1

A. 与主轴交于透镜与原光屏 S 之间

B. 与主轴交于原光屏 S 的右侧

C. 平行于主轴

D. 其反向延长线与主轴交于透镜左侧

6. 关于折射率（refractive index），下列说法正确的是（　）

A. 根据 $n=\frac{\sin i}{\sin r}$可知，介质的折射率与入射角的正弦成正比

B. 根据 $n=\frac{\sin i}{\sin r}$可知，介质的折射率可能为任何正数

C. 根据 $n=\frac{v}{c}$可知，介质的折射率与介质中的光速成反正

D. 以上说法都不对

7. 点光源照射一个障碍物，在屏上所成的阴影的边缘部分模糊不清，产生的原因是（　）

A. 光的反射（reflection）　　B. 光的折射（refraction）

C. 光的干涉（interference）　　D. 光的衍射（diffraction）

8. 绝对零度是（　）

A. 0℃　　B. 100℃　　C. 273℃　　D. －273℃

9. 氢原子周围的电子能级如图 2 所示，该电子的基态能量是 －13. 6eV. 若氢原子发射一个光子，该光子的能量不可能是（　）

A. 1. 9eV

B. 13. 6eV

C. 0. 65eV

D. 11. 1eV

图 2

10. 钍的同位素（isotope）$^{234}_{90}$Th 可以通过反应 $^{234}_{90}\text{Th} \longrightarrow {}^{A}_{Z}\text{X} + {}^{4}_{2}\text{He}$ 进行 α 衰变，其中元素 X 是（　）

A. $^{238}_{92}$U　　B. $^{230}_{88}$Ra　　C. $^{236}_{94}$Pu　　D. $^{238}_{88}$Ra

11. 两电荷 q_1、q_2 相距 r，其相互作用力为 F. 若两个电荷的电量分别增加一倍，同时距离缩短为原来的一半，那么它们之间的作用力为（　）

A. 0. 25F　　B. 4F　　C. 8F　　D. 16F

12. 两块带电极板平行放置，如图 3 所示．下面将这些粒子依次放入极板中间，分别是：Ⅰ. 电子，Ⅱ. 质子，Ⅲ. 中子．它们从静止开始运动，会向右运动的粒子是（　）

A. Ⅰ和Ⅱ　　B. Ⅰ和Ⅲ

C. Ⅱ和Ⅲ　　D. Ⅱ

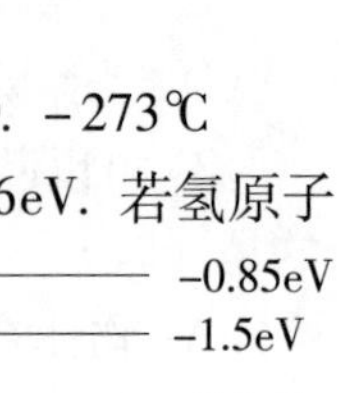

图 3

13. 两电阻 $R_1=3\Omega$ 和 $R_2=6\Omega$ 与 6V 的电源并联．三个电流表和两个电压表按图 4 所示的方式接入电路（假设电压表和电流表都是理想的）. 下列说法正确的是（　）

A. V_1 和 V_2 读数相同

B. V_1、A_2 的读数分别为 6V、1A

C. A_1、A_3 的读数分别为 2A、1A

D. A_2、A_3 的读数分别为 2A、1A

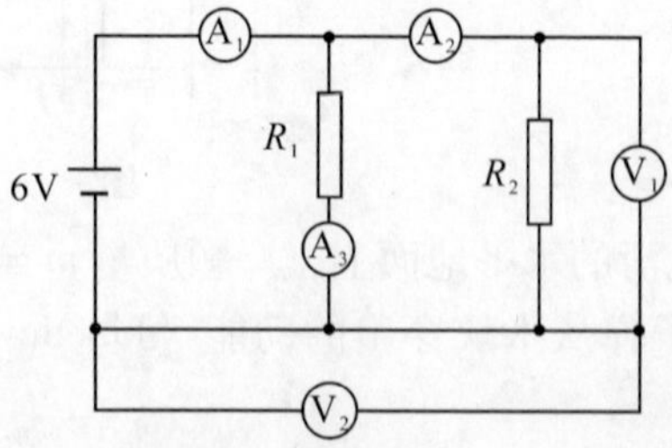

图 4

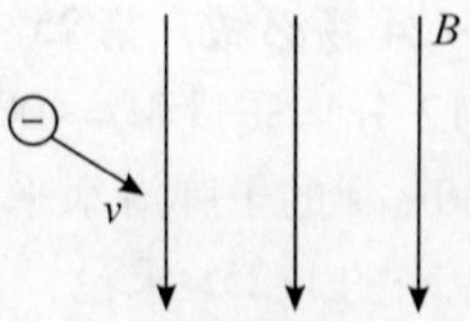

图 5

14. 一个电子进入磁场（magnetic field），如图 5 所示．该电子进入磁场之初的受力方向为（　）

A. 垂直纸面向里　　B. 垂直纸面向外

C. 向上　　D. 向下

15. 有一台理想变压器的原、副线圈（the primary，secondary coil）的匝数比为 4∶1，若原线圈上加 $u = 100\sqrt{2}\sin 100\pi t$（V）的交变电压，则在副线圈两端用交流电表测得的电压是（　）

A. 25V　　B. 35.25V　　C. 400V　　D. 564V

二、填空题（30 分）

在以下各小题横线上填入（写在答题纸上）你认为正确的答案（每空 3 分）．

16. 一个做匀速圆周运动的物体，如果轨道半径不变，转速变为原来的 3 倍，所需的向心力（centripetal force）就比原来的向心力大 40N，物体原来的向心力大小为______ N.

17. 每秒做 100 次全振动（complete cycles of the motion）的波源产生的波，以 10m/s 的速度传播，其频率为______ Hz，波长（wave length）为______ m.

18. 如图 6 所示，物体 M 受到两个水平推力：$F_1 = 20$N，$F_2 = 5$N，向右匀速运动，则摩擦力的大小是______ N，方向为______．若不改变 F_1 的大小和方向及 F_2 的方向，要使物体能向左匀速运动，F_2 应增大到原来的______倍.

图 6

19. 一个平行光源从地面竖直向上将光线投射到一块和光线垂直的平面镜上，平面镜离地面 3m 高，如果将平面镜绕水平轴转过 30°，则水平地面上的光斑离光源______ m.

20. 钴 $^{60}_{27}Co$ 的半衰期（half-life）为 5 年．现有 1kg 的钴样品，20 年后，该样品还

剩______ kg.

21. 一直导线上通有电流 I = 2A，放置在磁感应强度为 0.1T 的磁场中，如图 7 所示．导线长度为 0.3m，横截面半径为 0.5mm. 该导线在磁场中受力为______ N，方向为______.

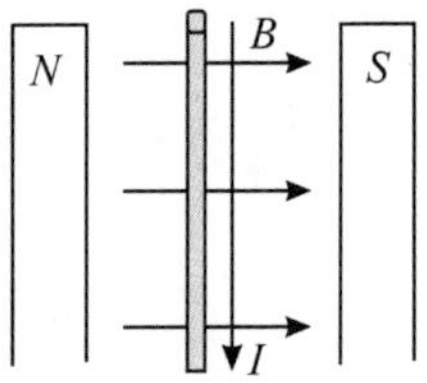

图 7

三、计算题（60 分）

第 22 ~24 题必做，第 25 ~28 题选做两题.

22. （12 分）质量 $M = 400$g 的木块静止在光滑的水平地面上，一颗质量 $m = 20$g，速度 $v = 500$m/s 的子弹沿水平方向射入木块，子弹从木块穿出的动能（kinetic energy）减为原来的 1/25. 求：

（1）子弹穿透木块的过程中，子弹克服阻力做的功；

（2）子弹穿透木块的过程中，子弹和木块组成的系统损失的机械能（mechanical energy）.

23. （12 分）两根光滑的长直金属导轨 MN、$M'N'$ 平行置于同一水平面内，导轨间距为 l，电阻不计，M、M' 处接有如图 8 所示的电路，电路中各电阻的阻值均为 R，电容器（capacitor）的电容（capacitance）为 C. 长度也为 l、阻值同为 R 的金属棒 ab 垂直于导轨放置，导轨处于磁感应强度为 B、方向竖直向上的匀强磁场中．ab 在外力作用上向右匀速运动且与导轨保持良好接触，在 ab 运动距离为 s 的过程中，整个回路中产生的焦耳热为 Q. 求：

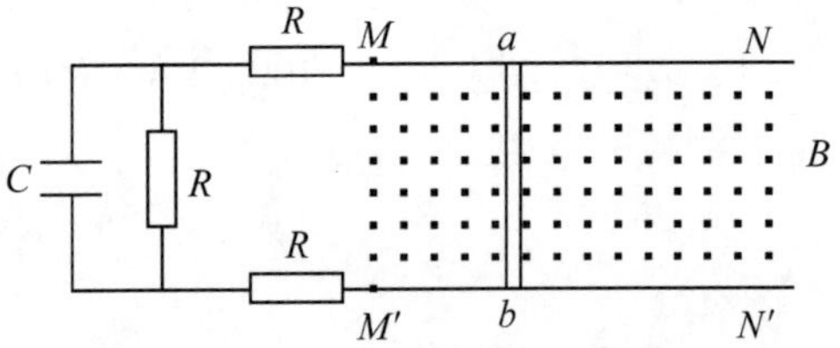

图 8

（1）ab 运动速度 v 的大小；

（2）电容器所带的电荷量 q；

（3）请判断电容器的上极板所带电荷的极性.

24. （12 分）如图 9 所示，一定质量的理想气体（ideal gas）被活塞封闭在可导热的气缸内，活塞相对于底部的高度为 h，可沿气缸无摩擦地滑动．取一小盒沙子缓慢地倒在活塞的上表面上．沙子倒完时，活塞下降了 $h/4$. 再取相同质量的一小盒沙子缓慢地倒在活塞的上表面上．若外界大气的压强和温度始终保持不变，求此次沙子倒完时活塞距气缸底部的高度．

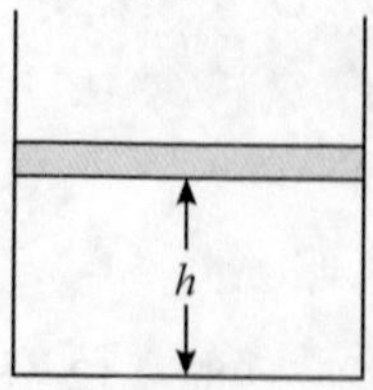

图 9

以下第 25 ~ 28 题选做两题．

25. （12 分）一个 T 形电路如图 10 所示，电路中的电阻，$R_1 = 10\Omega$，$R_2 = 12\Omega$，$R_3 = 40\Omega$. 另有一测试电源，电动势（electromotive force）为 100V，内阻忽略不计．

（1）当 ab 两端接测试电源时，cd 两端的电压是多少？

（2）当 cd 两端接测试电源，且 ab 两端短路时，电流表 A 的读数为多少？

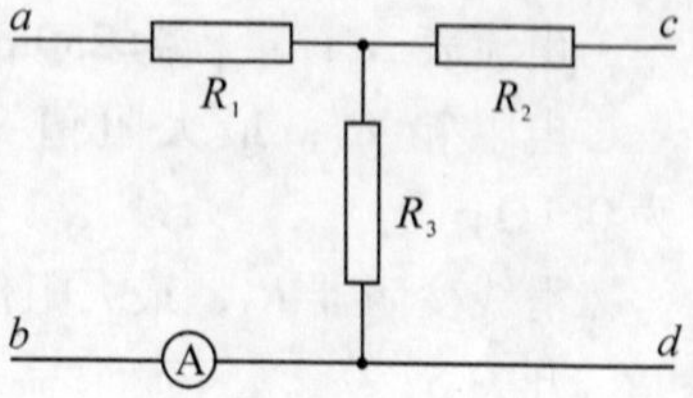

图 10

26. （12 分）某溶液的折射率 $n = \dfrac{5}{3}$，当在液面下 $h = 2\text{m}$ 深处放一强点光源时，看到透光液面的最大直径是多大？当此透光液面的直径变大时，光源正在上浮还是正在下沉？

27. （12 分）一列火车总质量 $M = 500\text{t}$，机车发动机的额定功率（rated power）$P = 6 \times 10^5\text{W}$. 在轨道上行驶时，轨道对列车的阻力 F_f 是车重力的 0.01 倍．求：

（1）火车在水平轨道上行驶的最大速度；

（2）在水平轨道上，发动机以额定功率 P 工作，当行驶速度 $v_1 = 1\text{m/s}$ 和 $v_2 = 10\text{m/s}$ 时，列车的瞬时加速度 a_1、a_2 各是多少？

（3）在水平轨道上以 36km/h 速度匀速行驶时，发动机的实际功率 P'.

28. （12 分）实验室中现有器材：

电池 E，其电动势约 10V，内阻约 1Ω；

电流表 A_1，量程为 10A，内阻 r_1 约为 0.2Ω；

电流表 A_2，量程为 300mA，内阻 r_2 约为 5Ω；

电流表 A_3，量程为 250mA，内阻 r_3 约为 5Ω；

电阻箱 R_1，最大阻值 999.9Ω，阻值最小改变量为 0.1Ω；

滑线变阻器 R_2，最大阻值为 100Ω；

开关 S；

导线若干.

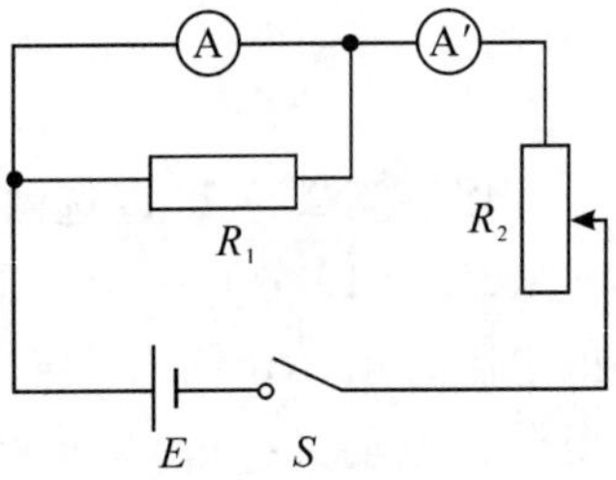

图 11

若要求用图 11 所示的电路测定图中电流表 A 的内阻，请回答以下问题：

（1）在所给的三个电流表中，哪几个可用此电路精确测出其内阻？________________________.

（2）测量电流表内阻需要读出的物理量有______个，分别是________________________.

（3）用这些物理量表示待测内阻的计算公式是________________________.

化 学

答卷时间：120 分钟

本卷用到的原子量

H：1　C：12　O：16　Cl：35.5　Na：23　N：14　S：32

Mg：24　Al：27　Ba：137　P：31　Cu：64　Zn：65.4

一、选择题（每小题只有一个正确答案，请将正确答案的代号填入答题纸，每小题 3 分，共 60 分）

1. 下列说法正确的是（　）

A. 牛奶是化合物

B. 所有室温下是气态的元素都是非金属

C. 铁生锈是物理变化

D. 氧气的最小粒子是原子

2. 原子内的质子数目等于（　）

A. 电子数目　B. 中子数目

C. 中子数目 + 电子数目　D. 中子数目 - 电子数目

3. 下列需贮存在石蜡油中的金属是（　）

A. 铜　B. 钠　C. 锌　D. 铝

4. 下列各组溶液混合，不产生沉淀的是（　）

A. $MgCl_2$ 和 $NaOH$　B. Na_2CO_3 和 $CaCl_2$

C. K_2SO_4 和 $NaCl$　D. $AgNO_3$ 和 KCl

5. 下列反应中属于氧化反应的是（　）

A. $CaCO_3 + 2HCl \longrightarrow CaCl_2 + CO_2 + H_2O$

B. $CaO + H_2O \longrightarrow Ca(OH)_2$

C. $2KMnO_4 \longrightarrow K_2MnO_4 + MnO_2 + O_2$

D. $CaCO_3 \longrightarrow CaO + CO_2$

6. 当熔融 KI 被电解时，阳极上的生成物是（　）

A. 碘　B. 钾　C. 氢气　D. 氧气

7. 压强变化不会使下列化学反应的平衡发生移动的是（　）

A. $H_2(g) + I_2(g) \rightleftharpoons 2HI(g)$

B. $3H_2(g) + N_2(g) \rightleftharpoons 2NH_3(g)$

C. $2SO_2(g) + O_2(g) \rightleftharpoons 2SO_3(g)$

D. $C(s)+CO_2(g) \rightleftharpoons 2CO(g)$

8. 准确量取25.00mL高锰酸钾溶液，可选用的仪器是（　）

A. 50mL 量筒　　B. 50mL 烧杯

C. 50mL 滴定管　　D. 250mL 容量瓶

9. 下列粒子不存在于HCl水溶液中的是（　）

A. H^+　　B. OH^-　　C. Cl^-　　D. HCl

10. 下列关于单质氯的说法不正确的是（　）

A. 常温常压下是黄绿色气体

B. 双原子分子

C. 沸点高于单质氟

D. 周期表中最活泼的非金属元素

11. 下列结论不正确的是（　）

A. 稳定性：$H_2O(g)>H_2S(g)$　　B. 酸性：$H_2SO_4>HClO_4$

C. 氧化性：$Cl_2>S$　　D. 半径：$S^{2-}>S$

12. 下列关于NO_2的叙述，不正确的是（　）

A. 可以用来制取HNO_3　　B. 大气污染物之一

C. 能与人体血红蛋白作用　　D. 溶于水

13. 以下化合物不是有机物的是（　）

A. $CoBr_2$　　B. CCl_4

C. CH_3COONa　　D. CH_3CH_2OH

14. 下列关于化合物的说法正确的是（　）

a. $CH_3CH_2OCH_2CH_3$　　b. $(CH_3)_2C=CH_2$　　c. 

d. CH_3CH_2OH　　e. CH_2Cl_2　　f. $CH_3C\equiv CCH_3$　　g. $CH_3\overset{O}{\overset{\|}{C}}CH_3$

A. a和b是烃　　B. a、b和d是烃

C. a、b、d和e是烃　　D. b、c和f是烃

15. 以下结构属同分异构的是（　）

A. $CH_3CH_2CH_2CH_2CH_3$　　$CH_3CH_2CH_2$（CH_2上连CH_2CH_3）

B. $CH_3CH_2CHCH_2CH_3$（CH上连CH_3）　　$(CH_3)_2CHCH_2CH_2CH_3$

C. $CH_3CH_2CHCH_3$（CH上连CH_2CH_3）　　$CH_3CH_2CHCH_2CH_3$（CH上连CH_3）

D. $CH_3CH_2CH_2CH_2CH_3$　　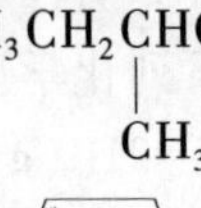

16. 以下属聚酯的是（ ）

A. $\left[CH_2CH_2O\right]_n$

B. $\left[CH_2CH\right]_n$（CH 上连 $COO(CH_2)_3CH_3$）

$\quad\quad\quad\quad |$

$\quad\quad COO(CH_2)_3CH_3$

C. $\left[O(CH_2)_4OOC(CH_2)_4CO\right]_n$

D. 以上皆不对

17. 以下不可能存在的结构是（ ）

A. $CH_3CH_2CHCH_2CH_3$

$\quad\quad\quad |$

$\quad\quad\quad CH_3$

B. $CH_3CHCH_2CBrCH_3$

$\quad\quad |\quad\quad\quad |$

$\quad\quad CH_3\quad CH_3$

$\quad CH_3$

$\quad |$

C. $CH_3CHCH_2CH_2CH_3$

$\quad |$

$\quad Br$

D. $CH_3CH_2CHCH_2CH_3$

$\quad\quad\quad |$

$\quad\quad\quad CH_2CH_3$

18. 右图所示的操作是（ ）

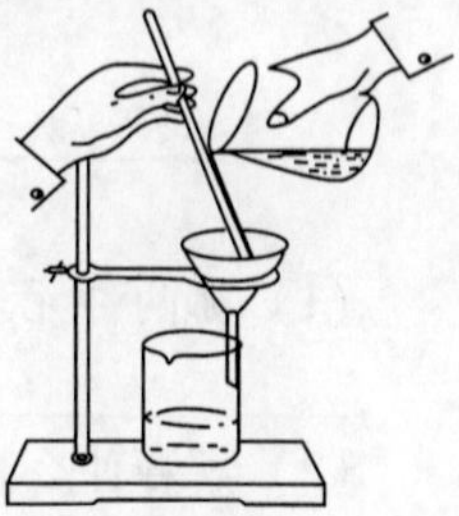

A. 蒸馏

B. 萃取

C. 过滤

D. 滴定

19. 在实验室里吃东西（ ）

A. 不允许

B. 午餐时间可以

C. 如果你够小心就行

D. 如果很饿就可以

20. 如果水银洒落到实验台上（ ）

A. 马上捡起来

B. 告诉你的指导老师

C. 推到台下没有人看得到的地方

D. 扫进垃圾桶

二、填空题（共 22 分）

1.（4 分）一块锌片和一片铜片放在硫酸铜溶液中构成一个简单电池，负电极是________，半反应式为________；正电极是________，半反应式为________。

2.（4 分）K、Na、Li 三种金属的活性序是（由大到小排列）________，Na、Mg、Al 三种金属的活性序是（由大到小排列）________。这说明周期表中的金属活泼性沿族由上而下是________（填“增大”或“减小”），同一周期由左至右是________（填“增大”或“减小”）。

3.（5 分）所有水溶液都含有氢离子和氢氧离子，化学家利用________来量度溶液里的氢离子浓度，其范围是________，当________时溶液呈酸性，当________时溶液呈碱性，当________时溶液呈中性。

4.（4 分）葡萄糖的结构简式是：

$HOCH_2CHOHCHOHCHOHCHOHCHO$

葡萄糖含有 5 个________基和 1 个________基，葡萄糖既是________也是________。

5.（5分）化合物 A（$C_6H_{12}O_2$）在酸性水溶液中受热得到化合物 B（$C_4H_8O_2$）和化合物 C（C_2H_6O），化合物 B 显酸性，推导化合物 A、B 及 C 可能的结构。

A：____；

B：____；

C：____。

三、问答题（共 38 分）

1.（本题 10 分）利用下表的资料回答问题。

元素	原子序数	相对原子质量
X	6	12
Y	17	35.5
Z	20	40

（1）哪两种元素可以形成共价化合物？预测该化合物的化学式。

____。

（2）解释什么是共价键？

____。

（3）给出 Y 元素的电子排布。

____。

（4）为什么 Y 的相对原子质量不是一个整数？

____。

（5）哪两种元素可以形成离子化合物？预测该化合物的化学式。

____。

2.（本题 12 分）某学生设计如下图所示的实验装置以除去 N_2 中的 H_2O、O_2、CO_2、H_2S，制得干燥的 N_2。所有试剂有 NaOH 溶液、浓 H_2SO_4、灼热的铜网、酸性溴水溶液（主要成分为 Br_2）。

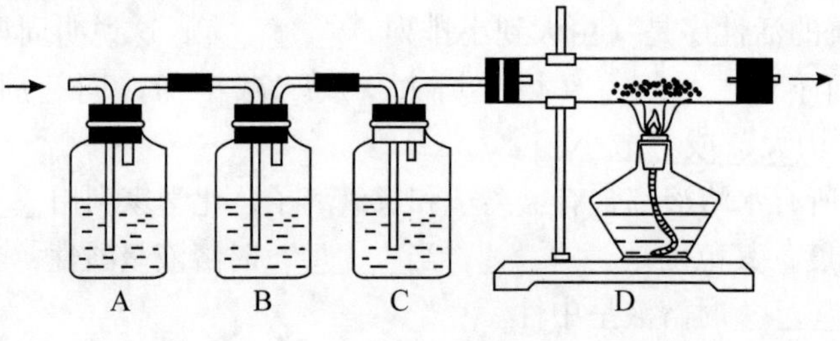

（1）指出 A 中应加入的试剂及所要除去的杂质。

____。

（2）指出 B 中应加入的试剂及要除去的杂质。

____。

（3）指出 C 中应加入的试剂及要除去的杂质。

____。

（4）指出 D 中应加入的试剂及要除去的杂质。

____。

（5）B 中所用试剂有多种选择，请再举一例。

____。

（6）写出问题（5）的相应化学方程式。

____。

3.（本题 6 分）2mol 镁与 1mol 氧气发生反应，放出 1200kJ 的热量。

（1）写出反应的热化学方程式。

____。

（2）能否用水来扑灭镁火？为什么？

____。

（3）1.2g 镁在充足的氧气中燃烧，放出的热量是多少？

____。

4.（本题 10 分）

（1）乙醇在碱性高锰酸钾溶液中转化为醋酸并形成 MnO_2 沉淀，写出这一反应的方程式。

____。

（2）2－丙醇在酸性重铬酸盐溶液中转化为丙酮，同时形成 Cr^{3+}，写出这一反应的离子方程式。

____。

（3）在这些反应中醇是被氧化还是被还原？

____。

（4）指出碱性高锰酸盐溶液中 1－丙醇反应的产物。

____。

（5）指出酸性重铬酸盐溶液中 2－丁醇反应的产物。

____。

四、计算题（从以下 3 题中任选 2 题，每题 15 分，共 30 分）

1. 一名学生有 $6mol \cdot L^{-1}$的硫酸溶液，若配置 800mL 的 $0.3mol \cdot L^{-1}$的硫酸。

（1）需要多少体积的浓酸？

（2）以 $0.3mol \cdot L^{-1}$的硫酸中和 12mL 的 $0.2mol \cdot L^{-1}$的氢氧化钠溶液，计算所需硫酸的体积。

（3）10mL 的 $0.3mol \cdot L^{-1}$的硫酸与 10mL 的 $0.2mol \cdot L^{-1}$的氢氧化钠溶液混合，

试计算混合液的 pH 值。

2. 工业上用接触法制硫酸，其流程为 $S \longrightarrow SO_2 \longrightarrow SO_3 \longrightarrow H_2SO_4$。

（1）假设所有的硫全转化为硫酸，制造 10mol 的硫酸需用多少摩尔的硫。

（2）24g 硫在空气中燃烧，计算产生的二氧化硫的体积（室温及常压）。

（3）在步骤 $SO_2 \longrightarrow SO_3$ 中，已知一定条件下 2mol SO_2 与 1mol O_2 在密闭容器中发生反应，达到平衡时，相同温度下测得混合气体的压强是反应前的 5/6，计算 SO_2 的转化率。

3. 1.0g Zn - Al 合金片与过量的稀盐酸作用放出氢气，收集到的氢气是 0.025mol。

（1）求氢气的体积（标况下）。

（2）求 Zn 的质量百分含量。

（3）求 Al 的质量百分含量。

生 物

答卷时间：120 分钟

一、选择题（每小题 2 分，共 60 分，每小题只有一个正确答案）

1. 下列选项中，分子与其功能正确匹配的是（ ）

A. 脂类——贮存遗传信息　　B. 维生素——为细胞提供能量

C. 酶——加快化学反应的速度　　D. DNA——为核糖体转运氨基酸

2. 科学家如在其他星球探寻可能存在的生命，他们会重点关注含有下列哪一种元素的分子（ ）

A. 碳　　B. 铁　　C. 钾　　D. 钠

3. 许多植物将能量贮存在淀粉中。当需要能量时，这些淀粉分子会很快被分解。这一化学反应产生的化合物是（ ）

A. 氨基酸　　B. 脂类　　C. 单糖　　D. RNA

4. 下列选项中，属于细胞壁主要功能的是（ ）

A. 贮存碳水化合物　　B. 保持细胞的形状

C. 蛋白质包装　　D. 进行光合作用

5. 下列哪一个是组成 DNA 分子的重复单位（ ）

A. 脂肪酸　　B. 核苷酸　　C. 氨基酸　　D. 染色体

6. 下列哪种生物不能独自合成自己的蛋白质，而需要一个寄主细胞（ ）

A. 蓝藻　　B. 细菌　　C. 原生动物　　D. 病毒

7. 许多植物的表面均具有一些蜡质的覆盖物。这些覆盖物是不透水的，因此可以减少水分损失。这些蜡质的覆盖物属于下列有机分子中的（ ）

A. 碳水化合物　　B. 脂类　　C. 核酸　　D. 蛋白质

8. 人体中的大多数碳水化合物（ ）

A. 用来作为构成蛋白质的原料

B. 用来作为细胞中化学反应的催化剂

C. 作为能量来源被消耗

D. 不容易被吸收到血液中

9. 下列物质中，通过渗透作用穿过细胞膜的是（ ）

A. 盐分　　B. 糖　　C. 水　　D. 蛋白质

10. 在有氧呼吸过程中，三羧酸循环发生在（ ）

A. 叶绿体　　B. 细胞核　　C. 中心体　　D. 线粒体

11. 下列生物属于真菌的是（ ）

A. 葡萄球菌　B. 酵母菌　C. 链球菌　D. 放线菌

12. 下列属于自养生物的是（　）

A. 硝化细菌　B. 大肠杆菌　C. 酵母菌　D. 草履虫

13. 下列叙述中，细胞结构与其功能匹配正确的是（　）

A. 细胞膜包装脂类　B. 线粒体进行光合作用

C. 高尔基体包装蛋白质　D. 细胞核产生能量

14. 处于有丝分裂后期的某细胞有 36 条染色体，那么此物种的染色体数目为（　）

A. 72　B. 36　C. 18　D. 9

15. 在减数分裂过程中交换发生在哪个分裂相（　）

A. 中期Ⅰ　B. 中期Ⅱ　C. 前期Ⅰ　D. 前期Ⅱ

16. 某生物的 DNA 中鸟嘌呤占碱基的比例为 30%，那么，腺嘌呤占碱基的比例是（　）

A. 0%　B. 10%　C. 20%　D. 30%

17. 下述适用于 tRNA 的是（　）

A. 将 mRNA 从细胞核运输至核糖体　B. 离开核糖体后降解成核苷酸

C. 由单链 RNA 组成　D. 是转录所必需的

18. DNA 和 RNA 都（　）

A. 是单链的　B. 含有相同的四种碱基

C. 含有相同的五碳糖　D. 含有磷酸基团

19. 一位研究者用两只黑毛老鼠进行杂交。黑毛基因对白毛基因为显性。杂交后代 75% 为黑毛，25% 为白毛。由此可以确定亲代的基因型最有可能为（　）

A. BB × BB　B. BB × Bb　C. BB × bb　D. Bb × Bb

20. 用蓝花和白花植物进行杂交。如果显性不完全，F_1 自交后代即 F_2 中将出现的表型比是（　）

A. 1∶0（只有一种表型）　B. 1∶1

C. 3∶1　D. 1∶2∶1

21. Kleinfelter 综合征患者含有 47 条染色体，其中有 3 条性染色体（XXY）。这种不正常的染色体数是由于减数分裂过程中发生错误而产生的。下列术语用来描述这种错误的是（　）

A. 交换　B. 不分离

C. 自由组合　D. 同源染色体配对

22. 科学家在海龟和鲨鱼的蛋白质中发现许多相同之处。这些相同之处表明海龟和鲨鱼（　）

A. 已经停止了进化　B. 有相同的祖先

C. 有完全相同的 DNA 序列　D. 含有相同的染色体数

23. 一个科学家克隆了一只山羊。下列各项正确地描述了该克隆羊的是（　）

A. 它有新的基因和性状　　B. 它缺少繁殖所需的基因
C. 它具有与亲代相同的基因　　D. 它的外表与亲代相同但基因不同

24. 海星个体在遗传上是各不相同的，与亲代也不同。这种遗传差异来自（　）
A. 有性生殖　　B. 无性生殖　　C. 有丝分裂　　D. 克隆

25. 从人体内排出代谢废物的生命过程称为（　）
A. 呼吸　　B. 排便　　C. 消毒　　D. 排泄

26. 人体内完成主要消化功能的器官是（　）
A. 小肠　　B. 肝脏　　C. 胃　　D. 大肠

27. 下列能被胃壁迅速吸收的化合物是（　）
A. 糖　　B. 酒精　　C. 脂肪　　D. 蛋白质

28. 研究表明吸烟会导致的疾病是（　）
A. 麻疹　　B. 百日咳　　C. 慢性肺气肿　　D. 肝炎

29. 下列消化器官中最长的是（　）
A. 食道　　B. 胃　　C. 小肠　　D. 大肠

30. 传染性疾病的原因是（　）
A. 有害的生活方式　　B. 污染物
C. 微生物　　D. 遗传

二、判断题（下列表述，正确的请写“T”，错误的请写“F”。每小题 2 分，共 20 分）

1. 叶绿体和内质网内都含有遗传物质。（　）
2. 大肠杆菌属于真核生物。（　）
3. 在大多数生物中遗传信息的传递方向是“蛋白质→DNA→RNA”。（　）
4. 两个隐性基因组合在一起（隐性纯合体）引起隐性性状的表达。（　）
5. 细胞壁的主要化学成分是纤维素和果胶质。（　）
6. 光合作用的暗反应发生在叶绿体类囊体膜中，光反应发生在叶绿体基质中。（　）
7. 在本质上，酶是生物催化剂。（　）
8. 20 种氨基酸中有 8 种是人体必需的。（　）
9. 群体是指不同种生物的集合体。（　）
10. 水不是人体的营养物。（　）

三、本大题共 8 小题，请将答案写在答题纸上（共 70 分）

1. （1）请标出下图中箭头所指染色体部位的名称。（3 分）

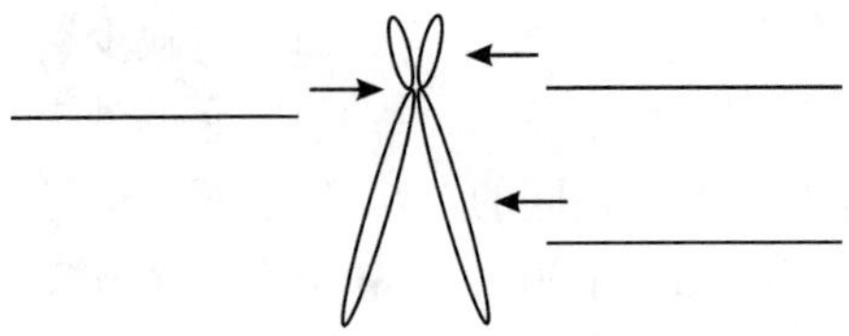

（2）圈出上图染色体中的一条姐妹染色单体。（1 分）

（3）三个 $2n=4$ 的细胞开始进行细胞分裂。一个进行有丝分裂，另外两个进行减数分裂。在下述分裂期中绘出你将看到的图像。（6 分）

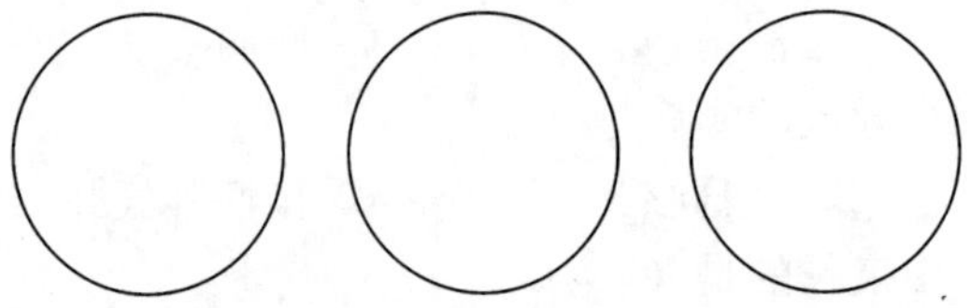

有丝分裂后期　减数分裂前期 Ⅰ　减数分裂中期 Ⅱ

2. 下表是一些 mRNA 密码子和其所编码的氨基酸。

mRNA 密码子表

密码子	GUG	CAC	CUC	ACU	CCU	GAG
氨基酸	缬氨酸	组氨酸	亮氨酸	苏氨酸	脯氨酸	谷氨酸

红细胞中的血红蛋白运输氧气。异常血红蛋白的氧气运输量少于正常血红蛋白。下述序列显示的是产生正常和异常血红蛋白的 DNA 序列片段。

	血红蛋白基因片段		
正常 DNA 序列	3'—GGA	CTC	CTC—5'
异常 DNA 序列	3'—GGA	CAC	CTC—5'

（1）写出以上述正常和异常 DNA 序列为模板转录产生的 mRNA 序列。（2 分）

（2）利用密码子表写出由上述正常和异常 DNA 序列产生的氨基酸序列。（2 分）

3. 两个用来杂交个体的基因型如下（基因对之间都是自由组合的）：

BbddEeGGHhNnrr × BbDdeeggHhNNRr

（1）杂交后代中可能有几种不同的基因型？(2 分)

（2）7 个性状全部都呈显性表型个体的概率是多少？(2 分)

（3）产生基因型为"bbDdEeGghhNnrr"个体的概率是多少？(2 分)

4. 某种鸟生活在一岛上。该鸟的种群中鸟喙的厚度是各不相同的。这种鸟主要以植物的种子为食。薄喙鸟只能吃小种子。只有厚喙鸟能够压碎和吃大种子。雨水较多的年份有许多小种子。干旱年份小种子非常少而大种子很多。大种子比小种子难压碎。下图显示了从 1979 年到 1985 年该种群的鸟喙的平均厚度。1980 年和 1982 年是干旱年份；1984 年是多雨的年份；1979、1981、1983 和 1985 年的雨量正常。

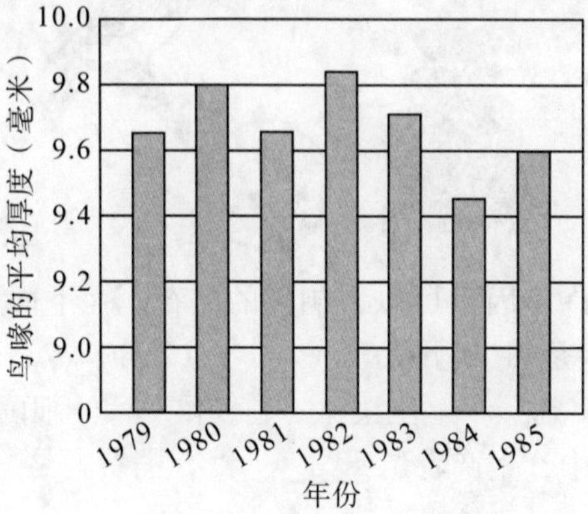

（1）解释鸟喙的平均厚度为什么在多雨水年份和干旱年份之间会发生变化。(2 分)

（2）如果随后的 10 年（1986 年到 1996 年）是多雨年份，请说明鸟喙的厚度将会如何变化。(2 分)

（3）命名导致这种变化产生的作用过程。(1 分)

5. 下表列出了人体中的一些消化酶。请写出它们的产生部位和所消化的化合物。

(10 分)

消化酶	产生的部位	所消化的化合物
唾液淀粉酶		
胃蛋白酶		
胰淀粉酶		
胰脂肪酶		
蔗糖酶		

6. 下图所示为某一生态系统中生物的关系。请根据此图回答下列问题。

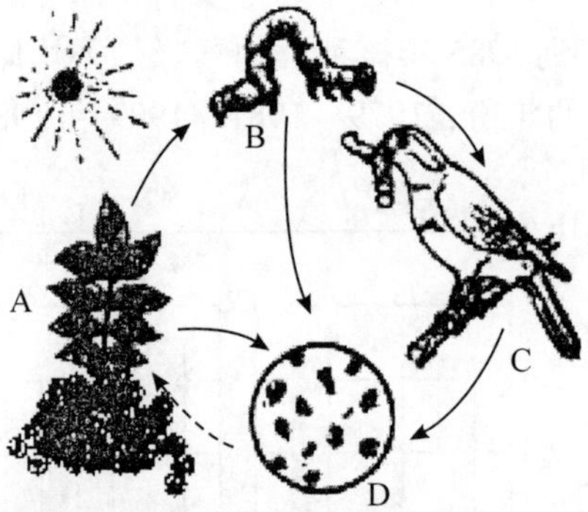

(1) 该生态系统有许多因子可以影响鸟的生存。在下面列出的因子中，哪些是生物因子?(　　) 哪些是非生物因子?(　　) (7 分)

昆虫　　水　　树　　土壤　　气候　　细菌　　阳光

(2) 在该生态系统中，生产者是__________，消费者是__________和__________。(3 分)

7. 右图所示为人体泌尿系统的结构示意图。请用给定的词标出所指部分的名称。给定的词为右肾、输尿管、膀胱、尿道、左肾。(5 分)

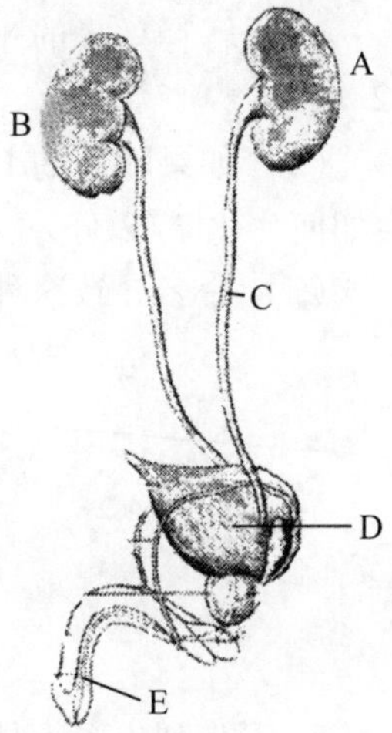

8. 下列为 20 个给定的专业术语和一细胞概念图。请将给定的专业术语填入图中的合适位置。注意每个给定的专业术语只能使用一次。(20 分)

20 个给定的专业术语为：

ATP	色素	白色体	细胞器	组蛋白
DNA	脂类	蛋白质	核基质	光合作用
RNA	核孔	核糖体	细胞核	细胞质基质
淀粉	质体	双层膜	有色体	粗面型内质网

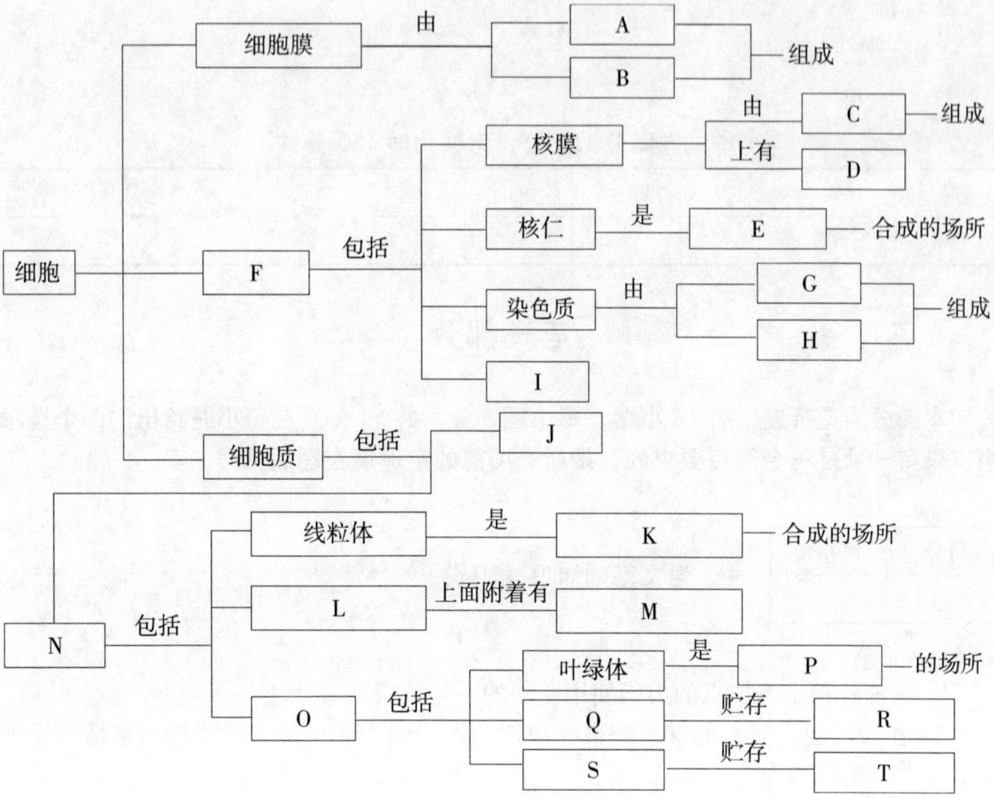

2009年中华人民共和国普通高等学校联合招收华侨、港澳地区、台湾省学生入学考试题目

语　文

本试卷满分150分，考试用时150分钟。

题号	一	二	三	四	五	六	总分
分数							

第一部分

本部分为选择题，有18小题，每小题3分，共54分。在每小题给出的四个选项中，只有一项是符合题目要求的，把所选项前的字母填在题后括号内。

得分	评卷人

一、语文基础知识（30分）

1. 下列各句中，加点的虚词使用正确的一句是（　）

A. 在人世间，只有能够掌握事物规律的人，因为不可能有对于任何事情的发展细节都未卜先知的人。

B. 如果各个经济区域之间、各个经济实体之间完全没有竞争，那么我们搞的就不是市场经济，而是计划经济了。

C. 大学生参加社会实践，关于社会会有更多的了解，关于人生也会有更深的体会，我们为什么要反对呢?

D. 医院要搞好医患关系，医生一方面要关心患者，要认真负责地为患者治病，另一方面患者也要主动配合治疗。

2. 依次填入下面横线处的词语，恰当的一组是（　）

①无论你评什么，怎样评，你都必须对所评论的事物有深入的了解和______的把握，这是起码的要求。

②这件事情历时长久，人物众多，盘根错节，个中______绝非三言两语能够同你

说得清楚的。

③春光明媚，草地碧绿，海棠嫣红，莺啼鸟啭，我们一个时辰就______在这花香鸟语之中了。

A. 准确　委屈　沉迷　　B. 正确　委屈　沉醉

C. 准确　委曲　沉醉　　D. 正确　委曲　沉迷

3. 下列句子中，加点的成语使用恰当的一句是（　）

A. 网络的开放性助长了剽窃者的胆量，一想到有那么多梁上君子在网上忙活着，我就感到害怕。

B. 国际金融危机尚未见底，一些地区时局充满变数，这令许多准备去国外的投资者和旅游者退避三舍。

C. 减轻小学生过重的负担，需要整个社会的关心，学校更要在教学工作中身体力行，把减负落到实处。

D. 他俩在中学同窗六载，像亲兄弟似的，一直相敬如宾，从来没有为琐事吵过嘴，更不用说打架了。

4. 下列各句中，没有语病的一句是（　）

A. 面对全球性的金融危机，我们对外投资，更要格外小心，以免少付出一些不必要的代价。

B. 不管事情难易，也不管分内分外，他总是知难而上，不推卸责任，出色地干好本职工作。

C. 要提高语文水平，除了上好课，做好作业，学生课外要多读书、多练笔是行之有效的办法。

D. 在新的一年，我们要面对复杂局面和严峻挑战，但是越是困难的时刻，越是要关注民生。

5. 下列各句中，语意明确的一句是（　）

A. 上午 9 时，市运动会开幕式开始，市长和分管体育的副市长以及其他市领导登上了主席台，运动员迈着整齐的步伐进场。

B. 对于能不能既提高教学质量，又减轻学生学业负担的问题，周校长说，我们的回答是肯定的。

C. 她没有听从别人的劝告，对那个男人提出控告，要求赔偿，真不知道当时她内心是怎样想的。

D. 两所本市和外国的中学，结成友好学校，有力地促进了两国文化和教育的交流，起到了互相学习的作用。

6. 下列句子中，标点符号使用不正确的一项是（　）

A. 大街上到处摆着水果摊，西瓜啊，香蕉啊，烟台苹果啊，库尔勒香梨啊……走到哪儿都能闻到诱人的香味。

B. 干扰素既是制服病毒的法宝，也是抗癌的“生力军”。近年来，医学临床试验证明：干扰素对淋巴癌、肺癌都有显著疗效。

C. 美国《时代》周刊称，奥巴马的《源自父亲的梦想：种族与继承的故事》一书为“美国政坛有史以来最好看的回忆录。”

D. 现在盛行的“山寨”一词源于广东话，它是指一种由民间 IT 力量发起的产业现象，主要表现为仿造性、快速化、平民化。

7. 下列句子中，没有运用“借代”修辞手法的一句是（　）

A. 今夏我被古典诗词吸引住了，都在和李白、杜甫、苏东坡打交道。

B. 下了一场雪，大地仿佛也怕寒冷，便整个儿缩到白地毯里去了。

C. 小张对小李说：“为了你们母子和好，你知道我费了多少唇舌？”

D. “你教的仍旧是‘子曰诗云’么？”我问久违了的老同学。

8. 下列有关文学常识的表述，不正确的一项是（　）

A. 词是诗歌的一种，最初是配合音乐来歌唱的；根据字数多少，词可分为小令、中调和长调。

B. “铁板铜琶，继东坡高唱大江东去；美芹悲黍，冀南宋莫随鸿雁南飞。”这副对联写的是苏轼。

C. 钱钟书是中国当代著名学者、小说家，代表作有学术论著《谈艺录》、《管锥篇》和长篇小说《围城》。

D. 巴尔扎克的《人间喜剧》以编年史的方式，广泛反映了 19 世纪上半叶法国的社会生活。

9. 下列有关中国文化常识的表述，不正确的一项是（　）

A. “五岳”是指我国的五大名山，即东岳泰山（又作“太山”）、西岳华山、南岳恒山、北岳衡山、中岳嵩山。

B. 古代文人，多有自取别号的，如李白别号青莲居士，陆游别号放翁。别号和名字在意义上不一定有什么联系。

C. 汉字的结构，传统有“六书”之说，即所谓六种造字的方法，其名称为象形、指事、会意、形声、转注、假借。

D. 我国古代对时辰的计算，根据天色变化把一昼夜分为几个时段，如将近日中时叫隅中，太阳西斜时叫昃。

10. 对下面这首唐诗的赏析，不恰当的一项是（　）

春山夜月　　于良史

春山多胜事，赏玩夜忘归。掬水月在手，弄花香满衣。

兴来无远近，欲去惜芳菲。南望鸣钟处，楼台深翠微。

A. 首联提纲挈领、统率全篇，两句之间还存有因果关系。

B. 颔联是“胜事”的具体描写，“掬”、“弄”二字既写景又写人。

C. 颈联承上“赏玩”、“忘归”而写，“欲去”还为下文埋下伏笔。

D. 尾联从声音引出画面，展示了远景，起到点题的作用。

得分	评卷人

二、白话文阅读（一）（12分）

阅读下面的文字，完成11～14题。

就一首首的诗说，我们得多吟诵，细分析；有人想，一分析，诗便没有了，其实不然。单说一首诗好是不够的，人家要问怎么个好法，便非先做分析的工夫不成。譬如《关雎》诗罢，你可以引《毛传》，说以雎鸠的“挚而有别”来比后妃之德，道理好。毛公原只是“章句之学”，并不想到好不好上去，可是他的方法是分析的，不管他的分析的结果切合原诗与否。又如金圣叹评杜甫《阁夜》诗说前四句写“夜”，后四句写“阁”，“悲在夜”，“愤在阁”，不管说得怎么破碎，他的方法也是分析的。现在看，他们似乎都将诗分析得没有了，然而一向很有势力，很能起信，就因为说得出个所以然。

语言作用有思想的、感情的两方面。如说“他病了”，直叙事实，别无涵义，照字面解就够，所谓“声音训诂”，属于前者。但如说“他病得九死一生”，便不能照字直解，只是“病得很重”的意思，却带着强力的情感，所谓“大义微言”，属于后者。诗这一种特殊的语言，感情的作用多过思想的作用。单说思想的作用吧，诗体简短，拐弯儿说话，破句子有的是，也就够捉摸的；加上情感的作用，比喻、典故，变幻不穷，更是绕手。

从分析下手，可不要死心眼儿，想着每字每句每篇只有一个正解；固然有许多诗是如此，但是有些却并不如此。不但诗，平常说话里双关的也尽有。又譬如我本名“自华”，家里给我起个号叫“秋实”，一面是“春华秋实”的意思，一面也因算命的说我五行缺火，所以取个半边“火”的“秋”字。这都是多义。

宋黄彻说杜甫《秋兴》“五陵衣马自轻肥”，虽出《论语》，总合其语乃范云“裘马悉轻肥”。《论语·雍也》篇“乘肥马，衣轻裘”，指公西赤的富而言；范云句见于《赠张徐州谡》诗，却指的张谡的贵盛。杜甫似乎不但受他句法影响；他这首诗上句云“同学少年多不贱”，原来他用“衣马轻肥”也是形容贵盛的。至于这两句诗的用意，看来是以同学少年的得意反衬自己的迂拙来。仇兆鳌《杜诗详注》说，“曰‘自轻肥’，见非己所关心”。多义中有时原可分主从，仇兆鳌这一解照上下文看，该算是从义。

多义也并非有义必收；搜寻不妨广，取舍却须严，不然就容易犯我们历来解诗时“断章取义”的毛病。我们广求多义，却全以“切合”为准，必须贯通上下文或全篇的才算数。从前笺注家也有一个典故引几种出处以资广证的。不过他们只举其事，不述其义，而所举既多简略，又未必切合，所以用处不大。

（摘编自朱自清《诗多义举例》）

11. 下列对于“一分析，诗便没有了”这一说法的批评，不符合作者原意的一项是（　）

A. 对于诗，既要吟诵，也要分析。单说一首诗好是不够的，还应该说得出怎么个好法，这就离不开分析。

B. 比如《诗经·关雎》，《毛传》说这首诗是用雎鸠的“挚而有别”来比喻后妃的美德，这个分析就很好。

C. 关于杜甫《阁夜》诗，金圣叹说前四句写“夜”，后四句写“阁”，虽然他说得支离破碎，但方法也是分析的。

D. 《毛传》和金圣叹似乎都把诗分析得没有了，但是人们还是相信他们，就是因为他们能说出诗为什么好。

12. 下列理解中，不符合原文意思的一项是（　）

A. “他病了”这样的句子，直叙事实，别无涵义，照字面解就够，这是起到了表达思想感情的作用。

B. 诗之所以难以捉摸，主要的原因就在于诗体简短，拐弯儿说话，再加上比喻、典故，变幻多端。

C. 分析诗的时候，不能以为所有的字、句、篇只有一个正确的解释；有一些诗并不如此，它是多义的。

D. 从前笺注家往往有一个典故引几种出处的，不过他们只举其事，不述其义，内容又未必切合，用处并不大。

13. 下列理解和分析，不符合原文意思的一项是（　）

A. 毛公的“章句之学”原来并不在意评论诗写得好不好，他的解释也有不切合原诗的，可是方法还是正确的。

B. 名“自华”号“秋实”，既包含“春华秋实”之意，又寓有五行缺火而借“秋”字补火之意。

C. 杜甫诗“五陵衣马自轻肥”虽典出《论语》，但其句法和用意却是受范云“裘马悉轻肥”的影响。

D. 仇兆鳌说“见非己所关心”，是说杜甫“衣马自轻肥”，因而并不关心同学少年的贵盛。

14. 根据原文内容，下列推断不正确的一项是（　）

A. 诗的语言，感情的作用多于思想的作用，所以诗的“大义微言”尤其是分析的难点。

B. 诗的意思有时是多义的，多义中有时可分主义从义，有时则两义或数义同等并列。

C. 自古至今，解诗的人经常有“断章取义”的毛病，诗的多义也就是因此而造成的。

D. 对于诗的分析，必须以“切合”为准，所以历来对于诗的分析，有正误优劣之分。

得分	评卷人

三、文言文阅读（12分）

阅读下面的文言文，完成15－18题。

王早，勃海南皮人也。明阴阳九宫□兵法，尤善风角。太宗时，丧乱之后，多相杀害。有人诣早求问胜术，早□设法，令各无咎。由是州里称之。时有东莞郑氏，因为同县赵氏□杀。其后郑氏执得仇人赵氏，又克明晨会宗族，当□墓所刑之。赵氏求救于早，早为占候，并授以一符，曰："君今且还，选壮士七人，令一人为主者，佩此符，于鸡鸣时伏在仇家宅东南二里许。平旦，当有十人相随，向西北行，中有二人乘黑牛，一黑牛最在前，一黑牛应第七。但捉取第七者将还，事必无他。"赵氏从之，果如其言，乃是郑氏五男父也。诸子并为其族所宗敬，故和解二家，赵氏竟免。后早与客清晨立于门内，遇有卒风振树。早语客曰："依法当有千里外急使。日中，将有两匹马，一白一赤，从西南来。至即取我，逼我，不听与妻子别。"语讫便入，召家人邻里辞别。语讫，浴，带书囊，日中出门候使。如期，果有二马，一白一赤，从凉州而至，即捉早上马，遂诣行宫。时世祖围凉州未拔，故许彦荐之。早，彦师也。及至，诏问何时当得此城。早对曰："陛下当移据西北角，三日内必克。"世祖从之，如期而克。与驾还都。时久不雨，世祖问早曰："何时当雨？"早曰："今日申时必大雨。"比至未时，犹无片云，世祖诏早诘之。早曰："愿更少时。"至申时，云气四合，遂大雨滂沱。世祖甚善之，而早苦以疾辞，乞归乡里，诏许之。遂终于家。或言许彦以其术胜，恐终妨己，故谲令归耳。

（节选自《魏书·王早传》）

15. 依次填入下列各句方框中的字，正确的一项是（　）

①明阴阳九宫□兵法　　②早□设法，令各无咎

③因为同县赵氏□杀　　④当□墓所刑之

A. ①及　②而　③所　④因　　B. ①及　②为　③所　④就

C. ①与　②而　③而　④因　　D. ①与　②为　③而　④就

16. 对下列各句中加点的词的解释，不正确的一项是（　）

A. 有人诣早求问胜术　　诣：拜访

B. 郑氏执得仇人赵氏　　执：抓获

C. 又克明晨会宗族　　克：约期

D. 伏在仇家宅东南二里许　　许：处所

17. "诸子并为其族所宗敬，故和解二家，赵氏竟免。"这个复句的类型是（　）

A. 因果复句　　B. 假设复句

C. 递进复句　　D. 转折复句

18. 下列叙述和分析，不符合原文意思的一项是（　）

A. 王早是勃海南皮人，擅长阴阳之术。其时正值丧乱之后，多相杀害。他使求

告的乡人设法免害，因此受到乡里的称赞。

B. 东莞赵氏是郑氏的仇家，在郑氏将要杀害仇人时，王早为赵氏设法捉得郑氏的五男父，并最终和解二家，赵氏免于难。

C. 王早善于预知未来，他清晨遇有急风振树，即知日中将有人自西南来取他外出，并不许与妻子辞别。后此事果然应验。

D. 世祖当时被围凉州，王早的学生许彦向世祖推荐王早。世祖咨询王早如何可破敌城，何时下雨，王早的回答全都正确。

第二部分

本部分为非选择题，有 7 小题，共 96 分。

得分	评卷人

四、文言文翻译、默写（13 分）

19. 把第一部分文言文阅读材料中画横线的句子翻译成现代汉语。（10 分）

（1）世祖甚善之，而早苦以疾辞，乞归乡里，诏许之。

译文：______________________________

______________________________。

（2）或言许彦以其术胜，恐终妨己，故谲令归耳。

译文：______________________________

______________________________。

20. 补写出下列名句的空缺部分。（任选三小题）（3 分）

（1）__________，行而不远。（《左传·襄公二十五年》）

（2）爱人者人恒爱之，__________。（《孟子·离娄下》）

（3）__________，宁静以致远。（诸葛亮《诫子书》）

（4）长风破浪会有时，__________。（李白《行路难》）

得分	评卷人

五、白话文阅读（二）（23 分）

阅读下面的文字，完成 21～24 题。

黎明前的北京

季羡林

前后加起来，我在北京已经住了四十多年，算是一个老北京了。北京的名胜古迹，北京的妙处，我应该说是了解的，其他老北京当然也了解；但是有一点，我相信绝大多数的老北京并不了解，这就是黎明时分以前的北京。

多少年来，我养成了一个习惯：每天早晨四点在黎明以前起床工作。我不出去跑步或散步，而是一下床就干活儿。因此，我对黎明前的北京的了解是在屋子里感觉到的。我从前在什么报上读过一篇文章，讲黎明时分天安门广场上的清洁工人。那情景必然是非常动人的，可惜我从来未能见到，只是心向往之而已。

四十年前，我住在城里的曾经是明朝特务机关的东厂里面。几座深深的大院子，在最里面三个院子里只住着我一个人。朋友们都说这地方阴森可怕，晚上很少有人敢来找我，我则怡然自得。每当夏夜，我起床以后，立刻就闻到院子里那些高大的马缨花树散发出来的阵阵幽香，这些香气破窗而入，我于此时神清气爽，乐不可支，连手中那一支笨拙的笔也仿佛生了花。

几年以后，我搬到西郊来住，照例四点起床，坐在窗前工作。白天透过窗子能看到北京展览馆那金光闪闪的高塔的尖顶，此时当然看不到了。但是，我知道，即使我看不见它，它仍然在那里挺然耸入天空，仿佛想带给人以希望，以上进的劲头。我仍然乐不可支，心也仿佛飞上了天空。

过了十年，我又搬家了。这新居既没有马缨花，也看不到金色的塔顶，但是门前却有一片清碧的荷塘。刚搬来的几年，池塘里还有荷花。夏天早晨四点已经算是黎明时分，在薄暗中透过窗子可以看到接天莲叶，而荷花的香气也幽然袭来，我顾而乐之，大有超出马缨花和金色塔尖之上的意味了。

难道我欣赏黎明前的北京仅仅由于上述的原因吗？不是的。三十几年以来，我成了一个“开会迷”。说老实话，积三十年之经验，我真有点害怕开会了。在白天，一整天说不定什么时候就会接到开会的通知。说一句过火的话，我简直是提心吊胆，心里不得安宁。即使不开会，这种惴惴不安的心情总摆脱不掉。只有在黎明以前，根据我的经验，没有哪里会来找你开会的。因此，我起床往桌子旁边一坐，仿佛有什么近似条件反射的东西立刻就起了作用。我心里安安静静，一下子进入角色，拿起笔来，“文思”（如果这也算是文思的话）如泉水喷涌，记忆力也像刚磨过的刀子，锐不可当。此时，我真是乐不可支，如果给我机会的话，我简直想手舞足蹈了。

因此，我爱北京，特别爱黎明前的北京。

21. 解释加点的成语在文中的意思。（4分）

（1）朋友们都说这地方阴森可怕，晚上很少有人敢来找我，我则怡然自得。

怡然自得：______________________________

（2）即使不开会，这种惴惴不安的心情总摆脱不掉。

惴惴不安：______________________________

22. 文中第3至第5段先后写到几次搬家，“黎明前”的时光都带给作者美的感受。请具体说明。（6分）

（1）四十年前，东厂大院中的黎明：________________________

（2）西郊的黎明：______________________________

（3）十年后新居的黎明：______

23. 作者在文末说“特别爱黎明前的北京”，为什么？请具体说明。(5 分)

答：______

______

24. 从全文看，作者具有什么样的性格特征？(8 分)

答：______

______

得分	评卷人

六、写作（60 分）

25. 请从下列两个题目中任选一题，写一篇不少于 600 字的文章。把所选的题目写在作文纸上。(60 分)

信心比金子还重要

微笑

数　学

本试卷满分150分，考试用时120分钟．

题号	一	二	三							总分
			21	22	23	24	25	26	27	
分数										

考生注意：这份试卷共三个大题，所有考生做第一、二题，在第三（21、22、23）题中任选两题；报考理工农医类的考生做第三（24、25）题，报考文史类的考生做第三（26、27）题．

得分	评卷人

一、选择题：本大题共12小题；每小题5分，共60分．在每小题给出的四个选项中，只有一项是符合题目要求的，把所选项前的字母填在题后括号内．

1. 设复数$z=1+i$，若$(z+a)(\overline{z}-a)$是纯虚数，则实数$a=$（　）

A. $\sqrt{2}$　　B. 2　　C. $\pm\sqrt{2}$　　D. ± 2

2. 设有平面α和任意直线m，则在α内必有直线n，使n与m（　）

A. 平行　　B. 相交　　C. 互为异面直线　　D. 垂直

3. 设$f(x)=\begin{cases} x^2-4x+c，当x<2 \\ \sqrt{x^2+5}，当x\geqslant 2 \end{cases}$，若$f(x)$是连续函数，则$c=$（　）

A. 7　　B. 6　　C. 4　　D. 3

4. 若方程$2x^2-y^2=m$表示的曲线是焦点在y轴上、焦距为4的双曲线，则$m=$（　）

A. $\frac{32}{3}$　　B. $\frac{8}{3}$　　C. $-\frac{8}{3}$　　D. $-\frac{32}{3}$

5. 若a、b、c是实数，且$a\geqslant b$，则（　）

A. $a(a+c)\geqslant b(b+c)$　　B. $a(a-c)\geqslant b(b-c)$

C. $|a+b|\geqslant|a-c|+|c-b|$　　D. $a|ac|\geqslant b|bc|$

6. 设数列$\{a_n\}$的前n项和$S_n=\frac{3}{2}(a_n-2)$，则$a_n=$（　）

A. $2\times 3^{n-1}$　　B. 2×3^n　　C. 3^n+3　　D. 3^n-3

7. 极坐标方程$2\rho\cos^2\frac{\theta}{2}=5$表示的曲线是（　）

A. 圆　　B. 椭圆　　C. 双曲线　　D. 抛物线

8. 在$\triangle ABC$中，已知$\sin A=\frac{3}{5}$，$\cos B=\frac{5}{13}$，则$\cos C=$（　）

A. $\frac{16}{65}$　　B. $-\frac{16}{65}$　　C. $\frac{16}{65}$或$\frac{56}{65}$　　D. $-\frac{63}{65}$

9. 函数$y=f(x)$的图像与$y=2^x$的图像关于直线$x+y=0$对称，则$f(x)=$（　）

A. $-\log_{\frac{1}{2}}(-x)$　　B. $\log_{\frac{1}{2}}(-x)$　　C. $-\log_2 x$　　D. $\log_2 x$

10. 设$f(x)=2-ab+(a+b)x-x^2$. 若$f(-2)=f(4)=0$，则以a、b为两根的二次方程可写为（　）

A. $x^2-2x-10=0$　　B. $x^2-2x-6=0$

C. $x^2-2x+6=0$　　D. $x^2+2x-10=0$

11. 若函数$f(x)=x^2-4x+\frac{a}{x}$在区间$(1, +\infty)$是增函数，则常数a的取值范围为（　）

A. $(-\infty, -2]$　　B. $(-\infty, -\frac{27}{4}]$

C. $(-\infty, -\frac{64}{27}]$　　D. $(-\infty, -\frac{32}{27}]$

12. 在$\triangle ABC$中，点D、E满足$\overrightarrow{AD}=2\overrightarrow{DB}$，$\overrightarrow{BE}=2\overrightarrow{EC}$. 设点$P=AE\cap CD$，$\overrightarrow{AP}=\lambda\overrightarrow{AB}+\mu\overrightarrow{AC}$，则$(\lambda, \mu)=$（　）

A. $(\frac{2}{7}, \frac{4}{7})$　　B. $(\frac{1}{7}, \frac{2}{7})$

C. $(\frac{1}{4}, \frac{1}{2})$　　D. $(\frac{4}{15}, \frac{8}{15})$

得分	评卷人

二、填空题：本大题共 8 小题；每小题 4 分，共 32 分．把答案填在题中横线上．

13. 在长方体$ABCD-A_1B_1C_1D_1$中，已知$AB=BC=1$，$AA_1=2$，则顶点A到对角线A_1C的距离为__________．

14. 抛物线$y^2=-10x$的准线方程为__________．

15. 函数$f(x)=\cos(3x+\frac{\pi}{4})\cos(3x-\frac{\pi}{4})$的最小正周期为__________．

16. 函数$y=\log_{\frac{1}{2}}(\cos x+\sin x)$（$0\leqslant x\leqslant\frac{\pi}{2}$）的最小值为__________．

17. 在空间直角坐标系$O-xyz$中，经过$A(1, 0, 2)$，$B(1, 1, -1)$和$C(2, -1, 1)$三个点的平面方程为__________．

18. 设等差数列 $\{a_n\}$ 的前 n 项和为 S_n. 若 $5S_{12}-12S_5=42$，则其公差为__________.

19. 多项式 $x^4+2x^3-4x^2-2x+3$ 与 x^3+4x^2+x-6 的最大公因式为__________.

20. 某质检员检验一件产品时，把正品误判为次品的概率为 0.1，把次品误判为正品的概率为 0.05. 如果一箱产品中含有 8 件正品，2 件次品，现从中任取 1 件让该质检员检验，那么出现误判的概率为__________.

三、解答题：在第 21、22、23 题三个题目中任选两题作答．在第 24、25、26、27 这四个题目中按考生报考专业的类别完成两题．

得分	评卷人

21. （本题满分 14 分）

曲线 $x^2y=8$ 按向量 $e=(1,2)$ 平移后得到的曲线 C 与直线 l：$2x+y=a$ 相切，求 a 的值以及 C 与 l 公共点的坐标.

得分	评卷人

22. （本题满分 14 分）

如图所示，在三棱锥 $P-ABC$ 中，$PA\perp$ 平面 ABC，$\angle PCB=30°$，二面角 $P-BC-A$ 等于 $60°$，且 $PB=BC$. 求 $\tan\angle BAC$ 的值，并比较 $\angle BPC$ 与 $\angle BAC$ 的大小.

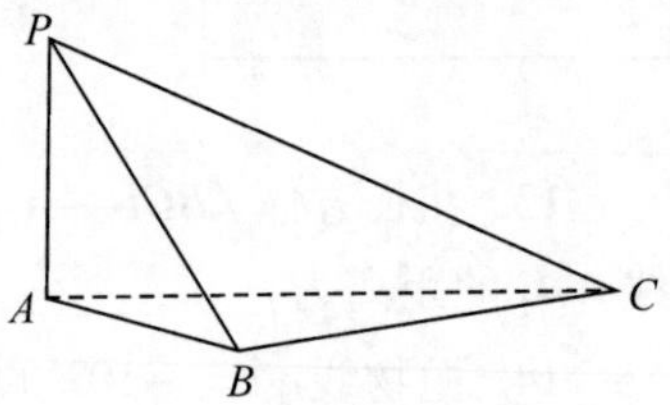

得分	评卷人

23. （本题满分14分）

在边长为4的正$\triangle ABC$中，点E、F分别在边AB、AC上，且$\triangle AEF$的面积等于$\triangle ABC$面积的一半．求$\overrightarrow{EF}\cdot\overrightarrow{BC}$的取值范围．

得分	评卷人

24. （本题满分15分，文史类考生不做）

设椭圆$\frac{x^2}{a^2}+y^2=1(a>1)$的左、右焦点分别为$F_1$、$F_2$，右准线$l$与$x$轴的交点为$E$.

（Ⅰ）当F_2是F_1E的中点时，求a；

（Ⅱ）若对于l上的任意点P，$\frac{|PF_2|}{|F_1F_2|}\neq 2$，求椭圆离心率$e$的取值范围．

得分	评卷人

25. （本题满分15分，文史类考生不做）

设$f_n(x)=(1+px)(1+p^2x)\cdots(1+p^nx)$，其中$n$是正整数，常数$p>0$. 用$a_n$和$b_n$分别表示$f_n(x)$展开式中$x$的系数和$x^2$的系数．

（Ⅰ）求数列$\{a_n\}$的通项公式；

（Ⅱ）当$p\neq 1$时，证明存在等比数列$\{c_n\}$和常数c满足$b_n=(c_n-c)(c_{n+1}-c)$，并求出该数列的通项c_n和常数c.

得分	评卷人

26.（本题满分 15 分，理工农医类考生不做）

设椭圆$\frac{x^2}{a^2}+y^2=1(a>1)$的左、右焦点分别为 F_1、F_2，右准线 l 与 x 轴的交点为 E.

（Ⅰ）当 F_2 是 F_1E 的中点时，求 a；

（Ⅱ）若对于 l 上的任意点 P，线段 F_1P 的中垂线都不经过点 F_2，求椭圆离心率 e 的取值范围.

得分	评卷人

27.（本题满分 15 分，理工农医类考生不做）

设$f_n(x)=(1+px)(1+p^2x)\cdots(1+p^nx)$，其中 n 是正整数，常数 $p>0$. 用 a_n 和 b_n 分别表示$f_n(x)$展开式中 x 的系数和 x^2 的系数.

（Ⅰ）求数列$\{a_n\}$的通项公式；

（Ⅱ）当 $p=2$ 时，证明存在等比数列$\{c_n\}$和常数 c 使得 $b_n=c(c_n-1)(c_{n+1}-1)$，并求出该数列的通项 c_n 和常数 c.

英 语

本试卷分第一卷（选择题）和第二卷（非选择题）两部分。考试时间 120 分钟。

第一卷

Ⅰ. 听力（共 20 小题，每小题 1.5 分；满分 30 分）

听完录音后，从各题所给的四个选项中选出能回答所提问题或完成所给句子的最佳选项。所有录音材料均仅读一遍。

例：（录音）Man：I wonder why the office is still not open.

Woman：But it's not yet eight. In fact，it's only a quarter to eight.

When does the office open?

A. At 8：30.　　B. At 8：15.　　C. At 8：00.　　D. At 7：45.

答案是 C。

听第 1 段材料，回答第 1 小题

1. What did the man say about the cell phone?

A. It was a gift.

B. He made it a gift.

C. He would sell it.

D. It got late calls.

听第 2 段材料，回答第 2 小题

2. Where does the conversation take place?

A. In a library.　　B. In an office.

C. In a bookstore.　　D. In a grocery store.

听第 3 段材料，回答第 3 小题

3. What will Olga do in the evening?

A. Go to see a play.　　B. Go to visit Susan.

C. Go to the disco.　　D. Go to meet his father.

听第 4 段材料，回答第 4 小题

4. Which book has Peter's brother got already?

A. English textbooks.
B. Chinese textbooks.
C. A chemistry book.
D. A history book.

听第5段材料，回答第5小题

5. Why does Jane eat a fruit for lunch?
A. She is on a diet.
B. She loves fruit a lot.
C. She can get nothing else.
D. She is in a rush for the work.

听第6段材料，回答第6至8小题

6. Why is Tom thinking of a part-time job?
A. To get some experience.
B. To make some money.
C. To meet people.
D. To get data for his school project.

7. What does Tom dislike about delivering newspapers?
A. Rising early.
B. Memorizing addresses.
C. Walking a lot.
D. Working alone.

8. Which of the following could Tom do while baby-sitting?
A. Meet friends.
B. Watch TV.
C. Drink beer.
D. Listen to music.

听第7段材料，回答第9至11小题

9. Which part of the party did Leila enjoy most?
A. Games.
B. Dancing.
C. Singing.
D. Eating.

10. What was the girl from Class Three usually like?
A. Determined.
B. Easy-going.
C. Confident.
D. Shy.

11. What did the speakers say about Tracy?
A. She had professional potential.
B. She was good but a bit nervous.
C. She learned singing from a professor.
D. She was famous for singing.

听第8段材料，回答第12至13小题

12. Why does Mary need a camera?
A. To photograph the weekend camping.
B. To photograph the landscape in Wales.
C. To take pictures of wild birds.
D. To improve her photography skills.

13. What must Mary do to borrow the camera?
A. Give John some batteries.
B. Invite John to camp together.
C. Make sure nothing goes wrong with it.
D. Show that she knows how to use it.

听第 9 段材料，回答第 14 至 17 小题

14. What does Rachel do at the present?
A. She edits films. B. She designs ads.
C. She composes music. D. She works as a film director.
15. Where did Rachel learn about the job?
A. From online ads. B. From her friends.
C. From the newspaper. D. From the movie studio.
16. What was Rachel advised to do to get the job?
A. Keep calling. B. Meet the boss.
C. Email the personnel officer. D. Deliver the resume personally.
17. Who helped Rachel a lot to get the job?
A. Her parents. B. Her teacher.
C. The interviewer. D. The career advisor.

听第 10 段材料，回答第 18 至 20 小题

18. What is most needed in the speaker's job?
A. Experience. B. Creative ideas.
C. Attractive appearance. D. Knowledge in advertising.
19. Why does the speaker like his job?
A. It is usually well-paid.
B. It has an excellent environment.
C. It brings a sense of achievement.
D. It offers an opportunity to travel abroad.
20. What do we know about the speaker's boss?
A. He is truly a good leader. B. He is an expert in advertising.
C. He is difficult to get along with. D. He is very strict with his employees.

Ⅱ. 英语运用（共 35 小题，每小题 1 分；满分 35 分）

A）单项填空（共 15 小题）

从 A、B、C、D 四个选项中，选出可以填入空白处的最佳答案。

21. —We've missed the train!

—______, there'll be another in ten minutes.

A. That's fine B. Never mind

C. Come on D. Don't mention it

22. I ______ my own living since I was seven, doing all kinds of jobs.

A. took B. brought C. obtained D. earned

23. ______ you call me to say you're not coming, I'll see you at the theatre.

A. If B. Unless C. Although D. Since

24. If you have computer problems, we suggest your ______ the company's helpline.

A. call B. to call C. called D. calling

25. ______ I like about Cambridge is that there's so much open space—there are parks and commons everywhere.

A. That B. Where C. Which D. What

26. After twenty-five years the town center had changed beyond all ______.

A. recognition B. examination C. impression D. identity

27. If Flora hadn't gone back for the letter, I'm sure she ______ have missed the bus.

A. wouldn't B. mustn't C. needn't D. shouldn't

28. I'm sorry I missed your birthday. I'll ______ to you, I promise.

A. send it over B. bring it out C. take it back D. make it up

29. You'd better phone home, ______ your parents will start to worry.

A. whereas B. otherwise C. while D. nevertheless

30. —When shall we meet again?

—Make it ______ day you like. It's all the same to me.

A. some B. another C. any D. one

31. My parents hold fond memories of ______ fashion and music of ______ 1980s.

A. /; a B. the; / C. a; the D. the; the

32. The pace of life in the city is rapid and busy, unlike in the country ______ it is more relaxed and slow.

A. when B. where C. that D. which

33. —Did you see a girl in white pass by just now?

—No, sir. I ______ a newspaper.

A. read B. have read C. was reading D. am reading

34. Your performance in the driving test didn't reach the required standard, ______, you failed.

A. after all B. in other words

C. in the end D. at the same time

35. Don started taking the bus to work every day after petrol prices rose ______ his means.

A. beyond　　B. without　　C. for　　D. through

B）完形填空（共20小题）

阅读下面短文，掌握其大意，然后从36至55各题所给的四个选项中选出一个最佳答案。

A few days after Christmas, my friend Zachary came over with his snowboard（滑雪板）to go to the hill near my house with me. He is very good at snowboarding, but I could __36__ do it at all. While I was __37__ my new board, Zachary was making run after run down the hill and having a great time.

On the hill, I struggled to stay up. I had __38__ a few times when a teenager I never met before __39__ that I was getting frustrated. He called over to me to give me some advice about how to snowboard. I don't __40__ strangers as a rule, but being out on the mountain with lots of other snowboarders around made me feel __41__. So I listened to what he had to say, and then I tried again. I was able to go __42__ down the hill than I had before. He __43__ as I made one more run, and then he came over to give me more __44__, like where to place my __45__ and what to do with my hands. He also told me that I __46__ lean（倾斜）a little bit forward once I got up. I tried what he __47__ me to do, and I was able to go all the way down the hills without falling! It seemed so much __48__ with the instructions that he gave me. He __49__ to help me a number of times and gave me lots of __50__ throughout the day.

I find it hard __51__ to listen to other people when they are telling me what to do, but this guy was very __52__ and nice about the way he instructed me. He could have __53__ to make a few more runs for the day, instead of taking the time to help me—a kid he didn't even __54__.

I'm a much better snowboarder now, __55__ a very helpful and considerate teenage stranger.

36. A. ever　　B. just　　C. barely　　D. seldom
37. A. dealing with　　B. struggling with　　C. playing with　　D. trying on
38. A. failed　　B. slipped　　C. moved　　D. fallen
39. A. admitted　　B. discovered　　C. noticed　　D. reported
40. A. admire　　B. respect　　C. talk to　　D. depend on
41. A. safe　　B. nervous　　C. ashamed　　D. excited
42. A. better　　B. farther　　C. quicker　　D. happier
43. A. shouted　　B. interrupted　　C. praised　　D. watched
44. A. consideration　　B. advice　　C. explanations　　D. opinions
45. A. feet　　B. body　　C. board　　D. legs
46. A. would　　B. should　　C. can　　D. might
47. A. challenged　　B. told　　C. ordered　　D. forced

48. A. convenient	B. comfortable	C. cleverer	D. easier
49. A. continued	B. tried	C. demanded	D. managed
50. A. encouragement	B. examples	C. ideas	D. skills
51. A. now	B. forever	C. sometimes	D. once
52. A. interesting	B. honest	C. lucky	D. helpful
53. A. chosen	B. afforded	C. left	D. prepared
54. A. remember	B. recognize	C. like	D. know
55. A. in addition to	B. thanks to	C. except for	D. as well as

Ⅲ. 阅读理解（共 20 小题，每小题 2.5 分；满分 50 分）

阅读下列短文，并做每篇后面的题目。从四个选项中，选出能回答所提问题或完成所给句子的最佳答案。

A

Harriet Tubman is well known for risking her life as a "conductor" in the Underground Railroad, which led escaped slaves to freedom in the North. But did you know that the former slave also served as a secret agent for the Union during the Civil War and was the first woman in American history to lead a military expedition?

Tubman decided to help the Union Army because she wanted freedom for all of the people who were forced into slavery, not just the few she could help by herself. And she convinced many other brave African Americans to join her as secret agents, even at the risk of being hanged if they were caught.

In one of her most dramatic and dangerous roles, Tubman helped Colonel James Montgomery plan a surprise attack to free slaves from plantations (种植园) along the Combahee River in South Carolina. Early on the morning of June 1, 1863, three gunboats carrying several hundred male soldiers along with Harriet Tubman set out for their task. Tubman had gathered key information about the Confederate positions. She knew where they were hiding along the shore. She also found out where they had placed gunpowder in the water.

As the early morning fog lifted on some of the South's most important rice plantations, the Union expedition hit hard. The soldiers set fire to buildings and destroyed bridges, so they couldn't be used by the Confederate Army. They also freed about 750 slaves—men, women, children, and babies—and did not lose one soldier in the attack.

Allen, who writes about this adventure and many others, got to know Tubman well through the months of research he did for the book. The historic details he shares bring Tubman and many other important figures of her time to life. To find out more about this extraordinary woman, read the book, Harriet Tubman, *Secret Agent*.

56. Which of the following best describes Harriet Tubman?

A. Dangerous. B. Intelligent. C. Ambitious. D. Brave.

57. What do we know about the adventure of June 1, 1863?

A. Both the Union and the Confederate suffered a heavy loss.

B. Harriet Tubman persuaded many slaves to join the attack.

C. Harriet Tubman was the only woman in action.

D. The attack took place in the deep night.

58. What type of writing is this text?

A. A news report. B. A movie commentary.

C. A book review. D. A book chapter.

B

Every Friday night the clerk at the food store in the Chevron gas station on Eagle Rock Boulevard and Avenue 40 offers us a discount on all the leftover (剩余的) apples and bananas. To get the best selection possible, my mother and I pile into our 20-year-old car and pull up to the food store at 5 p. m. sharp, ready to get our share of slightly overripe fruits.

Chevron shopping started like this: One day my mother suddenly realized that she had maxed out (刷爆) almost every credit card, and we needed groceries for the week. The only credit card she hadn't maxed out was the Chevron card and the station on Eagle Rock Boulevard has a pretty big store attached to it.

Since our first visit there, I've learned to believe in flexibility (灵活性). In my life, it has become necessary <u>to bend the idea of grocery shopping</u>. My mother and I can no longer shop at real grocery stores, but we still get the necessities.

Grocery shopping at Chevron has its drawbacks. The worst is when we have so many items that it takes the checker (收银员) what seems like hours to ring up everything. A line of anxious customers forms behind us. It's that line that hurts the most—the way they look at us. My mother never notices—or maybe she pretends not to.

I never need to be asked to help the checker bag all the items. No one wants to get out of there faster than I do. I'm embarrassed to shop there, and I'm deathly afraid of running into someone I know. I once expressed my fear of being seen shopping at Chevron to my mother and her eyes shone with disappointment. I know that I hurt her feelings when I try to escape our weekly shopping trips.

And that is why I hold on to the idea of flexibility so tightly. I believe that being flexible keeps me going—keeps me from being ashamed of the way my family is different from other families. Whenever I feel the heat rise to my face, I tell myself that we won't always have to shop at Chevron—that just because at this point in my life I am struggling does not mean that I will always struggle. My belief in flexibility helps me get through the difficult times because I know that no matter what happens, my mother and I will always figure out a way to survive.

59. Why does the author's mother shop at the Chevron?

A. She couldn't afford to buy food at a regular grocery store.

B. She doesn't like the service at a regular grocery store.

C. She likes the variety of the food there.

D. She has many Chevron cards.

60. Which of the following words best describes the author's feeling while shopping with her mother?

A. Hurt. B. Angry. C. Ashamed. D. Disappointed.

61. By saying "to bend the idea of grocery shopping" (Paragraph 3), the author most probably means ______.

A. to change the idea of grocery shopping

B. to give up grocery shopping

C. to do shopping with her mother

D. to start to shop in a supermarket

62. What does the author learn from shopping at the Chevron?

A. Children should help out in the family.

B. People need mutual understanding.

C. Shopping is a valuable experience.

D. Survival is of the first importance.

C

"Heaven (天堂) is where the police are English, the cooks are French, the mechanics are German, the lovers are Italian and everything is organized by the Swiss. Hell (地狱) is where the police are German, the cooks are English, the mechanics are French, the lovers are Swiss, and everything is organized by the Italians."

Obviously the national stereotypes (模式化的思想) in this old joke are generalizations, but such stereotypes are often said to "exist for a reason". Is there actually a sliver of truth in them? Not likely, an international research team now says.

"National and cultural stereotypes do play an important role in how people see themselves and others, and being aware that these are not dependable is a useful thing," said study author Robert McCrae of the National Institute on Aging. "These are in fact unfounded stereotypes. They don't come from looking around you," McCrae said.

If national stereotypes aren't rooted in real experiences, then where do they come from? One possibility is that they reflect national values, which may become known from historical events. For example, many historians have argued that the spirit of American individualism has its origins in the experiences of the pioneers in the Old West.

Social scientists such as psychologist Richard Robins have given several other possible explanations for stereotypes and why they may be incorrect. Robins notes that some stereotypes may have been correct at one point in history and then remained unchanged while the culture changed.

We may be "hard-wired", to some extent, to keep incorrect stereotypes, since we are less likely to notice and remember information that is different from our stereotypes. Generally, according to Robins, when we meet people who are different from our stereotypes, we see them as unique individuals rather than typical national or cultural groups.

63. The stereotype about Italians is ______.

A. friendly and good-tempered B. romantic but disorganized

C. dreamy and impractical D. strict but thoughtful

64. National stereotypes are not always correct because ______.

A. they are formed by individual historians

B. what was true in the past may not be true at the present

C. generalizations are made through personal experience

D. people tend to have false idea about other cultures

65. According to the research team led by McCrae, national stereotypes are ______.

A. interesting B. harmful C. humorous D. unreliable

66. The underlined word "hard-wired" in the last paragraph probably means ______.

A. forgetful B. anxious C. helpless D. fixed

D

RIPTA at a Glance

The Rhode Island Public Transit Authority (RIPTA) (公共交通局) is a public, independent authority. Established in 1966, RIPTA is authorized to operate public transit services throughout the State of Rhode Island.

- RIPTA has provided 42 years of statewide service (1966 – 2008)
- Governed by an 8-member appointed Board of Directors
- Serves 38 of 39 Rhode Island communities
- Operates 7 days a week
- Operates 3,300 daily trips on 58 statewide fixed bus routes
- Manages the statewide ride program for seniors and people with disabilities
- Operates flexible service in 6 Rhode Island communities
- Provides Park & Ride Service at 27 sites around the State of Rhode Island
- Operates seasonal Ferry (渡船) (May 16 – October 16) service between Providence and Newport, Rhode Island
- Operates 9.3 million fixed route automobile miles annually
- Keeps a team of 241 fixed route buses, and 17 flexible vans
- Uses 2.5 million gallons of fuel per year

- Employs 844 people
- Offers free statewide service on Air Quality Alert Days
- Operates and maintains two facilities (设施) in Providence and one in Newport
- 2008 Ridership:

  Fixed Route Bus 24,130,167

  Providence LINK 704,301

  Providence/Newport Ferry 42,988

  Flexible Services 375,995

  Ride Senior/Disabled Program 690,432

  Total: 25,296,132

67. What service does RIPTA offer?

A. Public transit nationwide. B. Public transit across Rhode Island.

C. Public transit in Providence. D. Public transit in Newport.

68. How many communities does RIPTA serve?

A. 17. B. 38. C. 27. D. 58.

69. When does Providence/Newport Ferry service open to the public?

A. On workdays. B. On weekends.

C. All year round. D. From late spring to fall.

70. How many old and disabled people did RIPTA serve in 2008?

A. 690,432. B. 704,301. C. 24,130,167. D. 25,943,883.

E

The connections between mathematics and music are many, from the unproven Mozart effect (the idea that playing Mozart's music to children might improve their math abilities) to the music of the spheres (the ancient belief that the movements of the planets could be viewed as a form of music). Now scientists have created a mathematical system for understanding music.

Clifton Callender of Florida State University, Ian Quinn of Yale University and Dmitri Tymoczko of Princeton University outlined their "geometrical (几何的) music theory" in the journal *Science*.

The team designed a geometrical technique for mapping out music in space. For music made of chords (和弦) containing two notes, all musical space basically looks like a twisted rubber band. The team found that the shape of possibilities using three-note chords is a 3-D ice cream cone (锥形物), where types of chords, such as major chords and minor chords, are unique points on the cone. The space of four-note chords looks like a pyramid in our 3-D universe. Any piece of music can be mapped in these spaces.

"You can use these geometrical spaces to provide ways of viewing musical pieces," Tymoczko told *LiveScience*. "These spaces give us a much better and comprehensive picture of the space of all possible chords."

It's probably not surprising that mathematics and music are so deeply linked, he said. "When music doesn't have words, it doesn't necessarily look like anything in the real world," Quinn said. "This is a feature people have been amazed by and found unbelievable. Traditionally, paintings always looked like things, and poetry and literature were talking about things. But music is coming closer to pure truth. People who talk about mathematics say the same thing—it's not necessarily about anything, it's just truth."

71. Why is "Mozart effect" mentioned in the first paragraph?

A. To show some link between music and math.

B. To give examples of various kinds of music.

C. To persuade children to learn music by Mozart.

D. To show how music can improve children's math.

72. The underlined words "mapping out" (Paragraph 3) probably mean ______.

A. measuring B. examining C. identifying D. describing

73. Which of the following can be viewed as an ice cream cone in space?

A. Two-note chords. B. Three-note chords.

C. Four-note chords. D. Six-note chords.

74. According to Ian Quinn, which of the following deals with pure truth?

A. Math. B. Poetry. C. Literature. D. Painting.

75. What is the main topic of the text?

A. Different types of music resemble different shapes in the universe.

B. Pyramids were built from the inspiration of four-note chords.

C. Both math and music deal with things in the real world.

D. Scientists have proposed a mathematical system to understand music.

第二卷

题号	Ⅳ	Ⅴ	总分
分数			

得分	评卷人

Ⅳ. 短文改错（共 15 小题，每小题 1 分，满分 15 分）

此题要求你对一段文章改错。先对每一行作出判断是对还是错。如果是对的，在该行右边横线上画一个钩（√）；如果有错误（每行不会多于一个错误），则按具体情况改错如下：

此行多一个词：把多余的词用斜线（\）划掉，在该行右边横线上写出该词，也用斜线划掉。

此行缺一个词：在缺词处加一个漏字符号（∧），在该行右边横线上写出该加的词。

此行错一个词：在错的词下划一横线，在该行右边横线上写出改正后的词。

注意：原行没有错的不要改。

例：

When I have free time I go ∧ a long walk. Some	(a) for
people read ~~the~~ books or watch television while	(b) ~~the~~
others have sports. Charles and Linda Mason do all	(c) √
of these things as well as <u>climbed</u> buildings.	(d) climbing; climb

In February, my teacher told us on the Woodmen of	76. ________
America speech contest and made us to work hard for it.	77. ________
After the class gave its presentations, my teacher picked	78. ________
three to five students to go on to the next level. I am one of	79. ________
them! Then the top five from each of the three fifth-grade	80. ________
class competed. The top seven would be the finalists; again,	81. ________
I was one of them! The top seven worked hardly. We had	82. ________
one month to practise. March 15 rolled around. After I knew	83. ________
it, I was in our school gym with people all around, include	84. ________
the judges, listening every word I said. I was the sixth to	85. ________
present. I was soon done. How a relief! I knew the top seven	86. ________
got prizes, but I still wanted that honor. After the seven	87. ________
person finished, the judge made their final decisions. They	88. ________
announced winners. The first-place winner was Kelli! I	89. ________
finally win first place!	90. ________

得分	评卷人

V. 书面表达（共 1 题，满分 20 分）

假设你参加了一个名为“六艺俱乐部”(Liuyi Club)的学生社团。为了在网页上宣传自己的社团，请你用英语写一份俱乐部简介。

简介要点如下：

1. 成立时间：2003 年。

2. 六艺：中国传统的文化艺术，如书法、音乐、绘画等。
3. 俱乐部宗旨：宣传中国文化、交友。
4. 经常组织的活动：
   （1）中国书法、绘画竞赛。
   （2）免费中国书法课程。
   （3）中国文化讲座。
5. 俱乐部网页：www. liuyi12345. cn。

注意：

1. 词数：100词左右。
2. 生词：
   （1）学生社团：student society。
   （2）中国书法：Chinese calligraphy。

Liuyi Club

____

____

____

____

____

____

____

____

____

____

历 史

本试卷满分 150 分，考试用时 120 分钟。

题号	一	二	三	总分
分数				

得分	评卷人

一、选择题：本大题共 20 小题，每小题 3 分，共 60 分。在每小题给出的四个选项中，只有一项是符合题目要求的，请把所选项前的字母填在题后的括号内。

1. “宝贝”之称，最早是指（ ）

A. 珍珠　　B. 玉石　　C. 金银　　D. 货币

2. 在一批战国竹简中，有《尚书》等重要内容，引起学术界的普遍关注。据测定这批简抄写年代在公元前 305 年左右，活跃于这一时期的思想家是（ ）

A. 老子　　B. 孟子　　C. 墨子　　D. 孙武

3. “喜则连衡而叛上，怒则以力而相并”，这种状况指的是（ ）

A. 春秋五霸　　B. 战国七雄

C. 唐末藩镇　　D. 五代十国

4. 魏晋南北朝时期江南农业迅速发展的最主要原因是（ ）

A. 南方气候适宜农业生产　　B. 南方少数民族与汉人融合

C. 先进生产技术的推广和应用　　D. 政府实行有利于农业发展的措施

5. 导致地方割据势力更加强大的历史事件是（ ）

A. 西汉七国之乱　　B. 唐代安史之乱

C. 明代靖难之役　　D. 清代三藩之乱

6. 最早将近代天文、数学、理化等科技知识传入中国的西方传教士是（ ）

A. 郎世宁　　B. 南怀仁　　C. 利玛窦　　D. 汤若望

7. 鸦片战争后，清朝为加强与外国联系而设立的第一个外交机构是（ ）

A. 总理衙门　　B. 理藩院

C. 海关总税务司　　D. 外务部

8. 读图 1，指出中日甲午战争期间黄海大战的所在海域是（ ）

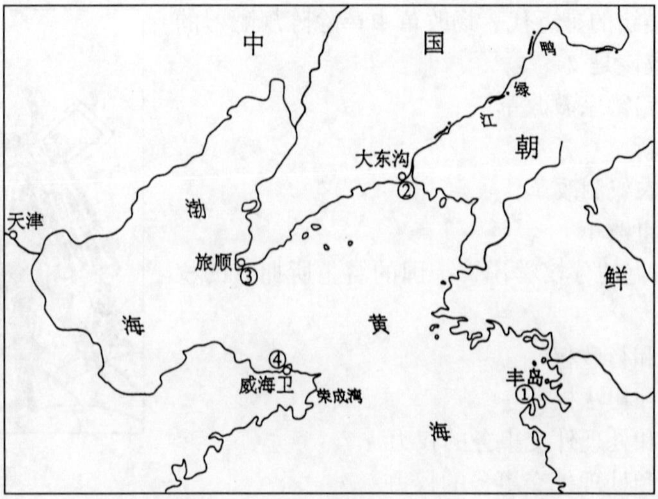

图 1

A. ①　　B. ②　　C. ③　　D. ④

9. 20 世纪初期，中国民族工业中规模最大、发展速度最快的是（　）

A. 采矿业　　B. 造纸业　　C. 面粉业　　D. 纺织业

10. 日本侵华战争期间，对沦陷区的矿业、钢铁工业和交通运输业等实行“统制事业”的目的是（　）

A. 掠夺中国的资源　　B. 扩大商品输出

C. 使之成为日本的经济附庸　　D. 扩大资本输出

11. 有一副对联的上联为“放开肚皮吃饱饭”，下联为“鼓足干劲搞生产”，横批为“多快好省”。这副对联最早应出现于（　）

A. 20 世纪 50 年代初　　B. 20 世纪 50 年代末

C. 20 世纪 60 年代中期　　D. 20 世纪 70 年代初

12. 民族区域自治制度是我国的基本政治制度。20 世纪 60 年代我国成立的省级自治区是（　）

A. 内蒙古自治区　　B. 新疆维吾尔自治区

C. 广西壮族自治区　　D. 西藏自治区

13. 促使 1972 年中日两国迅速实现邦交正常化的是（　）

A. 中美两国关系走向缓和

B. 中苏两国关系破裂

C. 中华人民共和国恢复在联合国的合法权利

D. 中美两国正式建交

14. 上海合作组织的主要成员国是中国和（　）

A. 俄罗斯、中亚国家　　B. 印度、东南亚国家

C. 巴基斯坦、东盟国家　　D. 韩国、日本、蒙古

15. 图2描绘的是近代一场改革中革除陈规陋习的场景，该改革应该是（　）

A. 马丁·路德宗教改革

B. 明治维新

C. 1861年农奴制改革

D. 彼得一世改革

图2

16. 按照洛克的分权学说，一国的君主所拥有的权力是（　）

A. 立法权和行政权

B. 行政权和司法权

C. 行政权和处理外交事务的权力

D. 立法权和处理外交事务的权力

17. 林肯在1854年的一次演讲中指出："奴隶制是建立在人性中的自私自利上面的，是与人热爱正义的天性相违背的。"这段话表明，林肯（　）

A. 主张立即废除奴隶制　　B. 主张限制奴隶制

C. 从伦理道德角度批判奴隶制　　D. 从经济角度否定奴隶制

18. 拉丁美洲独立运动是18～19世纪革命浪潮的重要组成部分，最先获得独立的是（　）

A. 墨西哥　　B. 海地　　C. 哥伦比亚　　D. 阿根廷

19. 第一次世界大战前夕，帝国主义国家之间的矛盾主要是（　）

A. 美西矛盾　　B. 英德矛盾

C. 日俄矛盾　　D. 法意矛盾

20. 下列各项中，属于罗斯福新政内容的是（　）

A. 限制过度竞争　　B. 实行计划经济

C. 降低关税　　D. 建立福利社会

得分	评卷人

二、材料解析题：本大题共2小题，每小题15分，共30分。

21. 阅读下列材料：

土地改革的基本目的，不是单纯地为了救济穷困农民，而是为了要使农村生产力从地主阶级封建土地所有制的束缚之下获得解放，以便发展农业生产，为新中国的工业化开辟道路。

——《刘少奇选集》

结合材料与所学知识，简述20世纪50年代中国农村土地所有制的变化及其对工业化建设的作用。（15分）

22. 阅读下列材料：

材料一

中国人在道德和政治经济学、农业、生活必需的技艺等方面已臻完美境地，其余方面的知识，倒是我们传授给他们的；但是在道德、政治经济、农业、技艺这方面，我们却应该做他们的学生了。

——伏尔泰《哲学辞典》

材料二

中国的专制主义，在祸患无穷的压力之下，虽然曾经愿意给自己带上锁链，但都徒劳无益；它用自己的锁链武装了自己，而变得更为凶暴。

——孟德斯鸠《论法的精神》

材料三

应该看到，科学和艺术在中国没有任何进步，这个民族既无高大的建筑，也没有美丽的雕像，更无诗歌、音乐、绘画和雄辩术。

——狄德罗《狄德罗全集》

根据材料并结合所学知识，回答下列问题。

（1）指出启蒙思想家们对中国的态度出现了怎样的分野，他们眼中的中国具有哪些特征。(6 分)

（2）根据中国的历史实际，评价启蒙思想家们对中国的认识。(9 分)

得分	评卷人

三、问答题：本大题共 3 小题，任选 2 题，每小题 30 分，共 60 分。

23. “山外青山楼外楼，西湖歌舞几时休？暖风熏得游人醉，直把杭州作汴州。”指出这首《题临安邸》创作的朝代、反映的历史背景和诗人对时局的态度。(30 分)

24. 19 世纪下半叶到 20 世纪初期，中华民族在政治现代化和经济现代化方面进行了哪些探索？促成这些探索的主要原因有哪些？（30 分）

25. 第一次世界大战后，德国和日本分别出现法西斯运动。比较德、日法西斯运动的不同，指出德、日法西斯政权造成的危害。（30 分）

地　理

本试卷满分 150 分，考试用时 120 分钟。

题号	一	二	三	四	总分
分数					

得分	评卷人

一、选择题：本大题共 20 小题，每小题 3 分，共 60 分。在每小题给出的四个选项中，只有一项是符合题目要求的，请把所选项前的字母填在题后的括号内。

一般情况下，电网供应的电能相对稳定，而用电量常常是不稳定的。目前解决这一问题的最有效办法是，在条件允许的地方修建抽水蓄能发电站。完成 1 ~2 题。

1. 下列抽水蓄能水电站中，最先建设的是（　）

A. 广东从化电站　　B. 浙江天荒坪电站

C. 台湾日月潭电站　　D. 浙江桐柏电站

2. 下列发电方式中，供电最稳定、持续时间最长的是（　）

A. 火电站　　B. 水电站　　C. 核电站　　D. 风力发电站

在印度洋中有一个海湾，两面连接大海，两面临陆。完成 3 ~6 题。

3. 该海湾是（　）

A. 孟加拉湾　　B. 亚丁湾　　C. 阿曼湾　　D. 波斯湾

4. 与其相连通的两个海分别是（　）

A. 红海、阿拉伯海　　B. 红海、黑海

C. 地中海、黑海　　D. 阿拉伯海、地中海

5. 该海湾与其中一个海之间通过海峡连通，这个海峡是（　）

A. 曼德海峡　　B. 霍尔木兹海峡

C. 土耳其海峡　　D. 直布罗陀海峡

6. 只考虑海水表层盐度的因素，这个海峡表层海水长年流向为（　）

A. 西向东　　B. 东南向西北

C. 东向西　　D. 西南向东北

图 1 所示地区在当地时间 3 月 11 日 11 时许发生地震。读图 1，完成 7 ~9 题。

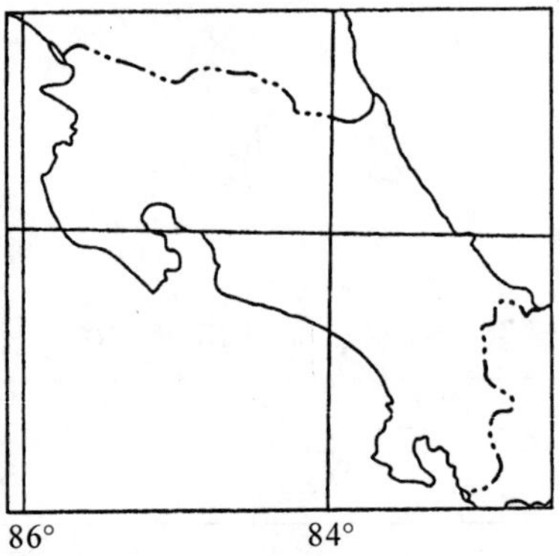

图 1

7. 该地区靠近的两大板块是（　）

A. 太平洋板块和亚欧板块
B. 印度洋板块和亚欧板块
C. 太平洋板块和美洲板块
D. 印度洋板块和非洲板块

8. 地震发生时，北京时间约为 3 月（　）

A. 12 日 13 时
B. 12 日 1 时
C. 11 日 23 时
D. 10 日 23 时

9. 该段时间这个地区盛行（　）

A. 西北风　B. 西南风　C. 东南风　D. 东北风

图 2 表示某地月降水量和平均气温的年变化，点的标号代表月份。读图 2，完成 10～12 题。

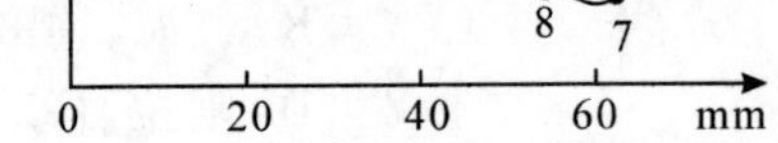

图 2

10. 该地气候属于（　）

A. 温带海洋性气候
B. 温带大陆性气候
C. 地中海气候
D. 亚热带季风气候

11. 该地可能位于（　）

A. 地中海沿岸
B. 澳大利亚西南部
C. 美国太平洋沿岸
D. 巴西东南部

12. 该地森林火险比较高的月份是（　）

A. 3、4、5 月
B. 6、7、8 月

C. 9、10、11月　　D. 12、1、2月

至2009年2月，我国已在两极地区建立了长城站、中山站、黄河站、昆仑站四座科学考察站。完成13～14题。

13. 四座极地科学考察站中，位于北极地区的是（　）

A. 长城站　　B. 中山站　　C. 黄河站　　D. 昆仑站

14. 四座极地科学考察站中，纬度和海拔都最高的是（　）

A. 长城站　　B. 中山站　　C. 黄河站　　D. 昆仑站

15. 2008年，我国被收入《世界遗产名录》的道教名山是（　）

A. 广东罗浮山　　B. 山东崂山

C. 安徽齐云山　　D. 江西三清山

16. 石油蕴藏量丰富，地跨两大洲的国家是（　）

A. 哈萨克斯坦　　B. 吉尔吉斯斯坦

C. 塔吉克斯坦　　D. 乌兹别克斯坦

17. 近几年开工兴建的大型水利枢纽工程溪洛渡位于（　）

A. 金沙江　　B. 雅砻江　　C. 红水河　　D. 澜沧江

18. 被誉为“波斯湾明珠”的城市迪拜所在的国家是（　）

A. 沙特阿拉伯　　B. 阿联酋

C. 卡塔尔　　D. 伊朗

19. 泰国最重要的农业出口商品是（　）

A. 稻米、兰花　　B. 小麦、棕榈油

C. 大豆、花生　　D. 棉花、香蕉

20. 已成为世界上第十一个人口超过1亿的国家是（　）

A. 墨西哥　　B. 尼日利亚　　C. 印度尼西亚　　D. 巴西

得分	评卷人

二、填充题：本题共4小题，20个空格，每填对一空得1分，共20分。

21. 与巴基斯坦相邻的海洋和国家，按顺时针方向依次为__________海，__________、__________、__________和__________。

22. 近年来，世界石油输出大国有亚洲的__________、__________，欧洲的__________，非洲的__________和南美洲的__________。

23. 亚洲是气候最为复杂多样的大洲。其中季风气候显著，自南向北依次分为__________季风气候、__________季风气候和__________季风气候；亚洲范围最广的气候类型是__________气候；亚洲还有全球最广的受非地带性因素影响而形成的__________气候。

24. 我国河流众多，其中最终注入印度洋的大河是__________和__________；最

终注入北冰洋的大河是__________；最大的内流河是__________；纬度最高的大河是__________。

得分	评卷人

三、读图、填图题（每项 2 分，共 40 分）

25. 读图 3 回答：

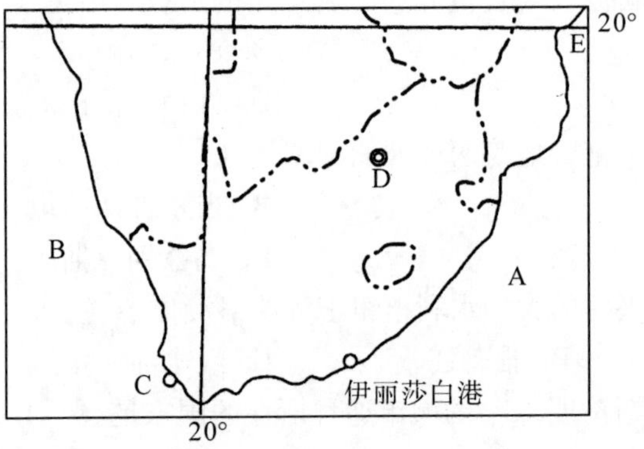

图 3

（1）A 是__________洋，B 是__________洋；

（2）C 城市是__________，D 城市是__________；

（3）E 是__________海峡。

26. 读图 4 回答：

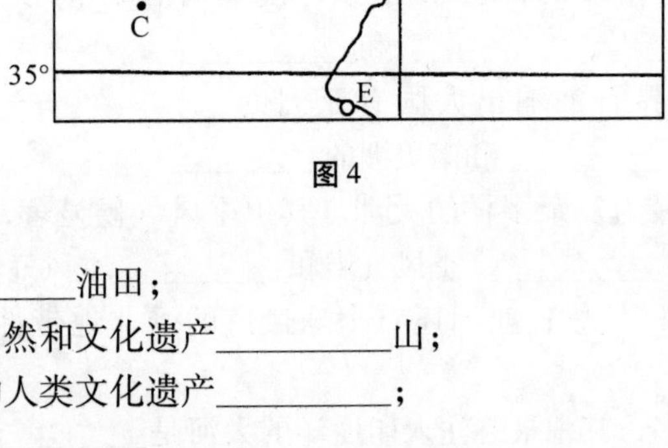

图 4

（1）A 是__________油田；

（2）B 是人类自然和文化遗产__________山；

（3）C 是著名的人类文化遗产__________；

（4）沿海开放城市、港口 D、E 分别是__________、__________。

27. 读图 5 回答：

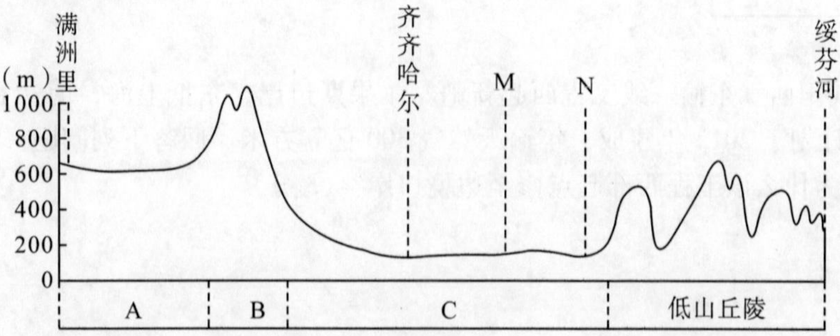

图 5

（1）A 是__________高原；

（2）B 是__________山脉；

（3）C 是__________平原；

（4）M 是著名的石油城__________；

（5）N 是省会城市__________。

28. 图 6 显示按亚洲、欧洲、非洲、大洋洲、北美、拉丁美洲统计的人口信息。根据图 6 中的信息判断：

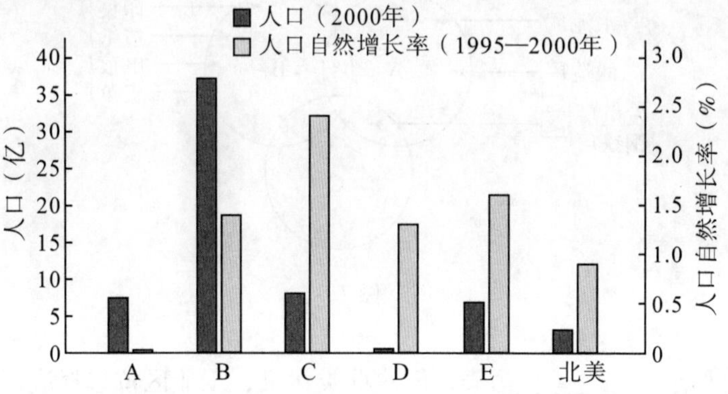

图 6

（1）A 是__________洲；

（2）B 是__________洲；

（3）C 是__________洲；

（4）D 是__________洲；

（5）E 是__________洲。

得分	评卷人

四、综合题（共 30 分）

29. 我国西气东输二线工程西起新疆霍尔果斯口岸，东抵上海，南达香港，2008 年开建，计划于 2012 年建成，年输天然气 300 亿立方米。回答下列问题。（15 分）

（1）为什么该工程西部起点修至边境口岸？（3 分）

（2）简述该工程的修建对珠江三角洲的意义。（12 分）

30. 图 7 示意一些工业的污染类型，读图回答下列问题。（15 分）

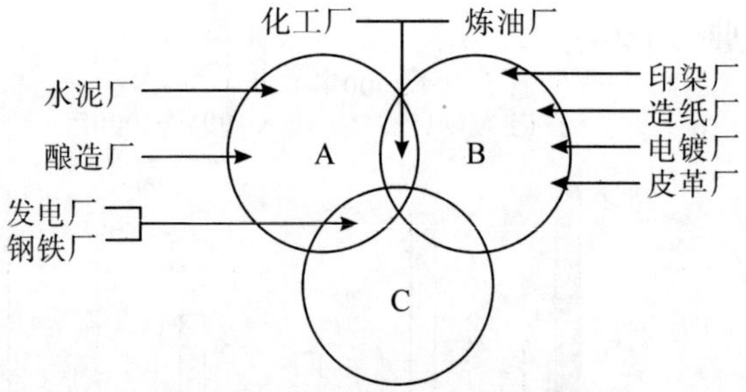

图 7

（1）A 类属于__________污染，解决此类污染，工业区位选择应______________________________。（5 分）

（2）B 类属于__________污染，解决此类污染，工业区位选择应______________________________。（5 分）

（3）C 类属于__________污染，解决此类污染，工业区位选择应______________________________。（5 分）

物　理

本试卷满分150分，考试用时120分钟.

题号	一	二								总分
		14	15	16	17	18	19	20	21	
分数										

得分	评卷人

一、选择题：本题共13小题；每小题4分，共52分．在每小题给出的四个选项中，只有一项是符合题目要求的，把所选项前的字母填在题后括号内．

1. 右图是一沿直线运动的质点在$t=0$到4s内的$v-t$图．从图中可以看出（　）

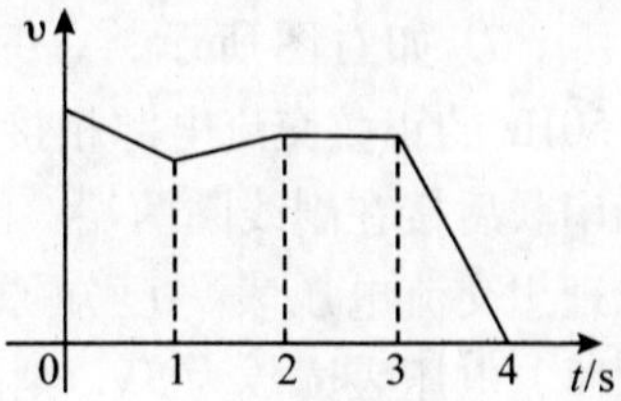

A. 质点的速度方向在0~4s内始终未变

B. 质点的加速度方向在0~4s内始终未变

C. 在1~2s内质点的加速度数值最小

D. 在3~4s内质点运动的距离最大

2. 一半圆柱形玻璃砖放置在竖直面内，其截面如右图所示．图中O为圆心，MN为竖直方向的直径，长为$2R$. 有一束细光线自O点沿水平方向射入玻璃砖，可以观测到有光线自玻璃砖内射出．现将入射光线缓慢平行下移．当入射光与O点的距离为d时，从玻璃砖射出的光线刚好消失．则此玻璃的折射率为（　）

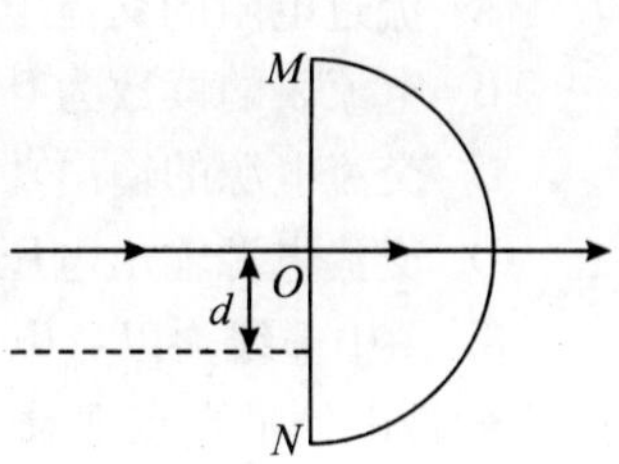

A. $\dfrac{R}{\sqrt{R^2-d^2}}$　　B. $\dfrac{\sqrt{R^2-d^2}}{R}$　　C. $\dfrac{R}{d}$　　D. $\dfrac{d}{R}$

3. 一张开的、竖直下降的降落伞下挂有一个弹簧秤，弹簧秤的另一端悬挂有一重物．已知重物质量为10kg，降落伞质量为1kg，弹簧秤质量忽略不计，其示数为80N. 重力加速度为$10\mathrm{m/s^2}$. 此时空气阻力为（　）

A. 30N　　B. 70N　　C. 88N　　D. 108N

4. 已知氢原子第n个定态的能量为$E_n=-\dfrac{13.6}{n^2}\mathrm{eV}$. 某个处于基态的氢原子（　）

A. 可以吸收可见光（波长为400~700nm）的光子，而跃迁到较高的能态

B. 可以在吸收12.1eV的能量以后，发射出可见光的光子

C. 可以在吸收12.1eV的能量以后，发射出红外光的光子

D. 不可能吸收大于13.6eV的能量

5. 如右图所示，光滑水平面上有一弹簧振子在纸面内左右振动．一小物块以向左的水平速度从右面飞来与振子小球正碰后粘在一起振动．若小球与物块均可看作质点，则与碰前相比，小球的（　）

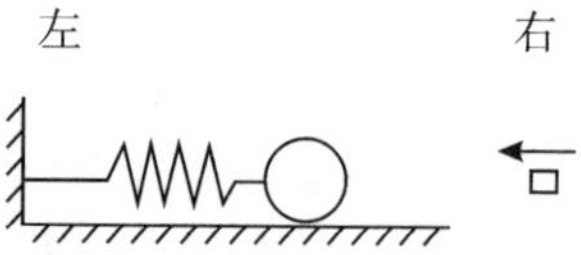

A. 振幅不变　　B. 平衡位置不变

C. 振动周期不变　　D. 周期、平衡位置和振幅都会改变

6. 光滑水平面上有两个质量相同、材质不同的物块p、q，处于静止状态．两个完全相同的子弹以相同的水平初速度分别射入两物块并留在物块中．子弹进入物块p的深度为d_p，与此物块一起运动的速度为v_p，从子弹接触物块p到它们刚开始以共同速度运动的一段时间内，物块p前进的距离为s_p；子弹进入物块q的深度为d_q，与此物块一起运动的速度为v_q，从子弹接触物块q到它们刚开始以共同速度运动的一段时间内，物块q前进的距离为s_q. 已知$d_p > d_q$，则（　）

A. $v_p > v_q$　　B. $v_p < v_q$　　C. $s_p > s_q$　　D. $s_p < s_q$

7. 如右图所示，一理想变压器原线圈与一频率为50Hz的正弦交流电源相接，两个阻值均等于20Ω的电阻串联后接在副线圈两端：图中Ⓐ为理想交流电流表，Ⓥ为理想交流电压表．已知原、副线圈分别为200匝和100匝，电压表读数为5V. 则（　）

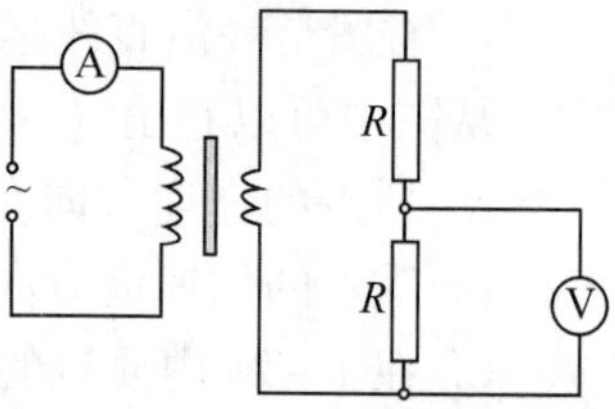

A. 流过电阻的交流电的频率为100Hz

B. 电流表的读数为0.5A

C. 交流电源的输出功率为10W

D. 交流电源输出电压的最大值为28V

8. 图中虚线为以点电荷O为圆心的同心圆．一具有初速度的带电粒子在点电荷O的电场中的运动轨迹如图中实线所示，箭头表示其运动方向．a、b、c、d为实线与虚线的四个交点．从图中可以看出（　）

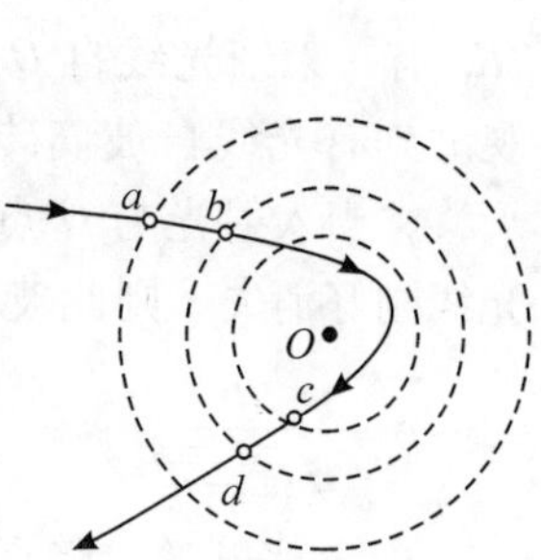

A. 带电粒子从a点运动到b点的过程中，电场力做正功

B. 带电粒子从c点运动到d点的过程中，电场力做正功

C. 带电粒子位于b点时的速率比其位于d点时的大

D. 带电粒子位于b点时的速率比其位于d点时的小

9. 在一倾角为α的斜面上同一点，分别以水平速度v_1和v_2抛出两个小物块．这两个小物块落到斜面上时速度方向与斜面的夹角分别用θ_1和θ_2表示．则$\theta_1 : \theta_2$（　）

A. 等于$v_1 : v_2$　　B. 等于$v_2 : v_1$

C. 等于 1 : 1　　　　　　　　　　　　D. 与 α 有关

10. 如右图所示，纸面内有一正方形导线框，其上下两边水平，边长为 a. 线框右方的平行四边形区域内有一方向垂直纸面向内的匀强磁场．此平行四边形的两条短边水平，边长为 $3a$；另外两条长边与水平方向成 45°角．线框以向右的水平速度匀速运动，当其右下角刚刚进入磁场区域时开始计时．用 t 表示时间，I 表示导线框中的电流，且设电流方向以顺时针为正，则下面 4 个图中可能正确的是（　）

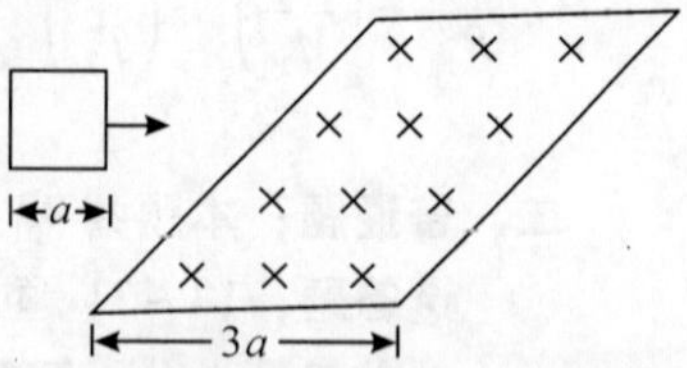

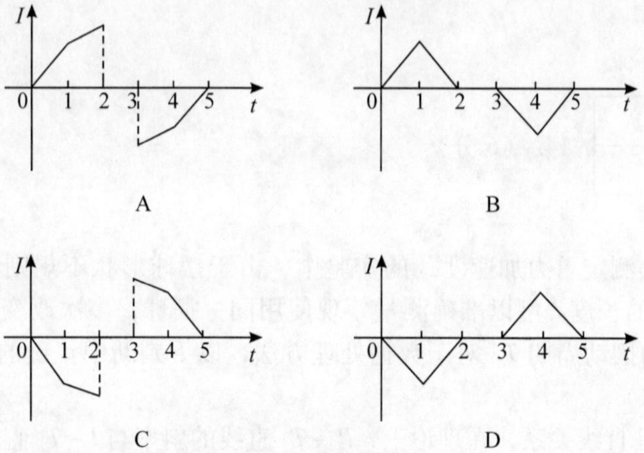

11. 右图为两分子间作用力 F 与其间距 r 的关系图线，力为正时表示斥力．从图中可以看出（　）

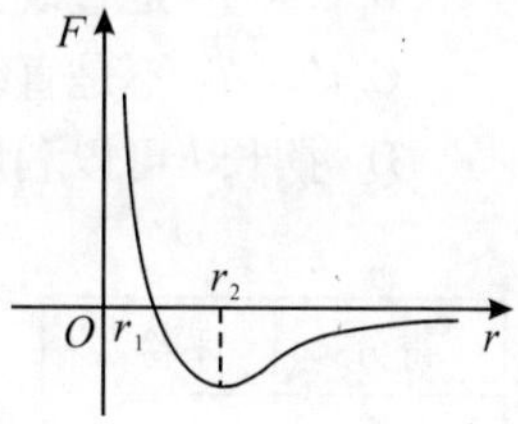

A. $r=r_1$ 时，两分子间势能最小

B. $r=r_2$ 时，两分子间势能最小

C. $r<r_2$ 时，两分子间的作用力为斥力

D. $r>r_2$ 时，两分子间的引力随 r 的减小而减小

12. 两个质量为 m_1 的氘核（${}_1^2\text{H}$），结合成一个质量为 m_2 的氚核（${}_2^3\text{H}$），同时生成另一粒子 X. 在这一核反应过程中释放的能量为 ΔE. 用 c 表示光速，由此可知（　）

A. 粒子 X 是质子　　　　　　　　　　B. 粒子 X 是正电子

C. 粒子 X 的质量为 $2m_1-m_2+\dfrac{\Delta E}{c^2}$　　　　D. 粒子 X 的质量为 $2m_1-m_2-\dfrac{\Delta E}{c^2}$

13. 设地球、火星的质量分别为 $M_{地}$、$M_{火}$，自转周期分别为 $T_{地}$、$T_{火}$，地球同步卫星距地心的距离为 $R_{地}$．假设火星也有一同步卫星，它与火星中心的距离为 $R_{火}$．则（　）

A. $\dfrac{R_{火}}{R_{地}}=\left(\dfrac{M_{火}}{M_{地}}\right)^{\frac{1}{3}}\left(\dfrac{T_{火}}{T_{地}}\right)^{\frac{2}{3}}$　　　　B. $\dfrac{R_{火}}{R_{地}}=\left(\dfrac{M_{火}}{M_{地}}\right)^{\frac{2}{3}}\left(\dfrac{T_{火}}{T_{地}}\right)^{\frac{1}{3}}$

C. $\frac{R_{火}}{R_{地}}=\left(\frac{M_{火}}{M_{地}}\right)^{-\frac{1}{3}}\left(\frac{T_{火}}{T_{地}}\right)^{\frac{2}{3}}$　　　　D. $\frac{R_{火}}{R_{地}}=\left(\frac{M_{火}}{M_{地}}\right)^{\frac{1}{3}}\left(\frac{T_{火}}{T_{地}}\right)^{-\frac{2}{3}}$

二、普通题：本题共 98 分，分为两组：第一组为必答题，14 ~ 17 题；第二组为选答题，18 ~ 21 题．从四题中任选做三题．请按各题要求作答．如多做，则按前三题计分．解答 16 ~ 21 题时应写出必要的文字说明、方程式和主要演算步骤．只写出最后答案，不能得分．有数值计算的题，答案中必须明确写出数值和单位．

第一组：

得分	评卷人

14. （6 分）

在“用单摆测定重力加速度”的实验中，由于摆球形状不规则，无法准确测量摆长 l，但摆线的长度 l'可以准确测量．现使用同一摆球，多次改变摆线长度 l'并测得每一次相应的摆动周期 T. 对于数据处理方法，以下判断中正确的是______．（填入选项前的字母）

A. l'与 T^2 是直线关系，在理论上，$l'-T^2$ 直线的斜率与 $l-T^2$ 直线的相同

B. l'与 T^2 是直线关系，在理论上，$l'-T^2$ 直线的斜率与 $l-T^2$ 直线的不同

C. l'与 T^2 不是直线关系

D. 摆长 l 可以利用 $l'-T^2$ 图线求出

得分	评卷人

15. （14 分）

实验室现有以下器材：直流电源 E，其电动势约为 6V，内阻可忽略不计；固定电阻 $R_1=2500\Omega$，固定电阻 $R_2=5000\Omega$；直流电流表Ⓐ₁，量程为 7.5mA，内阻 $R_{A_1}=50\Omega$；直流电流表Ⓐ₂，量程为 15mA，内阻 $R_{A_2}=25\Omega$；直流电流表Ⓐ₃，量程为 30mA，内阻 $R_{A_3}=12.5\Omega$；直流电压表Ⓥ，量程为 5V，内阻 $R_V=5000\Omega$；单刀开关 S；导线若干．现要在以上器材中选用直流电源、单刀开关、导线、一个固定电阻、一块电流表和一块电压表来测量一个阻值约为 500Ω 的未知电阻 R_x. 为提高测量的准确程度，要求测量时电表读数超过其量程的 2/3.

（1）画出实验原理电路图，图中器材均需用题目中给定的符号标出．

（2）若连接好电路并将开关闭合以后，电流表与电压表的示数分别为 I 和 U，则可以推导出 $R_x=$______________．（需要修正电表接入引起的误差）

得分	评卷人

16. (15 分)

将一光源、一竖直狭缝、一凸透镜和一光屏依次放置，光源、狭缝中心、屏中心与透镜的主光轴处于同一直线上．将光源、狭缝及屏固定，在狭缝与光屏之间沿它们中心的连线移动透镜，可以在屏上两次观察到清晰完整的狭缝的像．若这两个像的长度分别为 l_1 和 l_2，求狭缝的长度 l.

得分	评卷人

17. (18 分)

一竖直放置的、长为 L 的圆筒下端封闭，上端与大气（视为理想气体）相通．初始时筒内气体温度为 T_1. 现将一可沿筒壁自由滑动的活塞从上端放进圆筒，活塞下滑过程中气体温度保持不变且没有气体漏出，平衡后圆筒内活塞上下两部分气柱长度比为 1∶3. 将圆筒下部气体温度降至 T_2，在保持温度不变的条件下将筒倒置，平衡后活塞下端与圆筒下端刚好平齐．已知 $T_1=2T_2$，大气压强为 p_0，重力加速度为 g. 求活塞厚度 l 和活塞密度 ρ.

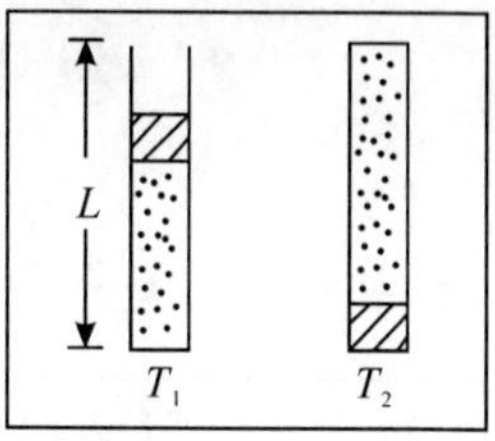

第二组：

得分	评卷人

18. (15 分)

如右图所示，xOy 平面（纸面）内，在 $x=-l$ 与 $x=0$ 之间有一沿 x 轴正方向的匀强电场；在 $x=0$ 与 $x=4l$ 之间存在磁场，在 x 轴上方磁感应强度方向垂直纸面向外，在 x 轴下方磁感应强度方向垂直纸面向内，整个磁场区域内磁感应强度的大小均为 B. 在 $x=-l$，$y=d$ 处有一质量为 m、电荷量为 q、初速度为零的粒子，在电场力的作用下开始运动. 粒子进入磁场后两次通过 x 轴，然后从 $x=4l$，$y=d$ 处离开磁场. 已知粒子在磁场中做圆周运动的半径 R 大于 d. 不计重力，求电场强度 E 的大小.

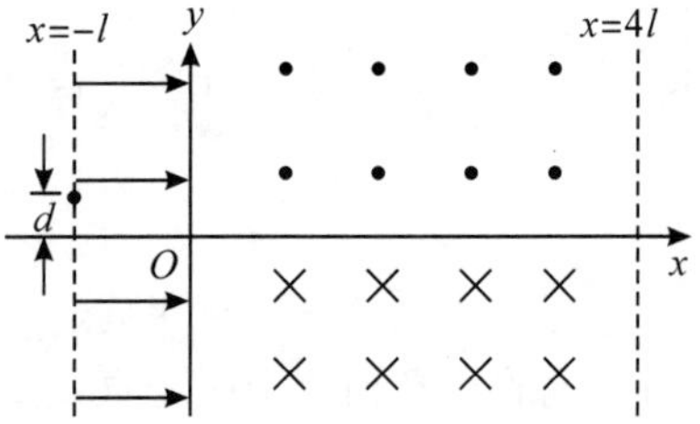

得分	评卷人

19. （15 分）

如右图所示，一由均匀材料制成的、电阻为 R 的矩形金属框 $abcd$ 位于磁感应强度为 B 的匀强磁场中，磁感应强度的方向与金属框所在的平面垂直. 一轻质金属棒放在矩形框上且与 ad 边平行. 在一变化的外力作用下，金属棒从 ad 边处开始，以平行于 dc 边的恒定速度 v 运动至 bc 边处. 运动过程中金属棒始终与矩形框保持良好接触. 若金属棒在 ab 与 cd 边之间的一段电阻为 r，此过程中外力的最小值 $F_{\min}$ 是多少？

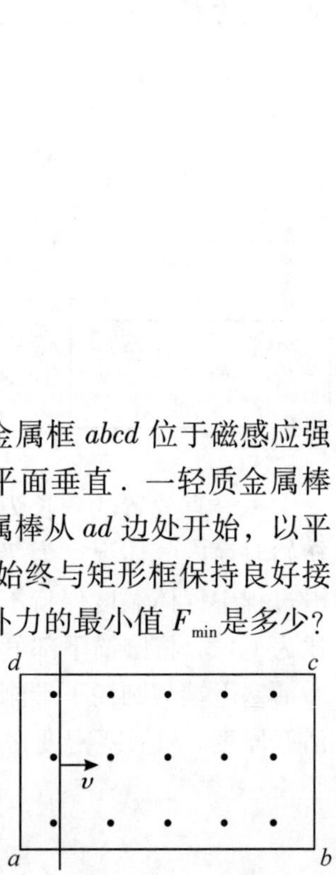

得分	评卷人

20. （15 分）

两个竖直放置的平行板电容器 C_a、C_b 串联后接在一直流电源两极，如右图所示. 初始时两电容器的电容数值相等. 电容器 C_b 内悬有一带电质点，平衡时悬线与竖直方向所成的角 $\theta=45°$. 现将电容器 C_a 的两板间距改变为初始时的 2 倍，则 C_b 内的带电质点再次平衡时，悬线与竖直方向所成的角 θ' 是多少？（不考虑带电质点的电场对 C_b 内电场分布的影响. θ' 可以用反三角函数来表示.）

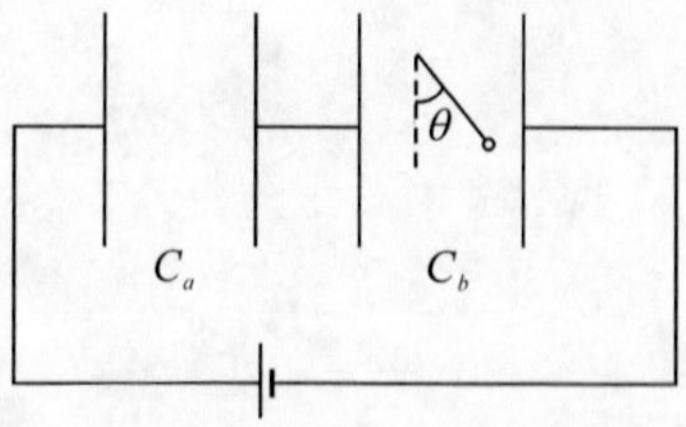

得分	评卷人

21. （15 分）

如右图所示，质量均为 m 的 A、B 两板中间固连一弹簧，B 板放置在水平地面上，A 板上放有一质量为 $2m$ 的物块 C. 初始时 A、B、C 与弹簧均静止 . 现用力将物块 C 和板 A 下压一段距离并使 A、B、C 与弹簧仍为静止，此时力的大小为 F. 在突然将力撤掉后，物块 C 和板 A 弹回时弹簧刚好能将板 B 提离地面 . 重力加速度为 g.

（1）若物块 C 和板 A 是连在一起的，F 的值是多少？

（2）若物块 C 和板 A 不是连在一起的，F 的值是多少？

（3）已知弹簧弹性系数 k，在第二种情况下，与初始时相比，物块 C 上升的最大高度 H 是多少？

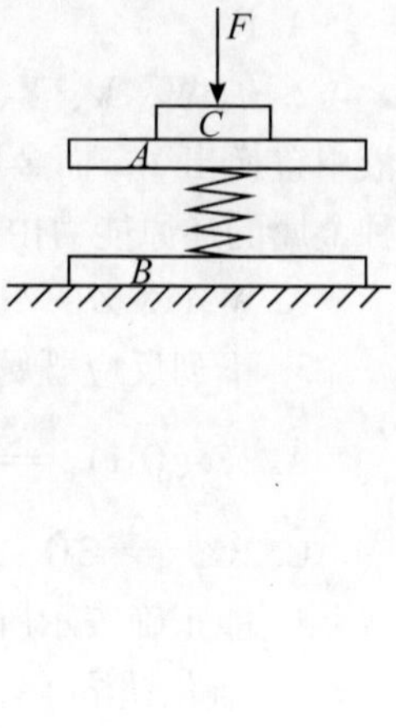

化　学

本试卷满分150分，考试用时120分钟。

题号	一	二	三	四	五	六	总分
分数							

可能用到的原子量：H 1　C 12　N 14　O 16　Na 23　Cl 35.5

得分	评卷人

一、选择题：本题共18小题；每小题3分，共54分。在每小题给出的四个选项中，只有一项是符合题目要求的，把所选项前的字母填在题后括号内。

1. 某原子得到电子后形成核外有18个电子的离子，该原子不可能是（　）

A. F　　B. P　　C. S　　D. Cl

2. 有W、X、Y、Z四种金属和它们的硝酸盐溶液，已知金属W仅能从Y的盐溶液中置换出Y，而金属X能分别从其他三种盐溶液中置换出相应的金属，由此判断四种金属的还原能力由强到弱的顺序是（　）

A. W Y X Z　　B. X Z W Y　　C. Y W Z X　　D. X W Y Z

3. 下列反应既属于分解反应又属于氧化还原反应的是（　）

A. $2Fe(OH)_3 \xlongequal{\triangle} Fe_2O_3 + 3H_2O$　　B. $CaC_2O_4 \xlongequal{\triangle} CaO + CO\uparrow + CO_2\uparrow$

C. $2O_3 \xlongequal{\triangle} 3O_2$　　D. $4Al + 3MnO_2 \xlongequal{\triangle} 2Al_2O_3 + 3Mn$

4. 能正确表示所发生反应的离子方程式是（　）

A. 氧化铁溶于盐酸　$Fe_2O_3 + 6HCl = 2Fe^{3+} + 6Cl^- + 3H_2O$

B. 小苏打溶解于烧碱溶液　$HCO_3^- + OH^- = CO_3^{2-} + H_2O$

C. 铁屑加至含6mol/L H^+离子的$FeCl_3$溶液中　$Fe + 2H^+ = Fe^{2+} + H_2\uparrow$

D. 少量硫化氢通入氢氧化钾溶液中　$H_2S + OH^- = H_2O + HS^-$

5. 下列可逆反应达到平衡后，增大压强和降低温度使平衡移动方向相同的是（　）

A. $CaCO_3(s) \rightleftharpoons CaO(s) + CO_2(g)$　　$\Delta H > 0$

B. $C(s) + \frac{1}{2}O_2(g) \rightleftharpoons CO(g)$　　$\Delta H < 0$

C. $CO(g) + NO_2(g) \rightleftharpoons CO_2(g) + NO(g)$　　$\Delta H < 0$

D. $Cl_2(g) + H_2O(l) \rightleftharpoons HCl(aq) + HClO(aq)$　　$\Delta H > 0$

6. 下列物质按熔点由高到低顺序排列，正确的是（　）

A. NaCl　Na　HCl　HF　CH_4　　B. NaCl　Na　CH_4　HCl　HF

C. Na　NaCl　HCl　HF　CH_4　　D. NaCl　Na　HF　HCl　CH_4

7. 某液体能使锌粒溶解并放出无色气体，该无色气体燃烧时火焰呈淡蓝色，反应后的溶液中加入硝酸银溶液产生白色沉淀，则此液体是（　）

A. 氯化钠溶液　　B. 氨水　　C. 盐酸溶液　　D. 硝酸溶液

8. 在实验室用盐酸制取氢气和氯气时，盐酸的作用分别是（　）

A. 氧化剂　氧化剂　　B. 还原剂　还原剂

C. 氧化剂　还原剂　　D. 还原剂　氧化剂

9. 下列叙述错误的是（　）

A. 卤素在自然界都是以化合态存在　　B. 卤素的单质都是双原子分子

C. 卤素负离子的半径比卤原子大　　D. 室温下，卤素单质都易与水反应

10. 下列四种物质中，

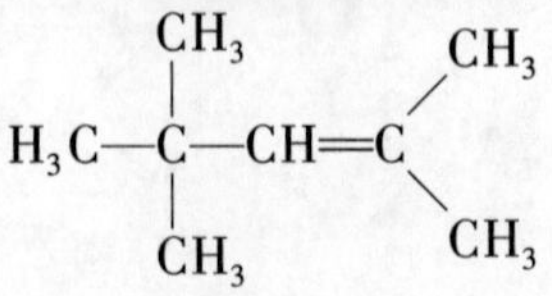
（i）

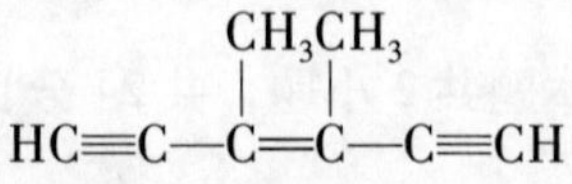
（ii）

（iii）

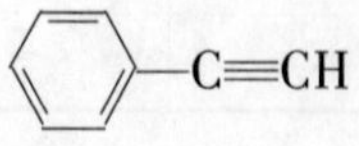
（iv）

互为同分异构体的是（　）

A.（i）和（ii）　B.（ii）和（iii）　C.（iii）和（iv）　D.（i）和（iv）

11. 下列反应中，属于加成反应的是（　）

A. 将小粒金属钠加入无水乙醇中，有气体放出

B. 将乙炔通入酸性高锰酸钾溶液中，溶液褪色

C. 将乙烯通入溴的四氯化碳溶液中，溶液褪色

D. 将甲烷与氯气的混合气体放在明亮的地方，氯气的黄绿色逐渐消退

12. 原硅酸（H_4SiO_4）可通过分子间的脱水生成一种新的硅酸，其反应式如下：（　）

$$2H_4SiO_4 = H_6Si_2O_7 + H_2O$$

在 $H_6Si_2O_7$ 分子中，硅氧键数目为（　）

A. 2　　B. 4　　C. 6　　D. 8

13. 下列说法正确是（　）

A. 化合反应都是氧化还原反应　　B. 分解反应都是氧化还原反应

C. 置换反应都是氧化还原反应　　D. 复分解反应都是氧化还原反应

14. 在两个体积相同的容器中，一个盛有 N_2 气体，另一个盛有 CO_2 和 H_2 的混合气体。在同温同压下，两容器中的气体一定具有相同的（　　）

A. 质量　　B. 密度　　C. 原子数　　D. 分子数

15. 下列叙述错误的是（　）

A. 工业盐酸显黄色是因为其中含有少量氯气

B. 久置的碘化钾溶液显黄色是因为碘离子被氧化成碘分子

C. 久置的氢氧化钠溶液中含有碳酸根离子是因为溶液吸收了二氧化碳

D. 浓硝酸显黄色是因为硝酸分解生成的二氧化氮溶于硝酸中

16. 等体积等浓度的两种溶液混合后，溶液的 pH 值最接近于 7 的是（　）

A. 盐酸溶液和碳酸钠溶液　　B. 盐酸溶液和碳酸氢钠溶液

C. 氢氧化钠溶液和醋酸溶液　　D. 氢氧化钠溶液和硫酸溶液

17. 将下列物质的溶液滴加到碘化钾淀粉试纸上，能使试纸变蓝的是（　）

A. 氯化氢　　B. 溴化钠　　C. 硝酸银　　D. 三氯化铁

18. 在下列溶液中分别加入少量二氧化锰，能产生气体的是（　）

A. 3% H_2O_2　　B. 1mol/L HNO_3

C. 1mol/L $KClO_3$　　D. 1mol/L HCl

得分	评卷人

二、（本题共 2 小题，共 24 分）

19. （12 分）在 U 形管中加入浓的 $CaCl_2$ 溶液和数滴石蕊试液。右管中插入石墨电极，左管中插入铁电极，按右图连接电源。

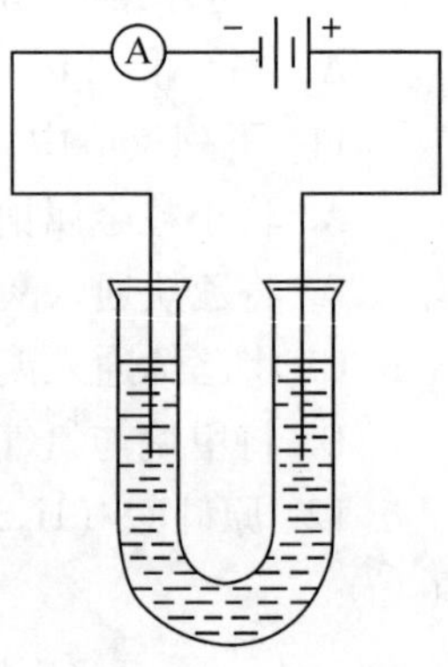

（1）右管中的电极反应式是____________________，检验此产物的方法是____________________；

（2）左管中的电极反应式是____________________，观察到的现象是____________________，其原因是____________________。

20. （12 分）已知 A、B、C、D、E 五种元素均为周期表中短周期元素。请填空：

（1）元素 A 和 B 可以形成离子化合物 AB_2，其中所有离子的电子层数相同，且电子总数为 30，则由此推断 AB_2 的化学式为________________，其电子式为____________________；

（2）元素 A 和 C 的原子序数之差为 4，它们可以形成 1：1 的化合物 AC，则 AC 的化学式为________________，其电子式为________________；

（3）D 元素原子 L 层的电子数是 K 层电子数的 2 倍，它可以与元素 E 形成共价化合物 DE_2，且其分子中电子总数为 22，则 DE_2 的化学式为________________，其电子式为________________。

得分	评卷人

三、（本题共 2 小题，共 34 分）

21.（16 分）某溶液中可能存在下列阴离子：SO_4^{2-}、CO_3^{2-}、OH^-、I^-、Cl^-、NO_3^-。请填空：

（1）若溶液呈强酸性，则溶液中一定不能大量存在的离子是________；

（2）若溶液中存在大量 Ba^{2+} 离子，则溶液中不可能大量存在的离子是________；

（3）若溶液中通入过量氯气，则得到的溶液中不可能大量存在的离子是________；

（4）若原溶液中存在大量________离子时（只答一种阳离子即可），则溶液中除 NO_3^- 离子外，其他阴离子均不可能大量存在。

22.（18 分）

已知硫粉跟亚硫酸钠溶液共热可制得硫代硫酸钠。下图是以硫化亚铁为主要原料来制取硫代硫酸钠的流程图。图中的 A、B、C、D 都是含有硫元素的无机物，其他需要添加的不含硫元素的试剂和生成物均被略去。

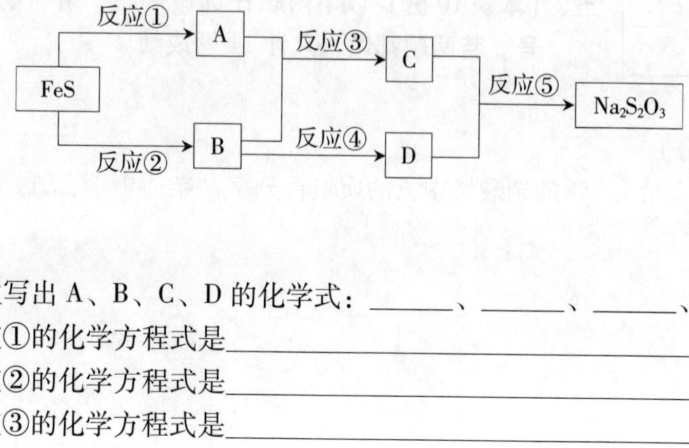

请填空：

（1）依次写出 A、B、C、D 的化学式：______、______、______、______；

（2）反应①的化学方程式是________________；

（3）反应②的化学方程式是________________；

（4）反应③的化学方程式是________________；

（5）反应④的离子方程式是________________；

（6）反应⑤的化学方程式是________________。

得分	评卷人

四、（本题 18 分）

23.（18 分）

由 A、B、C 三种化合物组成的混合气体只含有碳、氢两种元素。已知在室温下 A 是无色无味的气体，在标准状况下，A 的密度为 0.717g/L；B 是平面分子，分子量小于 30，能使溴的四氯化碳溶液褪色；C 是线形分子，在实验室可用电石和水反应制得。

请填空：

（1）A的分子式是________，电子式是________，其空间构型是________；

（2）B和盐酸反应的化学方程式是________________________；

（3）实验室制备C的化学方程式是________________________；

（4）已知A、B、C在混合气体中的质量百分组成是：A为22.9%，B为40%，C为37.1%，试问7.0g该混合气体在空气中充分燃烧时能放出多少克CO_2和生成多少摩尔H_2O？

得分	评卷人

五、（本题10分）以下两题任选做一题，请写明所选题的题号。若两题都做，只计24题成绩。

24.（10分）

试求杂质含量为8%的硝酸铵中氮的质量百分率（杂质中不含氮）。

25.（10分）

欲用电解食盐水的方法来制造烧碱，计算生产500kg烧碱理论上需要含85%氯化钠的食盐的质量。

得分	评卷人

六、(本题 10 分) 以下两题任选做一题，请写明所选题的题号。若两题都做，只计 26 题成绩。

26. (10 分)

为了测定某盐酸溶液的浓度，取称 0. 1500g 纯 Na_2CO_3 固体，溶于水后，以甲基橙为指示剂，用待测溶液进行滴定，共消耗盐酸 30. 00mL。计算该盐酸溶液的浓度。

27. (10 分)

某金属 (X) 3. 47g 与足量稀硫酸反应时生成 X^{3+} 的硫酸盐，并放出 2. 24L H_2 (标准状况)。计算该金属的相对原子质量 $A_r(X)$。

2009年暨南大学、华侨大学招收港、澳、台、华侨、华人及其他外籍学生入学考试题目答案

语　文

一、基础知识（共30分）

（一）单项选择题（每题2分，共14分）

1. D　2. A　3. B　4. A　5. D　6. C　7. C

（二）多项选择题（每题2分，共6分）

8. AD　9. ABE　10. BDE

（三）填空题（每空1分，共5分）

11. 子魂魄兮为鬼雄

12. 凄凄惨惨戚戚

13. 非淡泊无以明志

14. 南唐

15. 指事

（四）判断题（每题1分，共5分）

16. √　17. ×　18. ×　19. √　20. ×

二、阅读理解（共50分）

（一）文言文阅读（每题3分，共30分）

21. 用君王的赏赐，恩泽覆盖了（父、母、妻）三族，还扩大到了朋友。并用它赈济百姓，君王的赏赐已经很丰厚了！

22. 我想管仲失误的地方，或许是我想得对的地方。所以再次拜谢，不敢接受您的赏赐。

23. B　24. A　25. A　26. B　27. B　28. C　29. C　30. D

（二）现代文阅读（共20分）

31～32（共两小题，每题2分，共4分）

31. C　32. B

33.（共四小题，每题2分，共8分）

（1）C　（2）B　（3）A　（4）C

34.（共四小题，每题2分，共8分）

(1) × (2) √ (3) √ (4) ×

三、语言文字表达（共70分）

35.（3分）

下联：人间有爱，定挽旧貌换新颜

人寰有爱，誓变残垣为新城

36.（3分）

伸出你的援手，挽救同学的生命！

同学垂危！你能做点什么？

37.（4分）你们看，上升一个高度多么不易！生活中这样，写诗也这样！一次不成功没关系，再努力！

38. 作文（60分）

（略）

数　学

一、选择题（每小题4分，共60分．选错或不选的题得0分）

1. C　2. A　3. C　4. C　5. B　6. C　7. C　8. B　9. C　10. A　11. B　12. D　13. B　14. D　15. B

二、填空题（每小题4分，共20分）

16. $x \geqslant -1$　17. 216　18. $\frac{2}{3}\pi$　19. π　20. 6

三、解答题（本大题满分70分．在第21~25题中任选三题作答，若解答超过三题，按所答前三题计分．第26、27题为选考历史或地理的考生必做，第28、29题为选考物理、化学或生物的考生必做．解答时应写出文字说明、证明过程或演算步骤，按步计分）

21.（本小题满分14分）

解：$\sin\alpha\cos\alpha = \frac{\sin\alpha}{\cos\alpha} \times \cos^2\alpha$　（3分）

$= \frac{\sin\alpha}{\cos\alpha} \times \frac{1}{\sec^2\alpha}$　（7分）

$= \frac{\sin\alpha}{\cos\alpha} \times \frac{1}{1+\tan^2\alpha}$　（11分）

$= 3 \times \frac{1}{1+3^2} = \frac{3}{10}$　（14分）

22.（本小题满分14分）

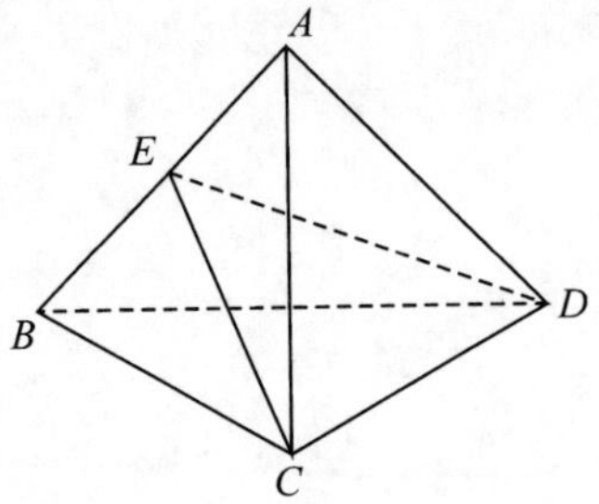

解：取 AB 的中点 E，连接 CE、DE.　（2分）

由于 $\triangle ABC$ 为等腰三角形，则 $CE = \sqrt{AC^2 - AE^2} = \sqrt{(\sqrt{2})^2 - 1^2} = 1$　（5分）

由于 $\triangle ADB$ 为等边三角形，则 $DE = \sqrt{AD^2 - AE^2} = \sqrt{(2)^2 - 1^2} = \sqrt{3}$　（8分）

由于平面 $ADB \perp$ 平面 ABC，则 $\angle DEC = 90°$，于是

$CD = \sqrt{CE^2 + DE^2} = \sqrt{1^2 + (\sqrt{3})^2} = 2.$　（14分）

23. （本小题满分 14 分）

解：由余弦定理及已知条件得，$a^2+b^2-ab=4$；（5 分）

又由于 $\triangle ABC$ 的面积为 $\sqrt{3}$，

所以 $\frac{1}{2}ab\sin C=\sqrt{3}$，得 $ab=4$.（10 分）

联立方程组 $\begin{cases}a^2+b^2-ab=4\\ab=4\end{cases}$，解得 $a=2$，$b=2$.（14 分）

24. （本小题满分 14 分）

解：由 $a_n=S_n-S_{n-1}$ 得（3 分）

$$a_n=\frac{1}{2}na_{n+1}-\frac{1}{2}(n-1)a_n$$

即 $\frac{a_{n+1}}{n+1}=\frac{a_n}{n}$，（8 分）

于是 $\frac{a_n}{n}=\frac{a_1}{1}=a_1=1$，则 $a_n=n$.（14 分）

25. （本小题满分 14 分）

解：显然函数 $f(x)$ 与 $g(x)$ 的定义域为 $\mathbf{R}$. 由于 $g(x)=f(x)-2$ 是奇函数，则 $g(0)=f(0)-2=0$，即 $f(0)=2$，（3 分）

得 $b=2$.（7 分）

又由 $g(-x)=-g(x)$ 得（10 分）

$ax^2=0$ 对任意 $x\in\mathbf{R}$ 成立，于是 $a=0$.（14 分）

26. （选考历史或地理的考生必做）（本小题满分 14 分）

解：如果直线 l 的斜率存在就设之为 k，因为直线 l 过点 $P(1,2)$，则直线 l 的方程可以写成：$y-2=k(x-1)$.（4 分）

由题意，圆心到直线 l 的距离为 $\sqrt{2^2-(\sqrt{3})^2}=1$，于是有

$$\frac{|-k+2|}{\sqrt{k^2+1}}=1 \qquad （8 分）$$

解得 $k=\frac{3}{4}$，直线 l 的方程为

$$y-2=\frac{3}{4}(x-1) \text{ 即 } y=\frac{3}{4}x+\frac{5}{4} \qquad （12 分）$$

如果直线 l 的斜率不存在，因为直线 l 过点 $P(1,2)$，则直线 l 的方程可以写为 $x=1$，该直线同样满足题意.（14 分）

27. （选考历史或地理的考生必做）（本小题满分 14 分）

解：该单位每月处理的问题奶可获得 $2x$ 万元，（3 分）

所以每月利润 $S=2x-(\frac{1}{4}x^2-3x+16)$

$$= -\frac{1}{4}(x-10)^2+9.$$ （10 分）

因为 $10\in[7,\ 12]$，所以当 $x=10$ 时，S 取得最大值 9. 因此该单位能获得利润，当每月处理 10 吨时，可获得最大利润 9 万元. （14 分）

28. （选考物理、化学或生物的考生必做）（本小题满分 14 分）

解：圆心为 M（0，2），易知一个切点为（2，2）. （4 分）

由于直线 MA 的斜率 $k_{MA}=\frac{-2-2}{2-0}=-2$，则直线 T_1T_2 的斜率为

$$k_{T_1T_2}=\frac{1}{2}$$ （10 分）

直线 T_1T_2 的方程为

$$y-2=\frac{1}{2}(x-2)，即 y=\frac{1}{2}x+1.$$ （14 分）

29. （选考物理、化学或生物的考生必做）（本小题满分 14 分）

解：（Ⅰ）总成本为 $c(x)=500+28x$， （3 分）

所以日销售利润 $Q(x)=f(x)g(x)-c(x)$

$$=\begin{cases}-\frac{1}{10}x^2+20x-500，& 0\leqslant x\leqslant 400\\ -28x+2700，& x>400\end{cases}$$ （8 分）

（Ⅱ）当 $x=100$ 时，函数 $y=-\frac{1}{10}x^2+20x-500$ 取得最大值 500；

当 $x>400$ 时，$-28x+2700<0$，即当 $x>400$ 时公司会赔钱.

于是，当每天生产 100 件产品时，该公司获最大利润 500 元. （14 分）

英 语

第一卷

Part Ⅰ

Section A (1 ×5)

1. My cousin Lerry lives at seventy-six thirty-two, twenty-seventh Avenue (7632, 27th), Chicago, USA.

2. The 2:15 train is coming in 14 minutes.

3. 6:15pm, March 27th is the time arranged for Mr. Stone to see Dr. Melton.

4. Your attention, please. Pan American Flight 546 for Madrid is now boarding at Gate 7.

5. The train standing at Platform 4 is the 8:36 for Louis and New Haven.

1. A 2. D 3. D 4. A 5. C

Section B (1 ×5)

6. You haven't written to your friends for quite a while, have you?

7. How much did the fine come to after he again broke the traffic rules?

8. Will Fanny be able to be transferred to a post she desires?

9. How will the Jackson brothers pay for their education?

10. Who has taken away my umbrella, do you know?

6. D 7. B 8. D 9. C 10. D

Section C (2 ×5)

11. W: Do you happen to know where the Job Center is?

M: Well, em... I've no idea really. But wait till I ask around in the post office. Someone there must know where it is.

Q: What is the man doing?

12. W: Hello, I'm enquiring about your ad for a secretary in today's newspaper. Do you still have that vacancy?

M: Yes, can you let me have your name and phone number. I'll make you an appointment for an interview.

W: Yes, my name is Bridge Smith.

Q: What do you learn about the woman?

13. M: It's been really wet lately. Nasty days, aren't they?

W: They sure are. The blackboards in the classroom are sometimes too wet to write anything on. I wonder how long these days will last.

Q: What did they complain about?

14. W: Hi, Ken. Fancy meeting you here!

M: Oh, Jean. Good to see you again.

Q: What did you learn from the conversation?

15. M: What do you want me to get? I'm ready to leave now.

W: Pick up a loaf of bread and a jar of peanut butter, please.

Q: Where is the man probably going?

11. D 12. A 13. C 14. A 15. A

Section D (2 ×5)

About a year ago I arrived at a Penn Hotel and made an arrangement to stay there. I had just cashed a check and didn't want to carry too much money with me. I asked the desk clerk to put a hundred-dollar bill in the safe for me overnight.

The next morning the clerk denied having taken the money. I had neither a receipt nor any other proof that I had given the man my money. There was nothing I could do but go to the nearest lawyer.

The lawyer advised me to return to the hotel with him and leave another hundred-dollar bill with the clerk. This we did. An hour later I went back to the desk and claimed the money. Since I had the lawyer with me when I handed the second hundred-dollar bill to the clerk, he dared not say he knew nothing about it.

Yet another hour later, I followed the lawyer's another piece of advice. This time both the lawyer and I went to the hotel. I asked for the hundred-dollar bill, and when the clerk insisted he had already given it to me, I denied it. The lawyer said, "I saw this man give you a hundred dollars. If you don't hand it over immediately, I'll be forced to call the police." The clerk realized he had been tricked, but he had no choice. He gave me back the first hundred-dollar bill. "I don't know how to thank you for getting my money back," I said to the lawyer. And what do you suppose he answered?

The lawyer replied, "That will be a hundred dollars for advice."

16. B 17. D 18. C 19. D 20. D

Part Ⅱ

21. C 22. D 23. D 24. A 25. C 26. D 27. D 28. D 29. A 30. B 31. A 32. B 33. D 34. A 35. B 36. C 37. C 38. B 39. D 40. D

Part Ⅲ

41. A 42. C 43. B 44. C 45. D 46. A 47. B 48. B 49. C 50. B 51. A 52. B 53. D 54. B 55. D 56. C 57. B 58. A 59. C 60. D

Part Ⅳ

61. C 62. A 63. A 64. B 65. C 66. D 67. C 68. C 69. D 70. D

Part Ⅴ

71. B 72. C 73. B 74. A 75. C 76. C 77. B 78. C 79. D 80. D 81. D 82. A 83. B 84. B 85. D 86. D 87. A 88. C 89. D 90. A

第二卷

Part Ⅵ

91. friends 92. √ 93. taught 94. a 95. √ 96. knew 97. for 98. √ 99. in 100. the

Part Ⅶ

（略）

历　史

一、单项选择题（每小题 2 分，共 40 分）

1. C　2. B　3. C　4. D　5. C　6. C　7. C　8. B　9. B　10. C　11. D　12. D　13. B　14. B　15. C　16. D　17. D　18. B　19. C　20. B

二、材料解析题（共 40 分）

21.（12 分）

（1）明代选官途径有进士、举贡、杂流三种；（3 分）科举，隋代。（2 分）

（2）明朝官办学校制度分为国子监、府学、州学、县学四级；（4 分）

明政府设立学校制度的目的一是行教化，二是育人才。（3 分）

22.（1）“戊戌变法自强之举”指百日维新（或戊戌变法运动）；（2 分）

“长江一带之骚动”指唐才常自立军起义（或庚子勤王）；（3 分）

“北方诸省之乱”指义和团运动（或庚子事变）。（3 分）

（2）康有为、梁启超等维新派的维新变法理论；

梁启超、严复等人“开民智、兴民德”的主张；

严复《天演论》（或“优胜劣汰、适者生存”的社会进化论）；

张之洞“中体西用”论。

以上四点，答对一点得 2 分，最多得 6 分。

23.（14 分）

（1）丘吉尔的演说中所说的“铁幕”是指苏联在东欧的军事扩张和政治渗透形成了一条对抗资本主义的防线。赫鲁晓夫所说的“铁幕”则是指资本主义对社会主义国家的经济和文化封锁。（4 分）二者的区别在于，前者指的是政治和军事上的，后者主要是经济和文化上的；前者指社会主义国家对资本主义国家的防线，而后者指资本主义对社会主义国家的围堵。（2 分）

（2）丘吉尔的演说发生在第二次世界大战结束，苏联和美英由战时合作向战后对抗的转变之中，冷战正在形成。而赫鲁晓夫的演说则发生在两大阵营的冷战已经完全形成之后。（4 分）

（3）意识形态上的相互攻击是两篇演说的共同点。丘吉尔指责苏联是新法西斯主义，而赫鲁晓夫指责资本主义“自由世界”的虚伪，并声称社会主义是“真正自由的”，而且必将取代资本主义。这种相互指责说明，冷战同时也是一种意识形态的战争。（4 分）

三、简答题（40 分）

24. 隋朝修建大运河过程：

为了加强南北交通，巩固隋朝的统治，公元 605 年，隋炀帝下令开凿一条贯通南北的大运河。(4 分) 大运河以洛阳为中心，东北通到涿郡，东南通到余杭，(4 分) 全程分为永济渠、通济渠、邗沟、江南河四段，全长四五千里。(5 分)

意义：

大运河成为南北交通的大动脉，有力地促进了南北经济的交流，是我国古代人民的伟大功绩，也是世界上最伟大的工程之一。(7 分)

25. 历史意义：

(1) 戊戌维新运动是中国资产阶级的政治代表维新派领导的爱国救亡运动，顺应了中国近代历史的发展趋势。(4 分)

(2) 戊戌维新运动不仅是一场政治变革运动，也是一场思想解放运动，具有资产阶级启蒙运动的重要意义。(4 分)

失败原因：

(1) 和封建守旧势力相比较，维新派及所代表的中国资产阶级力量过于弱小，缺乏政治经验，变法策略失当。(6 分)

(2) 维新派试图依靠皇帝进行自上而下的改革，而没有依靠广大的下层民众，最终导致了运动的失败。(6 分)

26. 其一，英国殖民体系存在内部矛盾。白人自治领与英国本土的矛盾，以及宗主国与殖民地、半殖民地的矛盾。(4 分)

其二，科技方面，英国完成第一次工业革命后丧失了创新和进取的动力，国内投资衰退，在德国等率先展开的第二次工业革命中处于落后地位。(4 分)

其三，英国国内政策方面，英国完成工业革命后执行自由主义的经济政策，既不重视通过保护性的关税阻止其他国家的工商业竞争，也无法通过国家的力量推动资本家的工业改造和国内投资。(4 分)

其四，国际格局的变化。美国，尤其是德国的统一和崛起改变了世界以及欧洲大陆的国际格局。英国在经济实力上落后于这两个国家，而在军事上受到了来自德国的挑战。(4 分)

其五，社会文化方面，英国整个社会食利者阶层增加，浮华奢靡，文化上保守持重。(4 分)

四、论述题 (30 分)

评分标准

得分	评分准则
27 ~ 30	立场明确，内容均衡，引用史料丰富、准确，评论详细深入，意见或评论精辟
21 ~ 26	立场清晰，内容较为均衡，能略引史实支持论点，援引史实无重大错误，意见或议论较为中肯

（续上表）

得分	评分准则
15～20	有一定的立场，能说出自己的看法，史实及分析能力一般，援引史实有一定错误，意见或评论切题
7～14	立场不定，有一定的看法，但史实及分析能力严重不足，援引史实大部分有错漏，意见或议论与题旨有一定关联
0～6	答案凌乱，内容贫乏，空洞无物，远离题旨

地 理

一、填空题（共20分，填对一空得1分）

1. 苏伊士 巴拿马 2. 地中海 温带海洋性 3. 温带海洋性 欧 4. 莱茵 鹿特丹 5. 纽约 底特律 芝加哥 圣弗朗西斯科（旧金山） 6. 湿润 半湿润 7. 西高东低 太平 8. 高原 盆地 9. 构造 火山

二、单项选择题（共60分，选对1题得3分）

1. D 2. A 3. C 4. B 5. A 6. B 7. A 8. D 9. C 10. C 11. A 12. C 13. A 14. A 15. A 16. B 17. B 18. C 19. C 20. C

三、判断改正题（共10分，判断对一题得2分，具体为1+1分）

1. ×，阿拉斯加州

2. √

3. ×，东南季风

4. ×，冰雪融水

5. ×，愈来愈早

四、读图填空或连线题（共40分，画对一线或填对一空得2分）

1. 天山 昆仑山 秦岭 大兴安岭 太行山 武夷山

2. ①－B ②－D ③－A ④－C

3. 低于 高于 甲 乙

4. B或乙 E C A 100米 约2.5

五、读图分析题（共20分，每小题10分）

1. （第三空3分，其他每空1分）

1）冲积扇 河流流出山口处 河流流速减慢，泥沙沉积而成

2）三角洲 河流入海口处

3）风蚀蘑菇 沙漠等干旱地区 风力侵蚀

2. （每空2分）

② 降低 降低 0 24

物　理

一、选择题（60 分，每小题 4 分）

1. C　2. C　3. B　4. B　5. A　6. D　7. D　8. D　9. D　10. B　11. D　12. D　13. B　14. B　15. A

二、填空题（30 分，每空 3 分）

16. 5

17. 100　0. 1

18. 15　向左　7

19. 5. 2 或 $3\sqrt{3}$

20. 1/16 或 0. 0625

21. 0. 06　垂直纸面向外

三、计算题

22. （12 分）

（1）子弹克服阻力所做的功 = 子弹动能的减少

$$W=\left(1-\frac{1}{25}\right)\cdot\frac{1}{2}mv^2=2400\text{J}\qquad（4 分）$$

（2）设子弹穿出后的速度为 v'，木块速度为 v''

由题意，$\frac{1}{2}mv'^2=\frac{1}{25}\times\frac{1}{2}mv^2$，可解得 $v'=100\text{m/s}$　（2 分）

由动量守恒有 $mv=mv'+Mv''$，解得 $v''=20\text{m/s}$　（4 分）

系统机械能损失 $\Delta E=\frac{1}{2}mv^2-\frac{1}{2}mv'^2-\frac{1}{2}Mv''^2=2320\text{J}$　（2 分）

23. （12 分）

（1）方法一：ab 匀速运动，所受外力与磁场力平衡，大小为 $F=BIl$　（2 分）

外力做功全部转化为焦耳热：$Q=Fs=BIls$　（2 分）

回路电流由感应电动势产生：$I=\frac{Blv}{4R}$，代入上式可得 $v=\frac{4RQ}{B^2l^2s}$　（2 分）

方法二：ab 匀速运动距离 s 所用的时间 $t=s/v$　（2 分）

该时间内电流在电阻上产生的焦耳热 $Q=I^2(4R)t=\frac{4I^2Rs}{v}$　（2 分）

回路电流由感应电动势产生：$I=\frac{Blv}{4R}$，代入上式可得 $v=\frac{4RQ}{B^2l^2s}$　（2 分）

（2）ab 两端的感应电动势 $\varepsilon=Blv$，电容与 R 并联，两端电压 $U=\varepsilon/4$

电容器带电量 $q=UC$，将（1）中结论代入得 $q=\dfrac{RQC}{Bls}$　（3 分）

（3）根据楞次定律，回路中电流沿顺时针方向，因此上极板带负电荷．（3 分）

24．（12 分）

整个过程均为等温过程，设大气压为 P_0，活塞截面积为 S，一盒沙子的重力为 G

第一盒沙子倒完后，$P_0Sh=P_1S\cdot\dfrac{3h}{4}$，则 $P_1=\dfrac{4}{3}P_0$　（3 分）

活塞受力平衡，$P_0S+G=P_1S$，可得 $G=P_0S/3$　（3 分）

第二盒沙子倒完后，活塞受力平衡，$P_0S+2G=P_2S$，解得 $P_2=\dfrac{5}{3}P_0$　（3 分）

设沙子倒完后活塞的高度为 h'，则 $P_0Sh=P_2Sh'$，解得 $h'=\dfrac{3}{5}h$　（3 分）

25．（12 分）

（1）$U_{cd}=\dfrac{R_3}{R_1+R_3}U_{ab}=80\text{V}$　（6 分）

（2）R_1 与 R_3 并联电阻 $R=\dfrac{R_1R_3}{R_1+R_3}=8\Omega$　（2 分）

R_3 两端电压为 $\dfrac{R}{R+R_2}U_{cd}=40\text{V}$　（2 分）

电流表 A 的电流即是通过 R_1 的电流 $I_A=4\text{A}$　（2 分）

26．（12 分）

全反射角 $\sin\theta=\dfrac{3}{5}$　（3 分）

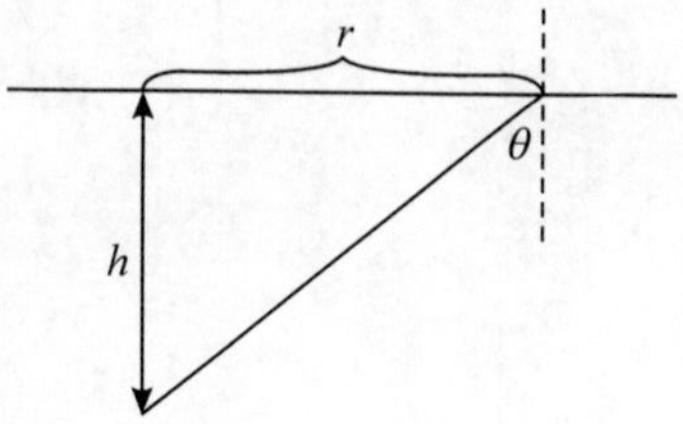

如右图所示，能看到的最大透光液面半径 $r=h\tan\theta$　（4 分）

透光液面直径 $d=2r=3\text{m}$　（1 分）

当此透光液面的直径变大时，由于全反射角不变，故 h 增大，即光源下沉．（4 分）

27．（12 分）

（1）火车加速过程中，速度增加，牵引力减小，功率保持不变．速度达到最大时，牵引力与阻力平衡，$v_{\max}=\dfrac{P}{F_f}=\dfrac{P}{0.01Mg}=12\text{m/s}$　（4 分）

（2）$F_1=\dfrac{P}{v_1}=6\times10^5\text{N}$，$F_2=\dfrac{P}{v_2}=6\times10^4\text{N}$　（2 分）

$a_1=\dfrac{F_1-F_f}{M}=1.1\text{m/s}^2$，$a_2=\dfrac{F_2-F_f}{M}=0.02\text{m/s}^2$　（2 分）

（3）$v'=36\text{km/h}=10\text{m/s}$

火车匀速行驶，牵引力与阻力平衡，$P'=F_fv'=5\times10^5\text{W}$　（4 分）

28. （12 分）

（1）A_2 和 A_3 （4 分）

（2）3 个，电源表 A 的读数 I_A，电流表 A′的读数 $I_{A'}$和电阻 R_1 （4 分）

（3）$r=\dfrac{(I_A-I_{A'})R_1}{I_A}$ （4 分）

化　学

一、选择题（每题 3 分，共 60 分）

1. B　2. A　3. B　4. C　5. C　6. A　7. A　8. C　9. D　10. D　11. B　12. C
13. A　14. D　15. B　16. C　17. C　18. C　19. A　20. B

二、填空题（共 22 分）

1. Zn 片　$Zn-2e^- \longrightarrow Zn^{2+}$　Cu 片　$Cu^{2+}+2e^- \longrightarrow Cu$

2. $K>Na>Li$　$Na>Mg>Al$　增大　减小

3. pH　0 ~ 14　$pH<7$　$pH>7$　$pH=7$

4. 羟　醛（羰）　醇　醛

5. $CH_3CH_2CH_2COOCH_2CH_3$ 或 $(CH_3)_2CHCOOCH_2CH_3$
$CH_3CH_2CH_2COOH$ 或 $(CH_3)_2CHCOOH$
CH_3CH_2OH

三、问答题（共 38 分）

1.（本题 10 分）

（1）X 和 Y；XY_4（CCl_4）

（2）分子中通过共用电子而形成的强化学键

（3）2，8，7

（4）Y（Cl）是同位素的混合物，同位素的平均质量不是一个整数

（5）Y 和 Z；ZY_2（$CaCl_2$）

2.（本题 12 分）

（1）溴水，除 H_2S

（2）NaOH，除 CO_2

（3）浓 H_2SO_4，除 H_2O

（4）铜网，除 O_2

（5）如 Na_2CO_3、$Ca(OH)_2$、KOH

（6）$Na_2CO_3+CO_2+H_2O \longrightarrow 2NaHCO_3$

3.（本题 6 分）

（1）$2Mg(s)+O_2(g) \longrightarrow 2MgO(s)$　$\Delta H=-1200kJ$

（2）不能；水会与燃烧的镁条起反应

（3）30kJ

4.（本题 10 分）

（1）$3CH_3CH_2OH+4KMnO_4 \xrightarrow{OH^-} 4MnO_2+3CH_3COOH+H_2O+4KOH$

(2) $3CH_3CHOHCH_3 + Cr_2O_7^{2-} + 8H^+ \longrightarrow 3CH_3COCH_3 + 2Cr^{3+} + 7H_2O$

(3) 被氧化

(4) 丙酸

(5) 2－丁酮

四、计算题（任选2题，每题15分，共30分）

1. 解：

(1) $M_1V_1 = M_2V_2$ (2分)

$6 \times V_1 = 0.3 \times 0.8$

所需浓硫酸的体积 $V_1 = 0.04L = 40mL$ (2分)

(2) $H_2SO_4 + 2NaOH = Na_2SO_4 + H_2O$ (2分)

1 2

$0.3 \times V_2 \times 2 = 0.2 \times 0.012$ (2分)

所需硫酸的体积 $V_2 = 0.004L = 4mL$ (2分)

(3) H_2SO_4 过量

反应掉的 H_2SO_4 的物质的量 $n_3 = \frac{0.01 \times 0.2}{2} = 0.001mol$ (1分)

剩余的 H_2SO_4 的物质的量 $n_4 = 0.01 \times 0.3 - 0.001 = 0.002mol$ (1分)

剩余的 H_2SO_4 的物质的量浓度 $= \frac{0.002}{0.01 + 0.01} = 0.1mol/L$ (1分)

$c(H^+) = 0.2mol/L$，$pH = 0.7$ (2分)

2. 解：

(1) $S \longrightarrow H_2SO_4$

1 1 (2分)

所需硫的物质的量 = 10mol

(2) $S + O_2 = SO_2$

1 1

产生的 SO_2 的物质的量 $= \frac{24}{32} = 0.75mol$ (2分)

$V = 0.75 \times 24 = 18L$ (2分)

(3) $2SO_2 + O_2 \rightleftharpoons 2SO_3$ (2分)

始 2 1 0

变 $-2x$ $-x$ $2x$ (2分)

平 $2-2x$ $1-x$ $2x$ (1分)

$\frac{(2-2x)+(1-x)+2x}{2+1} = \frac{5}{6}$ (2分)

$x = 0.5$

SO_2 的转化率 $= \frac{0.5 \times 2}{2} \times 100\% = 50\%$ (2分)

3. 解:

（1）产生的氢气的体积 $=0.025\times22.4=0.56\text{L}$ （2 分）

（2）（3）假设合金含 xg 的 Zn，则所含 Al 的质量为 $1-x$

$Zn+2HCl=\!=\!=ZnCl_2+H_2$ （2 分）

1　　　　1

$\frac{x}{64.5}$　　　　$\frac{x}{64.5}$ （1 分）

$2Al+6HCl=\!=\!=2AlCl_3+3H_2$ （2 分）

2　　　　3

$\frac{1-x}{27}$　　　　$\frac{3(1-x)}{27\times2}$ （1 分）

根据题意：$\frac{x}{64.5}+\frac{3(1-x)}{27\times2}=0.025$ （2 分）

$x=0.76$ （1 分）

所以 Zn 的质量百分含量 $=\frac{0.76}{1}\times100\%=76\%$ （2 分）

Al 的质量百分含量 $=\frac{1-0.76}{1}\times100\%=24\%$ （2 分）

生　物

一、选择题（每小题 2 分，共 60 分）

1. C　2. A　3. C　4. B　5. B　6. D　7. B　8. C　9. C　10. D　11. B　12. A　13. C　14. C　15. C　16. C　17. C　18. D　19. D　20. D　21. B　22. B　23. C　24. A　25. D　26. A　27. B　28. C　29. C　30. C

二、判断题（每小题 2 分，共 20 分）

1. F　2. F　3. F　4. T　5. T　6. F　7. T　8. T　9. F　10. F

三、

1.

（1）

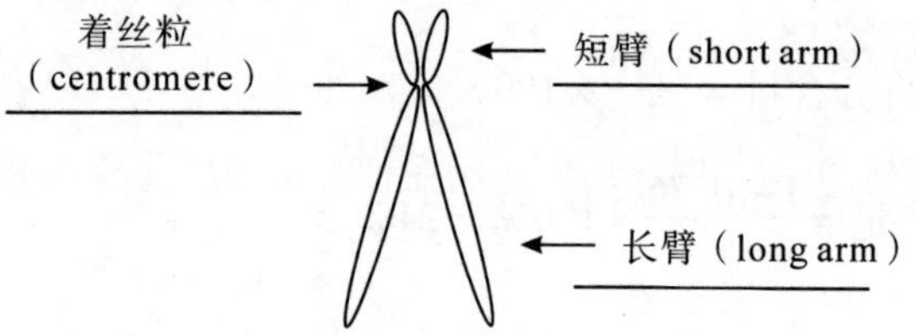

（2）

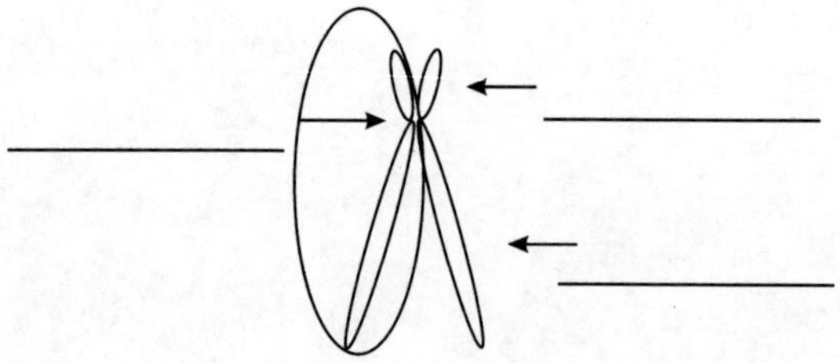

（3）

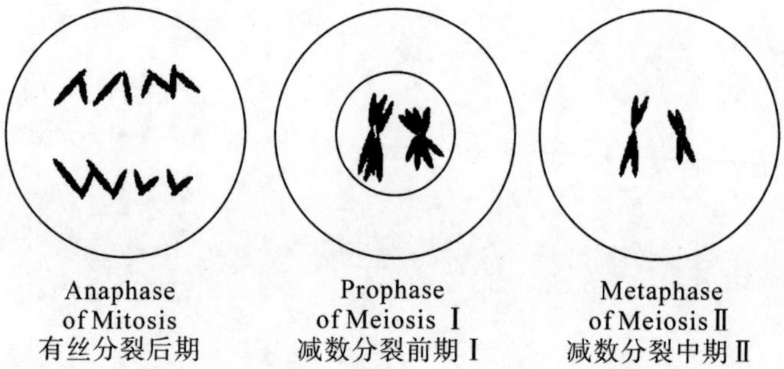

2.

（1）正常 mRNA 序列（Normal mRNA sequences）：

5'—CCU　GAG　GAG—3'

异常 mRNA 序列（Abnormal mRNA sequences）：

5'—CCU　GUG　GAG—3'

（2）正常氨基酸序列（Normal amino acid sequences）：

—脯氨酸(Proline）—谷氨酸(Glutamic acid）—谷氨酸(Glutamic acid）—

异常氨基酸系列（Abnormal amino acid sequences）：

—脯氨酸（Proline）—缬氨酸（Valine）—谷氨酸（Glutamic acid）—

3.

（1）$3 \times 2 \times 2 \times 1 \times 3 \times 2 \times 2 = 144$

（2）$(3/4) \times (1/2) \times (1/2) \times 1 \times (3/4) \times 1 \times (1/2) = 9/128$

（3）$(1/4) \times (1/2) \times (1/2) \times 1 \times (1/4) \times (1/2) \times (1/2) = 1/256$

4.

（1）由于多雨年份有许多小种子，只能吃小种子的薄喙鸟较易生存。它们在种群中的比例会上升并导致鸟喙的平均厚度减少。在干旱年份小种子少，大种子多，薄喙鸟不易生存，而厚喙鸟容易生存。厚喙鸟的比例在种群中增加并导致喙的平均厚度上升。

There are many small seeds during years with more rain, so that birds with thinner beaks which can eat only small seeds can live easily and their proportion in the population will rise. It decreases the average beak thickness. Whereas there are very few small seeds and many large seeds during dry years, only birds with thicker beaks can crush and eat large seeds and they live easily, so that their proportion in the population will rise and it increases the average beak thickness.

（2）由于随后的 10 年是多雨的年份，因此有许多小种子。这样薄喙鸟容易生存。它们的比例就会一年一年增加，鸟喙的平均厚度就会一年一年减少。

Because these years were wet years, there would be many small seeds and birds with thinner beaks lived easily and their proportion would increase year by year. So the average beak thickness would decrease year by year.

（3）自然选择。

Natural selection.

5.

消化酶 Digestive enzyme	产生的部位 Site of production	所消化的化合物 Digested compound
唾液淀粉酶 Salivary amylase	唾液腺 Salivary Glands	淀粉 Starch
胃蛋白酶 Pepsin	胃 Stomach	蛋白质 Protein

（续上表）

消化酶 Digestive enzyme	产生的部位 Site of production	所消化的化合物 Digested compound
胰淀粉酶 Amylopsin	胰脏 Pancreas	淀粉 Starch
胰脂肪酶 Pancreatic lipase	胰脏 Pancreas	脂肪 Fat
蔗糖酶 Sucrase	小肠 Small Intestine	蔗糖 Sucrose

6.

（1）生物因子包括昆虫、树、细菌；非生物因子包括水、土壤、气候、阳光。

（2）A　B　C

（1）The biotic factors include insect，tree，bacteria.

The abiotic factors include water，soil，weather，sunlight.

（2）In the ecosystem，the producer is A，the consumers are B and C.

7.

A：左肾（left kidney）

B：右肾（right kidney）

C：输尿管（ureter）

D：膀胱（urinary bladder）

E：尿道（urethra）

8.

A：蛋白质	B：脂类	C：双层膜	D：核孔
E：RNA	F：细胞核	G：DNA	H：组蛋白
I：核基质	J：细胞质基质	K：ATP	L：粗面型内质网
M：核糖体	N：细胞器	O：质体	P：光合作用
Q：白色体	R：淀粉	S：有色体	T：色素

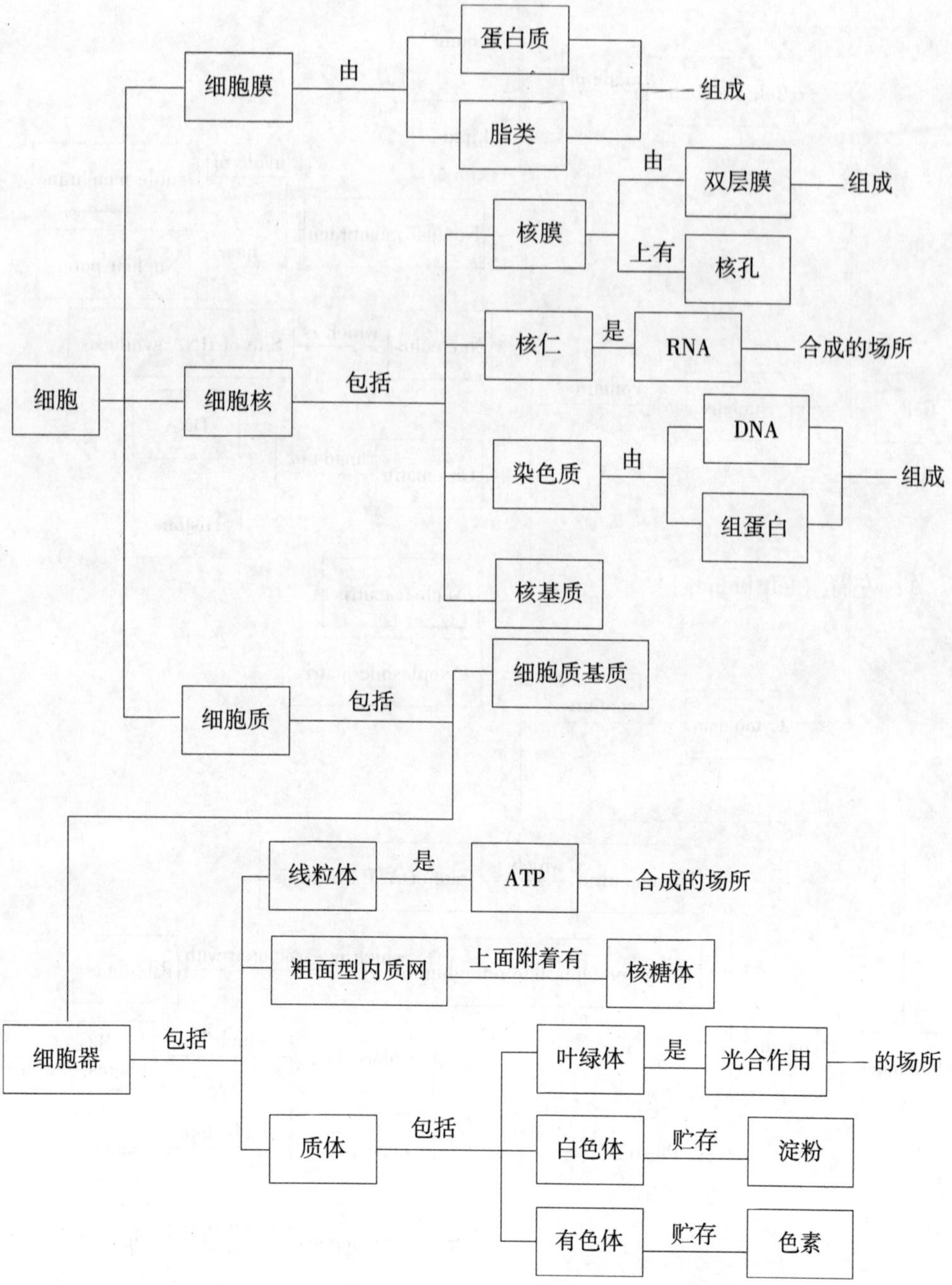
细胞
细胞膜
由
蛋白质
脂类
组成
细胞核
包括
核膜
由
双层膜
组成
上有
核孔
核仁
是
RNA
合成的场所
染色质
由
DNA
组蛋白
组成
核基质
细胞质
包括
细胞质基质
细胞器
包括
线粒体
是
ATP
合成的场所
粗面型内质网
上面附着有
核糖体
质体
包括
叶绿体
是
光合作用
的场所
白色体
贮存
淀粉
有色体
贮存
色素

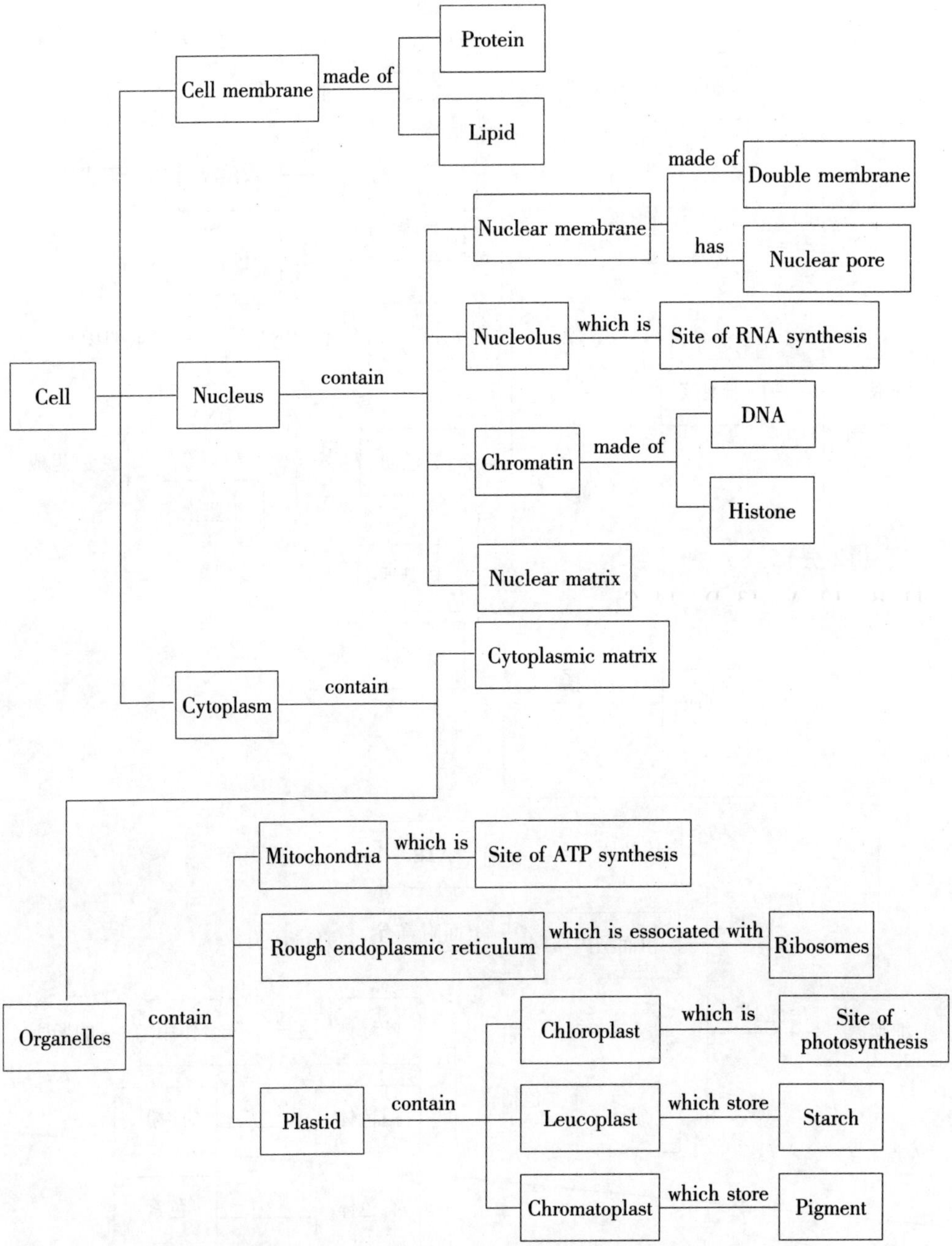
Cell
Cell membrane
made of
Protein
Lipid
Nucleus
contain
Nuclear membrane
made of
Double membrane
has
Nuclear pore
Nucleolus
which is
Site of RNA synthesis
Chromatin
made of
DNA
Histone
Nuclear matrix
Cytoplasm
contain
Cytoplasmic matrix
Organelles
contain
Mitochondria
which is
Site of ATP synthesis
Rough endoplasmic reticulum
which is essociated with
Ribosomes
Plastid
contain
Chloroplast
which is
Site of photosynthesis
Leucoplast
which store
Starch
Chromatoplast
which store
Pigment

2009 年中华人民共和国普通高等学校联合招收华侨、港澳地区、台湾省学生入学考试题目答案

语 文

第一部分（54 分，每小题 3 分）

一、(30 分)

1. B 2. C 3. A 4. D 5. B 6. C 7. B 8. B 9. A 10. D

二、(12 分)

11. B 12. A 13. D 14. C

三、(12 分)

15. B 16. D 17. A 18. D

第二部分（96 分）

四、(13 分)

19.（10 分）

(1)（5 分）

世祖认为他很好，而王旱却苦苦地以有病推辞，要求回归家乡，世祖下令同意了他。

译出大意给 2 分；“善”、“乞”、“许”三处，每译对一处给 1 分。

(2)（5 分）

有人说许彦因为王旱的法术高超，害怕最终妨碍自己，所以用诡诈手段让他回去而已。

译出大意给 2 分；“或”、“胜”、“谲”三处，每译对一处给 1 分。

20.（3 分）

(1) 言之无文

(2) 敬人者人恒敬之

(3) 淡泊以明志

(4) 直挂云帆济沧海

每答对一小题，给 1 分；如有错别字，该小题不给分。如四小题全做，据前三小题评分。

五、(23 分)

21. (4 分)

(1) 因为没有人打扰，能安心写作而自得其乐。

(2) 因担心随时可能开会而提心吊胆。

每答对一点给 2 分，意思答对即可。

22. (6 分)

(1) 因能闻到马缨花发出的幽香而神清气爽，乐不可支。

(2) 因耸入云天的塔尖带给人以希望和上进的劲头而乐不可支。

(3) 因透过窗子可以看到接天莲叶，荷花的香气也幽然袭来，顾而乐之。

每答对一点给 2 分，意思答对即可。

23. (5 分)

①美；②能让我安安静静地写作，很快进入角色，“文思”如泉涌，记忆力像刚磨过的刀子，锐不可当。

答出①给 2 分，答出②给 3 分。意思答对即可。

24. (8 分)

①珍惜时间；②勤奋刻苦；③朴实亲切；④真实自然。

每答出一个要点并加以说明给 2 分，意思答对即可。

六、写作 (60 分)

25. (60 分) 评分标准

等级分数	一等 (51~60)	二等 (41~50)	三等 (21~40)	四等 (0~20)
项目	切合题意 中心突出 内容充实 感情真挚 结构严谨 语言流畅 字迹美观 符合文体要求	符合题意 中心明确 内容较充实 感情真实 结构完整 语言通顺 字迹工整 符合文体要求	基本符合题意 中心基本明确 内容单薄 感情基本真实 结构基本完整 语言基本通顺 字迹清楚 基本符合文体要求	偏离题意 中心不明 内容不当 感情虚假 结构混乱 语言不通顺、语病多 字迹潦草难辨 不符合文体要求

说明：①评分以题意、内容、语言、文体为重点，全面衡量。符合文体要求，指符合考生根据题意和内容自选的文体的要求。

②缺题目扣 1 分；每 3 个错别字扣 1 分，重复的不计；不足字数的，每少 50 个字扣 1 分。

③确认为抄袭的作文，在四等之内评分。

数　学

说明：

一、本解答给出了一种或几种解法供参考，如果考生的解法与本解答不同，可根据试题的主要考查内容比照评分参考制定相应的评分细则．

二、对计算题，当考生的解答在某一步出现错误时，如果后继部分的解答未改变该题的内容和难度，可视影响的程度决定后继部分的给分，但不得超过该部分正确解答应得分数的一半；如果后继部分的解答有较严重的错误，就不再给分．

三、解答右端所注分数，表示考生正确做到这一步应得的累加分数．

四、只给整数分数．选择题和填空题不给中间分．

五、所有考生做第一、二题，在第三（21、22、23）题中任选两题；报考理工农医类考生做第三（24、25）题，报考文史类考生做第三（26、27）题．

一、选择题：每个小题选对给 5 分，不选、选错或者选出的代号超过一个，一律给 0 分．

1. C　2. D　3. A　4. C　5. D　6. B　7. D　8. A　9. B　10. B　11. C　12. A

二、填空题：每个小题满分 4 分，只要求直接填写结果．

13. $\frac{2\sqrt{3}}{3}$　　14. $x=\frac{5}{2}$

15. $\frac{\pi}{3}$　　16. $-\frac{1}{2}$

17. $4x+3y+z=6$　　18. $\frac{1}{5}$

19. x^2+2x-3　　20. 0. 09

三、解答题

21. （本题满分 14 分）

解：曲线 C 的方程为

$$y=\frac{8}{(x-1)^2}+2 \quad (x\neq 1)$$ （2 分）

求导得 $y'=-\frac{16}{(x-1)^3}$

设 $A(x_1, y_1)$ 为切点，则由 l 的斜率为 -2，得

$$\begin{cases}-\dfrac{16}{(x_1-1)^3}=-2\\ y_1=\dfrac{8}{(x_1-1)^2}+2\end{cases}$$

解得 $x_1=3$，$y_1=4$. 所以，切点 A 的坐标为（3，4）

故 $a=2x_1+y_1=10$ （8分）

于是 l 的方程为

$2x+y=10$

将 C 与 l 的方程联立，得

$$\begin{cases}2x+y=10\\ y=\dfrac{8}{(x-1)^2}+2\end{cases}$$

解得 $x_1=3$，$y_1=4$；$x_2=0$，$y_2=10$

所以 C 与 l 的公共点坐标为（3，4）和（0，10）. （14分）

22. （本题满分14分）

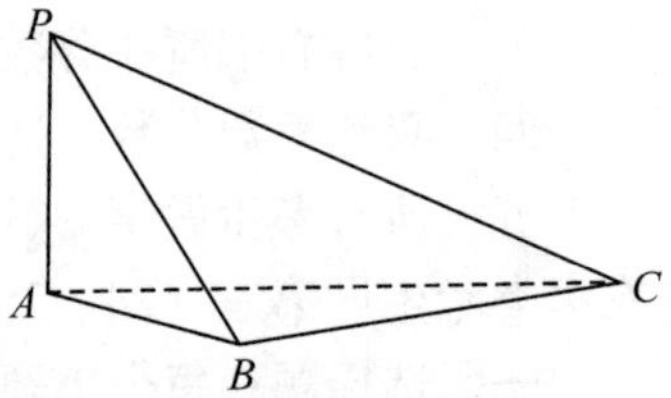

解：如右图所示，过 A 作 $AD\perp$ 直线 BC，垂足为 D，连接 PD. 因为 $PA\perp$ 平面 ABC，所以根据三垂线定理得 $PD\perp BC$，故 $\angle PDA$ 是二面角 $P-BC-A$ 的平面角. 依题设知 $\angle PDA=60°$. （4分）

在 Rt $\triangle PDC$ 中，由 $\angle PCB=30°$，$PB=BC$ 得

$\angle CPD=60°$，$\angle CPB=30°$，故 $\angle BPD=30°$，$BD=\dfrac{\sqrt{3}}{3}PD$，$CD=\sqrt{3}PD$.

由 $PA\perp$ 平面 ABC，知 $PA\perp AD$，故

$AD=PD\cos\angle PDA=\dfrac{1}{2}PD.$ （8分）

所以，在 Rt$\triangle ADC$ 中，

$$\begin{aligned}\tan\angle BAC&=\tan(\angle DAC-\angle DAB)\\&=\frac{\tan\angle DAC-\tan\angle DAB}{1+\tan\angle DAC\tan\angle DAB}\\&=\frac{(CD-BD)AD}{AD^2+CD\cdot BD}\\&=\frac{4\sqrt{3}}{15}\end{aligned}$$ （12分）

因为 $\tan\angle BPC=\tan 30°=\dfrac{\sqrt{3}}{3}>\dfrac{4\sqrt{3}}{15}$，

所以 $\angle BPC>\angle BAC$. （14分）

23. （本题满分14分）

解：由题设知 $|\overrightarrow{AB}|=|\overrightarrow{AC}|=4$

因为 $S_{\triangle ABC}=\dfrac{1}{2}|\overrightarrow{AB}|\cdot|\overrightarrow{AC}|\sin60°$，

$S_{\triangle AEF}=\dfrac{1}{2}|\overrightarrow{AE}|\cdot|\overrightarrow{AF}|\sin60°$，

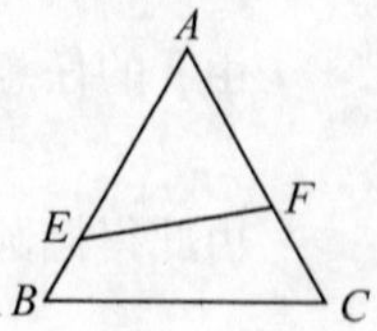

由 $S_{\triangle AEF}=\frac{1}{2}S_{\triangle ABC}$得

$$|\overrightarrow{AE}|\cdot|\overrightarrow{AF}|=\frac{1}{2}|\overrightarrow{AB}|\cdot|\overrightarrow{AC}|=8 \qquad (4分)$$

设$|\overrightarrow{AE}|=x$，$|\overrightarrow{AF}|=y$，则 $xy=8$，且$0<x\leqslant 4$，$0<y\leqslant 4$. 于是

$$x=\frac{8}{y}\geqslant\frac{8}{4}=2$$

由$\overrightarrow{EF}=\overrightarrow{EA}+\overrightarrow{AF}$知

$$\begin{aligned}\overrightarrow{EF}\cdot\overrightarrow{BC}&=\overrightarrow{EA}\cdot\overrightarrow{BC}+\overrightarrow{AF}\cdot\overrightarrow{BC}\\&=2x+2y\\&=2(x+\frac{8}{x})\end{aligned} \qquad (9分)$$

考虑函数$f(x)=2(x+\frac{8}{x})$（$2\leqslant x\leqslant 4$）

求导，得$f'(x)=2(1-\frac{8}{x^2})$

令$f'(x)=0$ 得 $x=2\sqrt{2}$. 当$2\leqslant x<2\sqrt{2}$时，$f'(x)<0$，$f(x)$单调递减；当$2\sqrt{2}<x\leqslant 4$时，$f'(x)>0$，$f(x)$单调递增. 又$f(2\sqrt{2})=8\sqrt{2}$，$f(2)=f(4)=12$，故$f(x)$在［2, 4］上的最小值为$8\sqrt{2}$，最大值为12，即$f(x)$的值域为［$8\sqrt{2}$, 12］，因此$\overrightarrow{EF}\cdot\overrightarrow{BC}$的取值范围是［$8\sqrt{2}$, 12］.（14分）

24.（本题满分15分）

解：（Ⅰ）设椭圆的半焦距为 c，则 $c=\sqrt{a^2-1}$，$F_1(-c,0)$，$F_2(c,0)$，$E(\frac{a^2}{c},0)$. 由 F_2 是 F_1E 的中点知

$$\frac{a^2}{c}-c=2c,$$

于是 $a^2=3c^2=3(a^2-1)$.

因此 $a=\frac{\sqrt{6}}{2}$.（5分）

（Ⅱ）由 $P\in l$ 可设 $P(\frac{a^2}{c},p)$. 从而$|PF_2|=\sqrt{(\frac{a^2}{c}-c)^2+p^2}$，$|F_1F_2|=2c$

（10分）

由题设知$\sqrt{(\frac{a^2}{c}-c)^2+p^2}\neq 4c$，

即 $p^2\neq 16c^2-(\frac{a^2}{c}-c)^2$.

由 p 的任意性知 $16c^2-(\frac{a^2}{c}-c)^2<0$，$4c<\frac{a^2}{c}-c$，故 $\frac{c^2}{a^2}<\frac{1}{5}$，

由此得椭圆离心率 e 的取值范围为 $(0,\frac{\sqrt{5}}{5})$． （15 分）

25. （本题满分 15 分）

解：（Ⅰ）由题设知

$$a_n=p+p^2+\cdots+p^n=\begin{cases}n，当 p=1 时\\ \frac{p-p^{n+1}}{1-p}，当 p\neq 1 时\end{cases}$$

所以，当 $p=1$ 时，数列 $\{a_n\}$ 的通项 $a_n=n$；当 $p\neq 1$ 时，数列 $\{a_n\}$ 的通项 $a_n=\frac{p}{p-1}(p^n-1)$．

（Ⅱ）证明：由题设知

$$f_n(x)=1+a_nx+b_nx^2+\cdots$$
$$f_{n+1}(x)=1+a_{n+1}x+b_{n+1}x^2+\cdots$$

又 $f_{n+1}(x)=(1+p^{n+1}x)f_n(x)$

$$=1+(a_n+p^{n+1})x+(b_n+a_np^{n+1})x^2+\cdots$$

所以 $b_{n+1}=b_n+a_np^{n+1}$

而由 $f_1(x)=1+px$ 知 $b_1=0$． （8 分）

（ⅰ）当 $n\geqslant 2$ 时，因为 $p>0$ 且 $p\neq 1$，所以

$$\begin{aligned}b_n&=(b_n-b_{n-1})+(b_{n-1}-b_{n-2})+\cdots+(b_2-b_1)\\&=a_{n-1}p^n+a_{n-2}p^{n-1}+\cdots+a_1p^2\\&=\frac{p^2}{p-1}\sum_{k=1}^{n-1}(p^{2k}-p^k)\\&=\frac{p^2}{(p-1)}\left(\frac{p^2-p^{2n}}{1-p^2}-\frac{p-p^n}{1-p}\right)\\&=\frac{p^2}{(p-1)^2}(p^n-p)\left(\frac{p^n+p}{p+1}-1\right)\end{aligned}$$

即得 $b_n=\frac{p^3}{(p-1)^2(p+1)}(p^{n-1}-1)(p^n-1)$． （12 分）

（ⅱ）当 $n=1$ 时，由 $b_1=0$，$p^0=1$ 知上式对于 $n=1$ 也成立．

综合（ⅰ）、（ⅱ），可取常数 $c=\sqrt{\frac{p^3}{(p-1)^2(p+1)}}>0$ 和等比数列 $c_n=cp^{n-1}$，便可满足 $b_n=(c_n-c)(c_{n+1}-c)$． （15 分）

26. （本题满分 15 分）

解：（Ⅰ）设椭圆的半焦距为 c，则 $c=\sqrt{a^2-1}$，$F_1(-c,0)$，$F_2(c,0)$，$E(\frac{a^2}{c},0)$．由 F_2 是 F_1E 的中点知

$\frac{a^2}{c}-c=2c$，

于是 $a^2=3c^2=3(a^2-1)$

因此 $a=\frac{\sqrt{6}}{2}$. (5 分)

（Ⅱ）线段 F_1P 的中垂线不经过点 F_2 的充要条件为 $|F_1F_2|\neq|F_2P|$.

由 $P\in l$ 可设 $P(\frac{a^2}{c}, p)$，故对任意实数 p

$$2c\neq\sqrt{(\frac{a^2}{c}-c)^2+p^2}$$

即

$$p^2\neq 4c^2-(\frac{a^2}{c}-c)^2.$$ (10 分)

故有 $4c^2-(\frac{a^2}{c}-c)^2<0$，$2c<\frac{a^2}{c}-c$，$\frac{c^2}{a^2}<\frac{1}{3}$.

所以离心率 e 的取值范围为 $(0, \frac{\sqrt{3}}{3})$. (15 分)

27.（本题满分 15 分）

解：（Ⅰ）由题设知

$$a_n=p+p^2+\cdots+p^n=\begin{cases}n, & \text{当 } p=1 \text{ 时}\\ \frac{p-p^{n+1}}{1-p}, & \text{当 } p\neq1 \text{ 时}\end{cases}$$

所以，当 $p=1$ 时，数列 $\{a_n\}$ 的通项 $a_n=n$；当 $p\neq1$ 时，数列 $\{a_n\}$ 的通项 $a_n=\frac{p}{p-1}(p^n-1)$. (4 分)

（Ⅱ）证明：当 $p=2$ 时，$a_n=2(2^n-1)$

$$\begin{aligned}f_{n+1}(x)&=(1+2^{n+1}x)f_n(x)\\&=(1+2^{n+1}x)(1+a_nx+b_nx^2+\cdots)\\&=1+(a_n+2^{n+1})x+(b_n+2^{n+1}a_n)x^2+\cdots\end{aligned}$$

所以，$b_{n+1}=b_n+2^{n+1}a_n=b_n+2^{n+2}(2^n-1)$.

而由 $f_1(x)=1+2x$ 得 $b_1=0$. (8 分)

（ⅰ）当 $n\geqslant2$ 时，

$$\begin{aligned}b_n&=(b_n-b_{n-1})+(b_{n-1}-b_{n-2})+\cdots+(b_2-b_1)\\&=2^{n+1}(2^{n-1}-1)+2^n(2^{n-2}-1)+\cdots+2^3(2-1)\\&=4\sum_{k=1}^{n-1}(2^{2k}-2^k)\\&=4(\frac{2^2-2^{2n}}{1-4}-\frac{2-2^n}{1-2})\end{aligned}$$

$$=4(2-2^{n})(1-\frac{2+2^{n}}{3})$$

即 $b_n=\frac{8}{3}(2^{n-1}-1)(2^n-1)$. (12分)

（ⅱ）当 $n=1$ 时，由 $b_1=0$ 和 $2^0=1$，知上式对于 $n=1$ 也成立.

综合（ⅰ）、（ⅱ），可取常数 $c=\frac{8}{3}$ 和等比数列 $c_n=2^{n-1}$，便可满足 $b_n=c(c_n-1)(c_{n+1}-1)$. (15分)

英　语

第一卷

Ⅰ.

1. A	2. C	3. C	4. D	5. C	6. B	7. A	8. B	9. C	10. D
11. A	12. C	13. C	14. A	15. C	16. A	17. D	18. B	19. C	20. A

Ⅱ.

21. B	22. D	23. B	24. D	25. D	26. A	27. A	28. D	29. B	30. C
31. D	32. B	33. C	34. B	35. A	36. C	37. B	38. D	39. C	40. C
41. A	42. B	43. D	44. B	45. A	46. B	47. B	48. D	49. A	50. A
51. C	52. D	53. A	54. D	55. B					

Ⅲ.

56. D	57. C	58. C	59. A	60. C	61. A	62. D	63. B	64. B	65. D
66. D	67. B	68. B	69. D	70. A	71. A	72. D	73. B	74. A	75. D

第一卷

Ⅳ.

In February, my teacher told us on the Woodmen of	76. about
America speech contest and made us to\ work hard for it.	77. to\
After the class gave its presentations, my teacher picked	78. their
three to five students to go on to the next level. I am one of	79. was
them! Then the top five from each of the three fifth-grade	80. √
class competed. The top seven would be the finalists; again,	81. classes
I was one of them! The top seven worked hardly. We had	82. hard
one month to practise. March 15 rolled around. After I knew	83. Before
it, I was in our school gym with people all around, include	84. including
the judges, listening ∧ every word I said. I was the sixth to	85. to
present. I was soon done. How a relief! I knew the top seven	86. What
got prizes, but I still wanted that honor. After the seven	87. seventh
person finished, the judge made their final decisions. They	88. judges
announced ∧ winners. The first-place winner was Kelli! I	89. the

finally win first place! 90. won

V.

一、评分原则

1. 本题总分为 20 分，按 5 个档次给分。

2. 评分时，先根据文章的内容和语言初步确定其所属档次，然后以该档次的要求来衡量，确定或调整档次，最后给分。词数少于 80 或多于 120 个，扣 1 分。

二、各档次的给分范围和要求

第五档：(17 ~ 20 分) 能写明全部或绝大部分要点；语言基本无误；行文连贯，表达清楚。

第四档：(13 ~ 16 分) 能写明全部或绝大部分要点；语言有少量错误；行文基本连贯，表达基本清楚。

第三档：(8 ~ 12 分) 能写出基本要点；语言虽有较多错误，尚能达意。

第二档：(4 ~ 7 分) 能写出部分要点；语言错误多，影响意思表达。

第一档：(0 ~ 3 分) 白卷，或文不对题，或错误百出，不知所云。

A possible student text:

Liuyi Club

Founded in 2003, Liuyi Club is a student society on Chinese traditional culture, especially the Chinese calligraphy. "Liuyi" means "the six arts", a general term referring to a variety of the traditional Chinese arts.

Since 2003, Liuyi Club has organized various activities aiming at promoting traditional Chinese arts. Some of the regularly held events include Chinese calligraphy and painting competitions, free Chinese calligraphy courses for students in the university, lectures on Chinese culture and traditions.

Liuyi Club is also a place for students from different departments to make friends who have common interests in the Chinese arts. Through various activities, members enjoy rich opportunities to improve communication and teamwork abilities.

For further information about Liuyi Club, please visit: www. liuyi12345. cn.

历 史

一、选择题

1. D　2. B　3. C　4. C　5. B　6. D　7. A　8. B　9. D　10. C　11. B　12. D　13. A　14. A　15. D　16. C　17. C　18. B　19. B　20. A

二、材料解析题

21. 答案要点：

（1）土地所有制的变化：1950 年，中央人民政府颁布《中华人民共和国土地改革法》，废除封建剥削的土地所有制，实行农民土地所有制，在全国农村开展了大规模的土地改革运动；（4 分）从 1953 年开始，在农业合作化浪潮中，农村实行了土地公有制（或集体所有制）。（4 分）

（2）作用：为工业生产开辟了广阔市场；为工业发展提供了大量原料、劳动力，并为之积累了大量资金。（7 分）

22. 答案要点：

（1）赞扬、批判和贬斥。道德和政治经济、农业等方面已臻完美；专制主义；科学和艺术落后。（6 分）

（2）对中国的赞扬带有美化的色彩，把中国视为楷模，为自己的学说提供依据；对中国的批评基本符合实际；对中国的贬斥表现出傲慢和偏见，说明对中国缺乏真切的了解。（9 分）

三、问答题

23. 答案要点：

（1）南宋时期。（3 分）

（2）“靖康之变”后，宋室南渡定都临安；与金签订《绍兴和议》，换取偏安；不思恢复，沉溺于歌舞升平中。（18 分）

（3）忧愤时局；抨击南宋朝廷苟安江南；痛心时人对危局无动于衷。（9 分）

24. 答案要点：

探索：戊戌变法，尝试建立君主立宪政体；辛亥革命，推翻帝制，实现民主共和；洋务运动，推动近代工业的出现；开展实业救国，发展民族经济。（18 分）

原因：西方列强侵略，民族危机深重；传统经济逐渐瓦解，民族资本实力逐渐增强；西方启蒙思想影响；民族意识不断觉醒。（12 分）

25. 答案要点：

德国：一个政党，一个领袖；运动基础广泛；活动以合法方式为主，成员基本为

社会中下层。(12 分)

日本：派别繁杂，没有绝对领袖；运动基础相对狭窄；暴力活动频繁；统治阶层是成员的重要组成部分。(12 分)

危害：对内恐怖统治；对外侵略扩张。(6 分)

地　理

一、选择题

1. C　2. C　3. B　4. A　5. A　6. B　7. C　8. B　9. D　10. C　11. B　12. D　13. C　14. D　15. D　16. A　17. A　18. B　19. A　20. A

二、填充题

21. （5分）阿拉伯　伊朗　阿富汗　中国　印度

22. （5分）沙特阿拉伯　伊朗　俄罗斯　尼日利亚　委内瑞拉

23. （5分）热带　亚热带　温带　温带大陆性　高原（山地）

24. （5分）雅鲁藏布江　怒江　额尔齐斯河　塔里木河　黑龙江

三、读图、填图题

每答对一项得2分。

25. 印度　大西　开普敦　比勒陀尼亚　莫桑比克

26. 胜利　泰　孔庙和孔府　青岛　连云港

27. 内蒙古（呼伦贝尔）　大兴安岭　东北（松嫩）　大庆　哈尔滨

28. 欧　亚　非　大洋　拉丁美

四、综合题

29. （1）（我国矿物能源蕴藏量不足,）可以利用中亚丰富的天然气资源。（3分）

（2）珠江三角洲地区经济发达，能源消耗量大，但本区能源资源缺乏。（3分）该工程可以缓解珠江三角洲地区能源短缺的状况，促进经济的发展；（3分）优化珠江三角洲地区能源消费结构（改变以煤炭为主的能源消费结构）；（3分）能减轻珠江三角洲地区环境污染状况，提高环境质量。（3分）

30. （1）大气；（2分）位于最小风频的上风地区、盛行风向的下风地区或垂直于盛行风向的郊外。（3分）

（2）水；（2分）远离城市水源地或在流经城市河流的下游。（3分）

（3）固体废弃物；（2分）尽量远离居民区和农田。（3分）

物 理

说明：

(1) 第一大题为选择题，只要求写出答案，不要求说明理由或列出算式，只根据答案评分.

(2) 第二大题为普通题，按照试题要求作答．解答题只有最后答案而无演算过程的，不给分；只写出一般公式但未能与试题所给的具体条件联系的，不给分.

(3) 第二大题解答中因前面错误而引起后面错误的，如属单纯的运算错误，不重复扣分；属概念错误的，按评分参考规定扣分.

(4) 对于计算题，答案的有效数字不作严格要求.

一、选择题：共52分，每小题4分．答错或不答的，都给0分.

1. A 2. C 3. C 4. B 5. B 6. C 7. D 8. A 9. C 10. D 11. A 12. D 13. A

二、普通题：共98分.

第一组：

14. AD（6分，选对一个选项给3分）

15. 参考解答：

(1) 方法一：

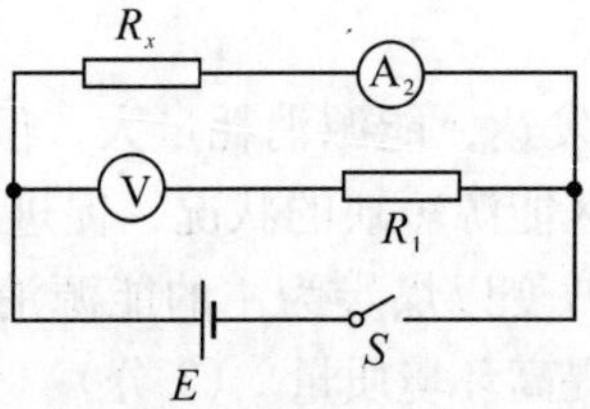

方法二：

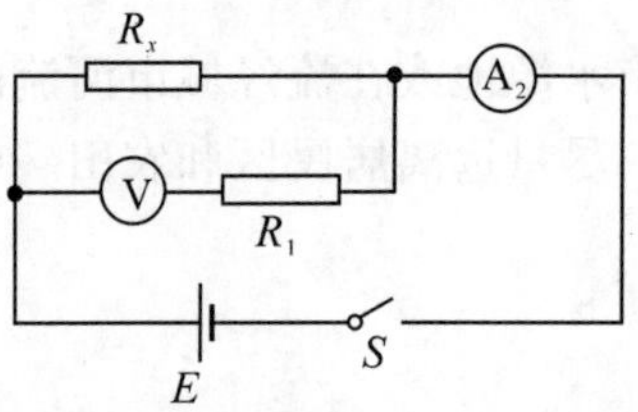

(2) 方法一：$\dfrac{(R_V+R_1)U}{R_V I}-R_{A_2}$

方法二：$\dfrac{(R_V+R_1)U}{IR_V-U}$

评分参考：本题共 14 分．第（1）问 6 分．第（2）问 8 分，将题中给出的数值代入式中的同样给分．没有修正电表接入引起的误差，只写出$\frac{(R_V+R_1)U}{R_V I}$的，适当给分．第（2）问的表达式要与第（1）问的电路图对应．

16. 参考解答：

设狭缝与屏的距离为 L，狭缝两次成像时相应的物距与像距分别为 u_1、v_1 与 u_2、v_2．由透镜成像关系式可知

$$\frac{u_1}{v_1}=\frac{l}{l_1} \quad ①$$

$$\frac{u_2}{v_2}=\frac{l}{l_2} \quad ②$$

由光路的可逆性可知

$$u_1=v_2 \quad ③$$

$$u_2=v_1 \quad ④$$

联合①、②、③、④式得

$$l=\sqrt{l_1 l_2} \quad ⑤$$

评分参考：本题 15 分．①②③④⑤式各 3 分．

17. 参考解答：

设圆筒横截面内圆面积为 S，初始时气体压强为 p_0，体积为

$$V_0=L\cdot S \quad ①$$

活塞下滑后圆筒下部气体压强为

$$p_1=p_0+\rho gl \quad ②$$

体积为

$$V_1=\frac{3}{4}(L-l)\cdot S \quad ③$$

圆筒倒置后，筒内气体压强为

$$p_2=p_0-\rho gl \quad ④$$

体积为

$$V_2=(L-l)\cdot S \quad ⑤$$

根据已知条件

$$T_1=2T_2 \quad ⑥$$

由理想气体状态方程有

$$Lp_0=\frac{3}{4}(L-l)(p_0+\rho gl) \quad ⑦$$

$$\frac{Lp_0}{T_1}=\frac{(L-l)(p_0-\rho gl)}{T_2} \quad ⑧$$

联立⑥、⑦、⑧式得

$l=\dfrac{L}{12}$ ⑨

$\rho=\dfrac{60p_0}{11Lg}$ ⑩

评分参考：本题 18 分．①②③④⑤⑥⑦⑧⑨⑩式各 2 分．

第二组：

18. 参考解答：

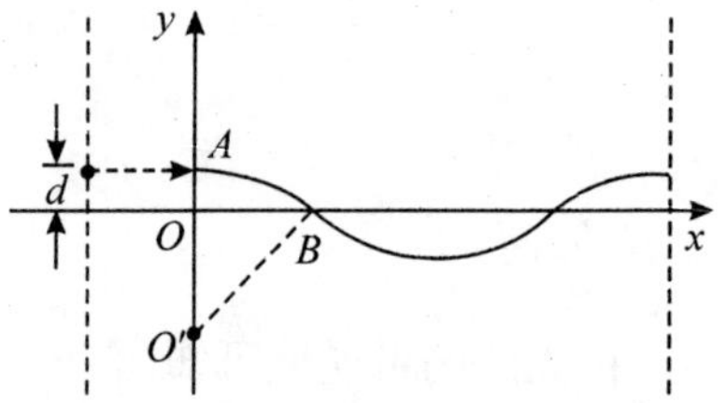

设粒子在电场力的作用下，从 A 点以速度 $\boldsymbol{v}$ 进入磁场区域，由能量守恒可得

$\dfrac{1}{2}mv^2=Eql$ ①

且

$OA=d$ ②

由题意可知，粒子在磁场中的运动轨迹如上图中曲线所示．由几何关系可知

$OB=l$ ③

弧$\overset{\frown}{AB}$所在圆的圆心 O' 在 y 轴上．由几何关系可以推出

$R^2=l^2+(R-d)^2$ ④

由洛伦兹力及匀速圆周运动公式得

$qvB=m\dfrac{v^2}{R}$ ⑤

联立①、④、⑤式可得

$E=\dfrac{qB^2(l^2+b^2)^2}{8ld^2m}$ ⑥

评分参考：本题 15 分．①式 3 分，④⑤⑥式各 4 分．

19. 参考解答：

设在金属棒运动过程中，棒中产生的感生电动势大小为 ε. 由法拉第电磁感应定律得

$\varepsilon=Blv$ ①

金属棒运动过程中将矩形框分为两部分．设这两部分的电阻分别为 R_1、R_2，电路中总电阻为 R_Z，则

$R_1+R_2=R$ ②

$R_Z=\dfrac{R_1R_2}{R_1+R_2}+r$ ③

当 $R_1=R_2$ 时，$\dfrac{R_1R_2}{R_1+R_2}$有最大值 R_M，且

$R_M=\dfrac{R}{4}$ ④

由欧姆定律得，电路中电流的最小值 I_{min} 为

$I_{\min} = \frac{\varepsilon}{R_M + r}$ ⑤

金属棒在运动过程中所受的安培力的最小值 $f_{\min}$ 为

$f_{\min} = BlI_{\min}$ ⑥

已知金属棒的速度始终未改变，所经外力 F 的大小与安培力在每一时刻都相等，其最小值

$F_{\min} = f_{\min}$ ⑦

联立①、④、⑤、⑥、⑦式得

$F_{\min} = \frac{4B^2l^2v}{R+4r}$ ⑧

评分参考：本题15分．①式1分，②式至⑧式各2分．

20. 参考解答：

分别用 Q_a、Q_b 表示电容器 C_a、C_b 极板所带的电量，U_a、U_b 表示电容器 C_a、C_b 两极板间的电压，用 ε 表示电源的电动势，根据电路的连接方式可知

$Q_a = Q_b$ ①

$U_a + U_b = \varepsilon$ ②

设电容器 C_a、C_b 的电容值分别为 C_a、C_b，由已知条件有

$C_a = C_b$ ③

根据①、②、③式及电容值的定义 $C = Q/U$，可得

$U_a = U_b = \frac{\varepsilon}{2}$ ④

设 C_b 内带电质点的质量为 m、电荷量为 q，C_b 两极板间的电场强度为 E，悬线的拉力为 T，在平衡时有

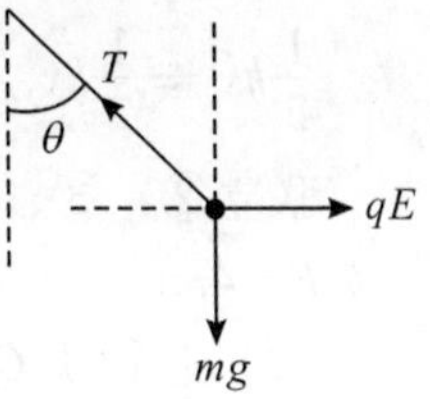

$T\cos\theta = mg$ ⑤

$T\sin\theta = qE$ ⑥

联立⑤、⑥两式并考虑已知条件，可得 $qE = mg$ ⑦

设在电容器 C_a 的两板间距改变为初始时的2倍以后，C_a 的电容值变为 C_a'，电容器 C_a、C_b 两极板间的电压分别变为 U_a'、U_b'，C_b 两极板间的电场强度为 E'，根据电容值与极板间距的关系可知

$C_a' = \frac{1}{2}C_a$ ⑧

且

$U_a' + U_b' = \varepsilon$ ⑨

联立①、⑧、⑨式得

$U_b' = \frac{1}{2}U_a' = \frac{1}{3}\varepsilon$ ⑩

$E' = \frac{2}{3}E$ ⑪

由共点力平衡条件可得

$$\tan\theta' = \frac{qE'}{mg} \quad ⑫$$

联立⑤、⑥、⑫式得

$$\theta' = \tan^{-1}\left(\frac{2}{3}\right) \quad ⑬$$

评分参考：本题15分．①②④⑤⑥式各1分，⑨⑩⑪⑫⑬式各2分．

21．参考解答：

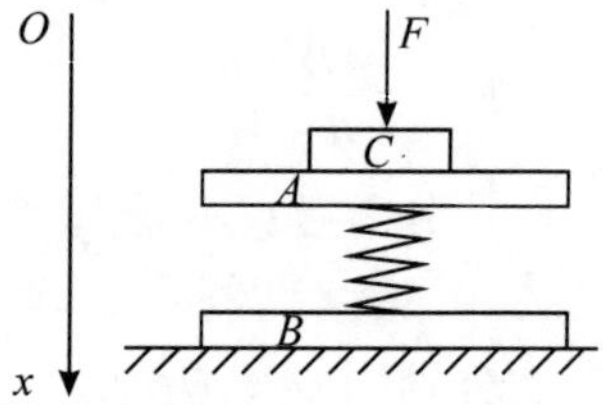

选取坐标系如右图所示．设弹簧上不压任何重物时，其上端所在位置为坐标原点 O.

设弹簧的弹性系数为 k，施加力前弹簧上端位置的坐标为 x_1，由已知条件和胡克定律有

$$mg + 2mg = kx_1 \quad ①$$

设在施加力 F 后系统再次静止时弹簧上端位置的坐标为 x_2，由已知条件和胡克定律有

$$3mg + F = kx_2 \quad ②$$

设弹簧刚好将板 B 提离地面时，其上端位置的坐标为 x_3，由胡克定律有

$$mg = k|x_3| \quad ③$$

此时板 A 恰运动至最高点，即

$$v_A = 0 \quad ④$$

（1）若物块 C 和板 A 是连在一起的，则始终有

$$v_A = v_C \quad ⑤$$

从撤掉力 F 至弹簧刚好将板 B 提离地面的过程中，根据系统机械能守恒，有

$$\frac{1}{2}kx_2^2 = \frac{1}{2}kx_3^2 + (mg + 2mg)\ (x_2 + |x_3|) \quad ⑥$$

联立②、③、⑥式得

$$F = 4mg \quad ⑦$$

（2）若物块 C 和板 A 不是连在一起的，在物块 C 和板 A 回弹、弹簧恢复至自然长度时 C 与 A 开始分离．设此时它们的运动速度为 v，由机械能守恒，有

$$\frac{1}{2}kx_2^2 = \frac{1}{2}(3m)v^2 + 3mgx_2 \quad ⑧$$

在以后的运动过程中，由 A、B 和弹簧组成的系统机械能守恒．当弹簧刚好将板 B 提离地面时，有

$$\frac{1}{2}mv^2 = \frac{1}{2}kx_3^2 + mg|x_3| \quad ⑨$$

联立②、③、⑧、⑨式得

$$F = 3\sqrt{2}mg \quad ⑩$$

（3）物块 C 与板 A 分离后的运动为竖直上抛运动，设 C 与 A 分离后上升的最大

高度为 h，由机械能守恒，有

$$\frac{1}{2}(2m)v^2=(2m)gh \qquad ⑪$$

由题意可知

$$H=h+x_1 \qquad ⑫$$

联立③、⑨、⑪、⑫式得

$$H=\frac{9mg}{2k} \qquad ⑬$$

评分参考：本题 15 分. ①②③式各 1 分，得出⑦式 4 分，得出⑩式 4 分，得出⑬式 4 分.

化　学

说明：

1. 本答案供阅卷评分使用，考生若写出其他正确答案，可参照评分参考给分。
2. 化学专用名词中出现错别字、元素符号书写错误，都要参照评分参考扣分。
3. 化学方程式、离子方程式未配平时，都不给分。
4. 在做计算题时，没有考虑有效数字的，可不扣分。

一、选择题（每题3分，共54分）

1. A　2. B　3. B　4. B　5. A　6. D　7. C　8. C　9. D　10. B　11. C　12. D　13. C　14. D　15. A　16. B　17. D　18. A

二、（本题含2小题，共24分）

19.（12分）

（1）$2Cl^- - 2e^- = Cl_2\uparrow$（2分）

将湿润的KI淀粉试纸放在右管口，观察其是否变成蓝色（3分）

（2）$2H^+ + 2e^- = H_2\uparrow$（2分）

有气体产生，电极附近的溶液变蓝色（2分）

氢离子还原成氢气后，溶液中的OH^-浓度相对较大，溶液呈碱性（3分）

20.（12分）

（1）MgF_2（2分）　$[:\ddot{\underset{\cdot\cdot}{F}}\times]^- Mg^{2+} [\times\ddot{\underset{\cdot\cdot}{F}}:]^-$（2分）

（2）MgS（2分）　$Mg^{2+}[\,{}^{\times}_{\times}\ddot{\underset{\cdot\cdot}{S}}:]^{2-}$（2分）

（3）CO_2（2分）　$\ddot{\underset{\cdot\cdot}{O}}::{}^{\times}_{\times}C{}^{\times}_{\times}::\ddot{\underset{\cdot\cdot}{O}}$（2分）

三、（本题含2小题，共34分）

21.（16分）

（1）CO_3^{2-}、OH^-（4分）

（2）CO_3^{2-}、SO_4^{2-}（4分）

（3）CO_3^{2-}、OH^-、I^-（6分）

（4）Ag^+（或Pb^{2+}）（2分）

22.（18分）

（1）H_2S（1分）　SO_2（1分）　S（1分）　Na_2SO_3（1分）

（2）$FeS + 2HCl = FeCl_2 + H_2S\uparrow$（3分）

（3）$4FeS + 7O_2 \xlongequal{燃烧} 2Fe_2O_3 + 4SO_2$（3分）

（4）$2H_2S + SO_2 = 3S\downarrow + 2H_2O$（3分）

(5) $SO_2 + 2OH^- \xlongequal{} SO_3^{2-} + H_2O$ (3分)

(6) $S + Na_2SO_3 \xlongequal{\triangle} Na_2S_2O_3$ (2分)

四、(本题18分)

23. (1) CH_4 (2分)　$H:\overset{\textstyle H}{\underset{\textstyle H}{\ddot{\underset{..}{C}}}}:H$ (2分)　正四面体 (2分)

(2) $CH_2{=}CH_2 + HCl \longrightarrow CH_3CH_2Cl$ (2分)

(3) $CaC_2 + 2H_2O \longrightarrow C_2H_2\uparrow + Ca(OH)_2$ (2分)

(4) $n(A) = 7.0g \times 22.9\% \div 16g/mol = 0.10mol$

$n(B) = 7.0g \times 40\% \div 28g/mol = 0.10mol$

$n(C) = 7.0g \times 37.1\% \div 26g/mol = 0.10mol$

$CH_4 + 2O_2 \xlongequal{} CO_2 + 2H_2O$

0.10　　　0.10　0.20

$CH_2{=}CH_2 + 3O_2 \xlongequal{} 2CO_2 + 2H_2O$

0.10　　　　0.20　0.20

$HC{\equiv}CH + 2.5O_2 \xlongequal{} 2CO_2 + H_2O$

0.10　　　　0.20　0.10

$m(CO_2) = 44g/mol \times (0.10 + 0.20 + 0.20)mol = 22g$

$n(H_2O) = 0.20mol + 0.20mol + 0.10mol = 0.50mol$　(8分)

五、(本题10分，任选一题)

24. 硝酸铵的分子式为NH_4NO_3，摩尔质量为80g/mol，氮的摩尔质量为14g/mol；硝酸铵中含2个N原子，纯净硝酸铵的含氮百分率为$\frac{2 \times 14g/mol}{80g/mol} \times 100\% = 35\%$，含杂质为8%的硝酸铵的含氮百分率为$35\% \times (1 - 8\%) = 32.2\%$。

25. 设生产500kg烧碱需要纯氯化钠的质量为x

$2NaCl + 2H_2O \xlongequal{电解} 2NaOH + Cl_2\uparrow + H_2\uparrow$

2×58.5　　　2×40

x　　　　　500kg

$x = \frac{2 \times 58.5 \times 500kg}{2 \times 40} = 731kg$

需要含85%氯化钠的食盐为$731kg \div 85\% = 860kg$

六、(本题10分，任选一题)

26.

$Na_2CO_3 + 2HCl \xlongequal{} 2NaCl + H_2O + CO_2\uparrow$

1　　　2

$\frac{0.1500g}{106.0g/mol}$　$c mol/L \times 0.03000L$

$$c(HCl)=\frac{0.1500g\times 2}{0.03000L\times 106.0g/mol}=0.0943mol/L$$

27.

$2X+3H_2SO_4 = X_2(SO_4)_3+3H_2\uparrow$

$2M$ $3\times 22.4L/mol$

$3.47g$ $2.24L$

$$M(X)=\frac{3.47g\times 3\times 22.4L/mol}{2\times 2.24L}=52.0g/mol$$

所以$A_r(X)=52.0$

2009年两校联招、全国联招试题比较分析

语 文

一、基础知识分析

（一）两校联招

2009年两校联招语文试题的基础知识部分紧扣《暨南大学、华侨大学招收港、澳、台、华侨、华人及其他外籍学生入学考试复习大纲》的要求。

与去年一样，两校联招语文基础知识总分值为30分，共20小题，有四种题型：单项选择题、多项选择题、填空题和判断题。单项选择题有7小题，每小题2分，共14分，主要考查字形辨识、成语运用、病句及表意明确辨析、同义词辨析、结合语境的语义理解、上下文衔接、代表作家的相关文学常识。多项选择题有3小题，每小题2分，共6分，主要考查修辞手法的辨析、虚词的运用、诗歌文体知识。填空题有5小题，每小题1分，共5分，主要考查名言名句补全、文化常识、造字方法的辨识。判断题有5小题，每小题1分，共5分，主要考查对文学常识的了解、文章内容的理解及文字演变的知识等。

（二）全国联招

2009年全国联招语文试题的基础知识部分也是严格依据《中华人民共和国普通高等学校联合招收华侨、港澳地区、台湾省学生入学考试大纲》的要求。

与往年一样，全国联招语文基础知识总分值为33分，共13小题，有两种题型：单项选择题（第一部分）和填空题（第二部分）。单项选择题有10小题，每小题3分，共30分，主要考查虚词运用、同义词辨析、成语运用、病句辨析、表意明确辨析、标点符号的使用、修辞手法辨析、文学常识的了解、文化常识的了解、唐诗的鉴赏。填空题3分，从给定4句名言名句中任选3句补全，每题1分（有错别字不得分），如4小题全做，按前3小题评分。

（三）两校联招、全国联招试题的比较

（1）相同之处：两套试卷的基础知识题分值相当（分别为30分和33分）；都包括单项选择题和填空题两种题型；都涉及虚词运用、同义词辨析、成语运用、病句辨析、表意明确辨析（两校联招此考点与病句辨析同题）、修辞手法辨析、文学常识了

解、文化常识了解等常用语文基础知识；都考查了名言名句的默写，且都为填空题，分值也都是 3 分。

（2）不同之处：①两校联招语文试卷的基础知识题型多样，分单选、多选、填空、判断四种题型，题量也稍多，共 20 小题；全国联招语文试卷的基础知识题型只有单选题和填空题，共 13 小题。两校联招单选题有 7 小题，每小题 2 分；全国联招单选题有 10 小题，每小题 3 分，不论题量还是分值都大过两校联招。两校联招的填空题为必答题，5 小题，共 5 分，除了名言名句的默写外，还涉及其他考点；全国联招的填空题为选答题，全部是名言名句的默写，从 4 小题中任选 3 题作答，共 3 分。②除了前面提到的两套试题都涉及的考点外，全国联招还考查了标点符号的使用和唐诗鉴赏，且每年的题型及考点相对稳定，考生备考时可加强专项；两校联招还考查了字形辨识、结合语境的语义理解、上下文衔接、造字法的辨识、文字演变的知识等，考查范围较广。即使是都涉及的考点，在两套试卷中所占的分值也有所不同（详见下表）。③全国联招试卷除唐诗鉴赏与名句默写涉及具体的文学作品外，其余很少涉及具体的文学作品，重在考查考生的语文积累及灵活运用能力，需要考生有相当的语文素养；两校联招试卷除考查考生的语文积累与灵活运用外，有不少题目还出自备考丛书《中国语文》（暨南大学出版社 2007 年版）。就 2009 年两校联招语文试题来看，在基础知识的 30 分中，出自《中国语文》的题目分值占一半多。

考点	全国联招		两校联招	
	分值	题型	分值	题型
虚词运用	3	单项选择题	2	多项选择题
同义词辨析	3	单项选择题	2	单项选择题
成语运用	3	单项选择题	2	单项选择题
病句辨析	3	单项选择题	2	单项选择题
表意明确辨析	3	单项选择题		（同上题）
标点符号使用	3	单项选择题		
修辞手法运用	3	单项选择题	2	多项选择题
文学常识	3	单项选择题	7	单选、多选、判断
文化常识	3	单项选择题	1	填空题
唐诗鉴赏	3	单项选择题		
名言名句默写	3	填空题	3	填空题
字形辨识			2	单项选择题
语义理解			3	单选、判断
上下文衔接			2	单项选择题
文字知识			2	填空、判断
总计	33	2	30	4

二、文言文阅读理解题分析

2009 年两校联招试题的文言文分值为 30 分，包括两篇文言短文，其中一篇为史传类作品，题型沿用了往年的选择题和翻译题。主要考点包括字词解释，筛选、整合文中的信息，文意和内容理解以及文言文翻译等。

全国联招试题的文言文分值为(12＋10)分，选材为史传类作品，题型为选择题和翻译题，考点包括填写缺词（多为虚词）、解释加点词语（实词）、判断复句类型、文意理解等。

两校联招、全国联招试题的比较：

同为对文言实词的考查，两校联招多考常用词，如“反”、“知”、“已”、“货”等，基本上是课文中语言材料的直接迁移，难度不大。全国联招则倾向于考查古今词义既有联系又有区别的部分，如“诣”、“执”、“许”等，学生需要结合原文语境或词语在句中的语法位置来推断。

关于文言虚词，两校联招将“之”、“其”、“于”、“以”、“而”作为考查对象，体现了命题不避基本考点的特点。文言常用虚词数量不多，但使用频率很高，考生应该很好地掌握它们的意义和用法，常用的虚词有“之”、“其”、“以”、“而”、“乃”、“即”、“因”、“于”、“则”、“故”、“且”、“既”。全国联招对文言虚词的考查相对显得更为灵活。

翻译题是历年文言文阅读理解中相对固定的一种考查方式。这种主观题型不仅考查学生对全文的准确理解，更重视考查学生对文中重要词句的掌握和自身的语言表达能力。因此，要求相对较高。全国联招翻译题的分值所占比例大于两校联招，但两套试题考查的都是语言现象比较集中的句子，包括对词的理解和词类的活用的考查。

文意和内容理解部分，全国联招和两校联招都选取了人物传记作品片断作为文言阅读材料，考查人物的言行经历及形象特点。两校联招意在考查考生对文言文内容的概括和分析能力，四个选项都是用现代文的语言形式对原文内容进行概述，题目设置的选项所需要的阅读区间不是很大（第 29 题）。全国联招对“文章内容的分析”，考题选项则是对原文内容的概述，或符合原文或不符合原文，考生只要仔细分析文章的内容，注意句间的关系，就不难作出正确的选择。

三、现代文阅读题分析

（一）两校联招

2009 年两校联招的现代文阅读材料，是一篇专业性较强的，关于“艺术魅力”的文章。为了对这个话题进行深入浅出的说明，文章运用了多种说明方法，尽量通俗地介绍了模糊思维在这个话题中的重要性。因此，对本文的阅读，难点主要在于概念的理解与运用。

在问题的设置上，题目以选择与判断为主，比主观问答形式在难度上有所降低。四个题目都紧扣文章。题目一可在文章第一段末尾找到依据。题目二、三则是概念的运用，需在读懂文章的基础上进行判断。题目四主要是对文段进行更深入的理解，是四个题目中较难的，要求学生在阅读之后形成自己的判断。

（二）全国联招

2009 年全国联招的现代文阅读材料，仍是两篇文章。前一篇重在对知识信息的解读，后一篇则重在情感的领悟。

阅读（一）是一篇关于诗歌多义的小品文。文章以大量的例子来阐释这个话题。问题是四个选择题，重点考查学生对文章所传达的信息是否能准确地接收。所有题目都紧扣原文的意思，以考查学生是否准确地理解并掌握了文章的内容，即考查阅读的基本功。

阅读（二）是一篇叙事抒情的散文。文章朴素自然，文字表面的阅读没有太大的障碍，更多的是要求对文章深意的把握及情感的领悟。题目以主观题出现，可以考查学生的主观领悟及表达的能力。题目一解释成语，要求结合文章来作答。题目二是对文章线索的梳理，考查学生对文章结构的把握。题目三、四要求对全文进行分析和归纳。

（三）两校联招、全国联招试题的比较

两校联招、全国联招试题相比，全国联招的阅读量要大于两校联招，考查的内容也更为宽泛，包括文段内容的理解、文章结构的把握及情感的领悟。考题形式多样，主客观题并重。两校联招由于篇幅有限，考查内容主要是对文段内容的掌握，题目全部都是客观题。

四、作文题分析

全国联招写作的题目一般都是两个，而且都是命题作文，考生从两个题目中任选一个写作即可。对于文章的体裁，试题没有提出要求，但所提供的题目往往内含了体裁的要求。比如，“微笑”一题可能写成叙事与抒情性文章会更合适些，而“信心比金子还重要”则既可写成议论性文章，也可写成叙事与抒情性文章。从全国联招多年的命题趋势分析，每年至少有一个题目是可以写成叙事与抒情性文章的，但不一定都有适合写成议论性文章的。

两校联招考试的作文题一般也是两个，但命题的形式比较灵活，曾经出现过两个都是命题作文的情况，但近年来多是一个命题作文加一个话题作文，如果出现两个都是话题作文的情况也不必感到奇怪。命题形式的多样性使试题对文章体裁的限制也更少。一般来说，话题作文可以用任何文体来写作，只是在试题中往往明确规定不能用诗歌这一文体。对此，全国联招试题倒是允许用诗歌体裁写作的。

两校联招是允许文言写作的，对于文言写作的字数提出了相对低的要求，只需400字即可，而用现代白话文写作的字数则要求达到700字。全国联招也是允许文言写作的，但对字数没有特别的要求，只统一要求600字。

不管是全国联招还是两校联招的作文题都不会太偏，每个考生都可以说上几句，而且绝大多数不会离题。但这并不意味着这样的作文题就好写，因为能写与写好是两回事。很多考生看到难理解的作文题会反复审题，因为怕离题，但看到好写的题目往往是不假思索提笔就写。这是不对的。容易写的题目要写出高分作文往往更难，因为大家都会写，所以要得到比别人更高的分数就必须在作文的思想深度和语言表达的准确与精确方面超出他人。不管是什么样的作文题，认真审题与构思都是非常重要的。

从近几年的考试情况来看，不管是全国联招还是两校联招，考生的作文普遍体现出思想没有深度，情感表达不真实的问题。有些考生的作文语言很花哨，结构虽然完整，但没有思想内容或情感不真实，这样的作文是不能得到比较理想的分数的。作文得高分者都是阅读量比较大而且善于思考的考生。有些考生在备考时过于关注写作的形式而不注重自己思想的提升，这是问题的症结所在。

作文考试时的一些细节也须注意。比如有些考生看到命题作文，往往不会在自己的作文前写上文章的题目，从而使自己的作文没有了题目。有些考生平时忽视对标点符号的学习应用，写作时便出现许多低级错误，比如有的给文章的题目也加上书名号，有的文章中标点符号的位置用得不当，有的文章只有逗号和句号两种标点符号，该用其他标点符号的地方一律不用。这反映了考生平时读书少而且不注重思考的毛病。有些考生书写太潦草，老师阅卷时很难读懂文章。考试时书写不一定要表现出书法的艺术性，但工整应是最基本的要求。

有些考生读书少，平时又不注意观察和思考，写作时便没有材料可用，于是文章写的内容都是大家耳熟能详的那几个历史故事，比如将相和、司马迁受辱或勾践卧薪尝胆等，把这些剩饭炒来炒去，让人觉得乏味之至。有些考生写作时实在没有内容可写，于是把话题作文或材料题中的内容大段大段地抄进自己的文章以充字数，其结果可能适得其反。

总而言之，重视对经典名篇的阅读并学会思考并在此基础上适当练笔是提高作文水平的不二法门。

数　学

一、两校联招试题分析

（一）试卷结构

本试卷文理合卷，考试时间为120分钟，满分150分，各有27道小题。2009年考试的题型仍如往届，客观题分值比重较大，共有三道大题，第一大题选择题计15小题，每小题4分，满分60分；第二大题填空题计5小题，每小题4分，满分20分；第三大题解答题计7小题，其中前三题为五题中任选三题作答，后四题分别为选考历史或地理的考生必答和选考物理、化学或生物的考生必答。具体题型及分值如表1所示。

表1　2009年两校联招数学试题类型与分值分布

试题类型	选择题	填空题	解答题	总计
试题数	15	5	7（5选3，文理各有2道必做题）	27
所占分值	60	20	70	150

（二）试卷内容

试题覆盖《考试大纲》规定的代数、三角、解析几何、立体几何以及排列组合与概率统计五大模块的基本内容，主要考查核心的基础知识（如第1、2、6、16、19小题，分别考查不等式求解、求交集、角度制与弧度制的转化、定义域求解、最小正周期）、基本技能（如第4、17小题，考查正弦函数图像的平移、图表数据处理）以及数学思想和方法（如第21、23小题，考查弦切函数互化的方法、新数列的构造思想），注重考查考生的运算能力（如第3、20小题，考查复数的计算、根式化简）和空间观念（如第14、22小题，考查异面直线、平面与平面垂直）及运用所学知识解决实际问题的能力（如第27、29小题，考查运用函数模型求解最大利润问题）。总之，2009年两校联招试题严格遵循考纲精神，重视对基础知识的考查，既覆盖全面又突出重点。具体的考查内容与分值分布如表2所示。

表 2　2009 年两校联招数学试题考查内容与分值分布

分值＼内容		代数	三角	解析几何	立体几何	排列组合与概率初步	总计
选择题（共 15 题）		6 题 24 分	3 题 12 分	2 题 8 分	1 题 4 分	3 题 12 分	60 分
填空题（共 5 题）		3 题 12 分	1 题 4 分	1 题 4 分			20 分
解答题（共 5 题）	文理 5 选 3	1 题 14 分	2 题 28 分	1 题 14 分	1 题 14 分		42 分
	文科 2 题	1 题 14 分		1 题 14 分			28 分
	理科 2 题	1 题 14 分		1 题 14 分			28 分
总计		64 分（文科）或 64 分（理科）	44 分	40 分（文科）或 40 分（理科）	18 分	12 分	150 分

（三）试题特色

2009 年两校联招试题对上严格遵循两校联招数学考试大纲的精神，对下体现了以考生为本的命题理念，试题重视对基础知识的考查，既覆盖全面又突出重点，重点内容在试题中占有较大的比重，注重学科知识的综合性和思维的灵活性，不刻意追求知识的覆盖面，全卷试题既保持常规，又适度创新。

1. 保持文理合卷的命题结构

试题文理合卷，其中绝大部分试题相同，体现了数学的共同基础，有利于对文理科考生数学基础的比较，文理科相同试题与分值分布如表 3 所示。

表 3　2009 年两校联招数学试题文理科相同试题与分值分布

试题类型	选择题	填空题	解答题	总计
相同试题数	15	5	5（5 选 3）	23
所占分值	60	20	42	122

2. 提供选考试题，保证有效区分

试题适当设置选考题目，供文理科考生自主选择，体现了对文理科考生的不同要求，反映了对理科考生数学思维能力有更高的要求，也体现了对文科考生的理解和关爱。况且选考题在全卷中所占比重不大，并注意了各选考题的等值性，从而保证了有效区分。

3. 注重数学双基与多种数学能力

本试卷从整体来看，知识面较广，内容较多。从命题重点上来讲，主要强调了对基础知识的牢固掌握，也非常重视考查学生的数学思维能力，同时也兼顾对空间想象、抽象概括、推理论证、运算求解、数据处理等基本数学能力的考查，为考生展示数学能力提供了广阔的空间。

4. 重视数学应用，贴近学生生活

两校联招一向注重考查学生的数学应用意识，而历年考生在应用题上失分甚多，这源于数学应用的多样性，数学问题情景的复杂性，以及学生生活环境的单一性等因素，为了减缓上述因素对学生的压力，2009 年试题对数学应用问题进行了精心设计与处理，以照顾海外考生的背景。

5. 降低试题难度，合理评价学生

2009 年两校联招试题在降低难度，提高区分度，保证评价的准确性和合理性方面做了很大的改善，考题入口朴素平实，加强分步设问，增加得分机会，甚至作出适当暗示，提供重要铺垫，而且大多问题以高中数学常见问题作为命题的背景，使大部分考生比较容易入手解决，便于考查学生的真实水平。

总之，2009 年两校联招试题淡化了特殊的技巧，全面考查通性通法，体现了以知识为载体，以方法为依托，以能力考查为目的的命题指向。全卷题型常规，但不失区分度，有助于检测学生对数学学科知识的理解、掌握、运用能力。试题多视点、多角度、多层次地考查了学生后续学习所应具备的数学素养和潜能，为高校录取新生提供了有效的数学评价。

二、全国联招试题分析

（一）试卷结构

本试卷满分 150 分，共三道大题，27 道小题。第一大题为选择题，共 12 小题，每小题 5 分，满分 60 分；第二大题为填空题，共 8 小题，每小题 4 分，满分 32 分；第三大题为解答题，共 7 小题。其中前三题为文理共答题，考生任选其中两题作答，每小题 14 分，后四题分别为选考理科或文科考生的必答题，各科必做两题，每小题 15 分。具体题型及分值如表 4 所示。

表 4　全国联招数学试题类型与分值分布

试题类型	选择题	填空题	解答题	总计
试题数	12	8	文理各 4 题	24
所占分值	60	32	58	150
所占比例（%）	40	21.3	38.7	100

从表4可明显看出，试题中客观题比例较大，满分92分，占试卷总分值的61.3%；选择题分值很大，每题5分，满分60分，占试卷总分值的40%，比考试大纲中规定的约占35%有所增加；文理科试卷的差别主要体现在最后两道解答题上（理科的24、25题要比文科的26、27题难度更大）。

（二）试卷内容

（1）试题从总体上贯彻了《考试大纲》的基本思想，并且在题目类型和题目分值上与前几年保持一致。

（2）试题覆盖的知识面广，涉及代数、三角、立体几何、解析几何、微积分和概率等方面，较全面地考查了考生的知识结构。

（3）试题紧扣《考试大纲》的要求，考查了考生对《考试大纲》所要求的数学的基础知识、基本技能和常用数学思想方法的掌握情况，注重考查学生的运算能力、思维能力和空间想象能力。

（4）试题文理同卷，其中绝大部分试题相同，说明对文理科考生的基本要求相同，只是在最后两道解答题上体现了文理科在难度上的差别。

（5）试题适当设置选考题，照顾不同地域考生的实际情况，有利于真实全面地考查考生的水平。

（6）值得考生注意的是，这两年的试题中几何题的分量都很重，解析几何题的分值在50至60分之间；特别是今年所出的解答题中，21、22、23、24、26均为几何题，考生须多加重视。

（7）数列知识也在这两年的考试中受到青睐，去年的24、26题，今年的25、27题都与数列有关。

（8）极坐标、概率、复数等方面的知识各只有一道客观题，从以往的情况看，考生对这些知识较生疏，可能是认为分值少，不太重视。其实，这些考得少的知识一般也较容易拿分，把这些分拿到，积少成多，对总分的提高是很有帮助的。

（9）试题中客观题的比例较大，占总分值的61.3%，其难度相对于解答题来说较小，但题量较大，这就要求学生灵活运用自己所掌握的知识，细致审题，把握关键字词，巧妙使用估算法、排除错误法、猜答等答题技巧，以较快的速度解题。

（10）解答题难度较大，不仅要求考生具有综合运用知识的能力（如第23题，要用到解三角形、向量和导数等知识），而且还要具有较高的解题技巧。从考试结果看，考生普遍在解答题上得分不高。因此，考生在考试时要根据自身的情况审时度势，即使在解答题上得不了多少分，也不要灰心和慌神，要尽量在客观题上多拿分，因为相对而言，客观题的分是较容易拿的。

（11）从总体看，整份试卷题量还是偏多，难度也偏大，因此考试时间会比较紧张，考生必须注意解题速度，注意合理分配时间。

三、两校联招、全国联招试题的对比分析

（一）两校联招与全国联招考试大纲的对比分析

两校联招考试大纲共分为五大部分：代数、三角、解析几何、立体几何、概率初步。全国联招考试大纲共分为六大部分：代数、三角、立体几何、解析几何、微积分、概率与统计。

从考试大纲来看，全国联招比两校联招考试范围广。全国联招和两校联招数学科知识点有70%左右相同，同时全国联招比两校联招多出的内容主要是解析几何中的"坐标平移"、"极坐标"和"空间解析几何"，概率与统计中的"统计"部分和整个"微积分"部分。

（二）试卷结构的对比分析

全国联招的试卷结构与两校联招的试卷结构是非常接近的，都是由选择题、填空题与解答题三种题型组成，也都设置了选做题。

表5　2009年两校联招与全国联招数学试卷结构比较

题型	两校联招	全国联招
选择题	15题，每题4分，共60分，占40%	12题，每题5分，共60分，占40%
填空题	5题，每题4分，共20分，占13%	8题，每题4分，共32分，占21%
解答题	五选三，加两道必做题。共70分，占47%	三选二，加两道必做题。共58分，占39%
总分	150分	150分

（三）试卷内容的对比分析

表6　2009年数学试题所考查的知识点分布

内容	代数	三角	立体几何	解析几何	微积分	概率与统计
两校联招	82分	48分	18分	26分	0分	4分
全国联招	61分	24分	23分	47分	5分	4分

1. 全国联招试题保持稳定，但稳中有新

2009年全国联招数学试题沿袭了前两年试卷的特点：重视基础，重视对数学思想方法、数学能力的考查；在题型、题量、难度分布上与前两年保持相对稳定。整套试题在稳定格局的前提下，也稳中有新、稳中有进，出现了一些富有新意的好题。例如解答题的第23题，将三角与向量以及求函数的最值有机融合，在知识的交汇处出题，突出了能力立意的命题思想，也使得该题显得新颖别致。

2. 两校联招注重对基础知识的全面考查

2009 年两校联招数学试题的起点低，入手容易，选择题、填空题的难度和计算量与去年相比都有所降低。这样有利于稳定考生情绪，使他们能迅速进入最佳状态。2009 年两校联招紧扣《考试大纲》，注重对基础知识的考查。试题所考查的知识点涵盖了高中数学的主要内容。很多试题的类型都能在“两校复习丛书”教材上找到出处，如解答题的第 21、23、26、28 题。重视基础，回归教材，在基础中考查能力，这些题目考查的都是现行高中数学中最基本、最重要的数学知识和数学思想方法。

(四) 试卷难度的对比分析

从两份试卷来看，全国联招对知识点的考查比两校联招的程度深，覆盖面广。全国联招的第 23 题与两校联招的第 28 题都是 14 分，所考查的都是解析几何的内容，但是全国联招的第 23 题要同时用到代数、三角、解析几何的知识，而两校联招的第 28 题所考查的只是解析几何的一些基础知识。很明显，全国联招的第 23 题难度更高，计算量更大，综合性更强。

多年来，全国联招数学试题的形式、结构和题量基本保持稳定，试题的难度基本保持不变。而 2009 年两校联招试题比以前的试题难度有所降低，提高了区分度，主要是为了照顾海外考生的背景，保证评价的准确性与合理性。

(五) 考生存在的主要问题

通过 2009 年两校联招和全国联招数学阅卷工作，反映出考生在高中数学学习中仍存在以下问题：

1. 基本概念掌握不牢固

数学概念学习是数学学习的基础，需要正确理解概念，正确、灵活运用概念解决数学问题。在这方面，教师在教学中已经作了很大努力，但考生对数学概念的掌握仍不理想。

2. 基本运算不过关

对运算能力的考查在数学考试中占有一定分量。但由于运算不过关，因而不能有效地对试题作答，出现这样情形的考生比比皆是。

3. 对题意不能正确理解造成失误

数学学习需要在日常生活语言、数学语言、图形语言间进行正确转换，最终以数学语言为载体解决数学问题。对这方面许多考生不能正确转换，因而无法下手或转换不正确造成失误。

4. 理性思维不深刻

数学思维能力是能力考查的重点。试题对理性思维进行了深刻的考查。许多试题突出了能力立意，但有的考生由于理性思维不深刻，致使无法完整解答。

英 语

一、全国联招试卷分析

(一) 试卷结构

题型	分值	各题型所占比例（%）
听力理解	30	20
英语运用：单项填空 完形填空	15 20	10 13.3
阅读理解	50	33.3
短文改错	15	10
作文	20	13.3
总分	150	

从各个题型分值所占比例来看，阅读理解和听力理解最高，作文和完形填空次之，而单项填空和短文改错最低。由此可见，全国联招的试题旨在考查考生对语言的实际运用能力，特别是听说和理解两个方面；而短文改错和单项填空分值所占比例低，说明考试意在淡化语法知识的细枝末节，引导学生从总体上对语言进行掌握。

(二) 各题型分析

第一部分：听力理解

该部分由 20 个小题组成，每小题 1.5 分，共 30 分，题目主要由短文和对话组成。该部分主要考查以下四个方面：

(1) 对对话或短文的主题的整体把握。

(2) 对对话或短文中具体的关键信息的把握，例如对时间、地点、人物、数字的提问。

(3) 通过对话中提供的语境或说话人的语气，推断相关的答案。

(4) 理解、领会说话人的观点、态度或意图。

第二部分：单项填空

题号	知识点
21	对话理解
22	短语 earn one's living
23	if 引导的条件状语从句
24	suggest + 动名词
25	what 作关系代词，引导主语从句
26	recognition 含义的理解
27	would not have done 表示对过去否定的推测
28	make it up to sb 对某人进行补偿
29	连词 otherwise 的用法
30	any 在特定语境中的用法
31	定冠词 the 的用法
32	定语从句
33	过去进行时
34	in other words 意为"换句话说"
35	考查 rise beyond 的意思，意为"超过"

第三部分：完形填空

该题型本身就是对考生语法知识、词汇知识、逻辑思维能力的一种综合考查，首先要求考生对整篇文章有一个综合的把握，例如文章的主要内容，作者的思想和态度，以及文章情节脉络的变化。在此基础上，再对考生语法和词汇进行考查。由于涉及语篇的理解，文章前后在内容和思想上都有着紧密的联系，因此完形填空有一定的解题技巧和解题规律，对于几个看似都正确的答案，运用相关知识和解题技巧都能找到最正确或者是最合适的答案。

第四部分：阅读理解

篇目	内容	题目分析
Text 1	有关历史人物（Harriet Tubman）主要生平事迹的介绍	主要对具体事件的细节进行考查（how, when, where, who），以及对文章体裁的判断
Text 2	关于自己购物的亲身经历	考查作者亲身经历的情感、态度上的状况
Text 3	关于民族心理文化的说明文	对文章主旨，以及几个民族文化心理的对比，还有各个专家对文化心理定式的看法

（续上表）

篇目	内容	题目分析
Text 4	关于公共交通局的职能介绍的公告	考查各种数据（时间、数量等）
Text 5	关于音乐和数学关系的科普说明文	推测题较多，没有直接明显的答案，需要通过上下文来理解

第五部分：短文改错

所有短文改错题基本上是围绕着语法、词汇和语篇来考查的，旨在培养学生准确使用英文的习惯和能力。语法方面包括时态、语态、动词人称、名词单复数等；词汇则包括动词短语的固定搭配、形容词和副词的区别等，而对语篇的考查主要集中在连词方面，例如考查文章前后是转折关系、并列关系、因果关系，还是递进关系等。具体而言，该篇短文考查了 3 题名词单复数、1 题时态、3 题动词搭配、1 题感叹句的用法、1 题副词（hard 和 hardly 的区别），以及定冠词、序数词的用法等。

第六部分：作文

2009 年全国联招的作文为命题作文，体裁是简介。要求考生写一篇关于一个中国传统文化俱乐部的简要介绍，要求要点全面而准确，行文连贯，语言基本无误，表达清晰。

二、两校联招试卷分析

（一）试卷结构

题型	分值	各题型所占比例（%）
听力理解	30	20
阅读理解	40	27
词汇	20	13
语法结构	10	7
完形填空	20	13
短文改错	10	7
作文	20	13
总分	150	

从各个题型分值可以判断出，两校联招的英语考试注重考查考生对英语的实际运用能力（听力和阅读分别占了 20% 和 27%，作文和完形填空都占了 13%）。

（二）各题型分析

第一部分：听力理解

题型	分值和题量	技巧
听辨数字	1×5	主要考查时间（年月日、小时、分钟的读法），以及街道门牌号等
回答问题	1×5	掌握四种疑问句的回答方式及一些日常用语
多层对话	2×5	根据设问内容和选项确定对话情景和主题、对话的场合、双方的关系等
短文独白	2×5	先看各个选项，根据选项内容预测可能出现的话题和问题

第二部分：阅读理解

篇目	主题	分析
Text 1	关于作者参加一个文化交流项目的见闻和感受	除了第一篇文章以外，其他文章的题目都考查了文章的主旨、大意或要求考生选择最合适的标题。几乎每篇文章都涉及关于时间、地点、人物、事件等细节问题。考题中较难的是推测题，要求考生根据文章内容推测作者的态度或结果，或者某个生词在文章中的意思，一共出现了6题。对于这种推测题，解题的关键在于对文章的理解
Text 2	关于年老工人和年轻工人之间的代沟问题	
Text 3	关于读书的作用	
Text 4	关于一个国家公园所面临的困境	

第三部分：词汇

题项	考查要点	分析
Section A	考查同义词或短语在具体语境中的运用以及习惯搭配	需要学生不仅了解单词的含义，而且还要了解单词的词性，以及关于该单词的固定搭配
Section B	考查多义词在具体语境中的运用	

第四部分：语法结构

题项	语言点
1	反意疑问句
2	with + 过去分词作伴随状语
3	suggest 表示建议时，用虚拟语气
4	only 引导的部分倒装句
5	比较级：the more... the more... 的用法
6	that 强调句
7	so that 如此……以至于

（续上表）

题项	语言点
8	情态动词 must 表示肯定的推测
9	连词 or，表示否则
10	过去完成时的用法

第五部分：完形填空

总体说来，两校联招的完形填空相对比较容易，主要考查考生对整个语篇内容和思想的把握，尽管也涉及对语法和词汇的考查，但是难度较低。例如 mean 接动名词作宾语，much，many，few 等修饰名词的用法；现在分词和过去分词修饰名词的区别等。只要把握整个语篇的意思，联系上下文，就能很容易地推导出正确的答案。

第六部分：短文改错

短文改错依然是围绕着词汇、语法、语篇来考查学生的英语应用水平的。在该短文中，涉及时态错误的有 2 题，单复数的有 1 题，介词用法的有 2 题，冠词的有 2 题。要做好这类题，除了要掌握基本的语法知识外，更要注意在整个篇章的宏观语境下来发现错误并改正错误。

第七部分：作文

两校联招的作文为命题作文和看图作文二选一，字数要求都为200字以上。在命题作文中，题目给出了每一段的开头一句，要求根据提示完成作文。三段的要求分别是：论述睡眠的重要性、睡眠不足的原因、一些健康睡眠的建议。这种题型较难，不但要求考生有一定的科学知识，较强的逻辑思维能力，还要求具有用复杂英文表达自己观点的能力。在看图作文中，题目给出了几种交通工具，要求考生比较几种交通工具的优劣，这种题型仍然比较难，首先要对各种交通工具有所了解，并且能比较它们之间的优劣。不论是对百科知识的要求，还是对语言能力的要求都是比较高的。

三、两校联招与全国联招试题比较分析

（一）听力理解

	相同点	不同点
全国联招	听力材料大多涉及英美国家日常生活的诸多方面，如吃穿住行等，以考查考生在不同环境下对英语的接受和反应能力；模式化的英文句子越来越少，大多取材于英美文化中的俚语和俗语	前五段对话需要根据问题回答问题，不仅考查考生对语言的理解能力，还考查考生的反应能力
两校联招		SectionA 难度较低，只需把听到的内容选择出来即可。SectionC、D 的分值较大（每题 2 分，而全国联招每题 1.5 分），如果考生出现失误，有可能失分较多

（二）语法结构

	相同点	不同点
全国联招	考试重点都没有超过考试大纲	总体而言，全国联招的语法题目要难于两校联招，即全国联招更注重对考生在特定复杂语境下语法的考查
两校联招		

（三）词汇题

词汇题总体来说，两者都比较简单，但两校联招的题目较多，有20题，而全国联招只有5题。从命题形式看，两校联招更注重对考生基础知识的考查，而全国联招则更强调对考生的英语运用能力的考查。

（四）阅读理解题

总体而言，全国联招的阅读理解题无论是在篇幅上、题量上，还是在语言难度上都要超过两校联招。

（五）短文改错题

相对来说，两校联招的试题要比全国联招的简单一些，大多数错误都集中在词汇的用法上，很少涉及语法和篇章理解，即使涉及也比较简单。两校联招试题中，大部分都是介词、冠词、时态的错误；而全国联招的试题却大量涉及从句、连词等复杂的语法知识。

（六）作文

两校联招的作文题目难于全国联招，前者不仅要求考生通过分析得出自己的观点，而且这种逻辑分析必然要求考生写出更为复杂的句型和词汇，而后者只是要求把一些要点罗列出来，前后通顺即可。

历　史

历史学科两校联招与全国联招两类考试的招考对象基本相同，即主要都招收华侨、港澳台地区的学生。稍有不同的是，两校联招的招生对象除上述考生外，还包括外籍学生。尽管如此，由于命题主体、招生学校范围等不同，这两类考试还是有较大区别的。

一、考试要求不同

两校联招的考试要求：

（1）历史学科两校联招考试内容包括中国历史和世界近现代史。本学科要求考生掌握最重要的历史事实；通过对历史基础知识的学习，理解历史事件的由来、发展及其相互关系。

（2）整理、分析、综合及评价史实，运用历史资料及有关论述得出适当结论。

全国联招的考试要求：

（1）历史学科高考内容包括古今中外最重要的历史事实，要求考生通过对历史基础知识的学习，初步认识人类文明和中华文明的发展演变以及中华民族在世界历史上的卓越贡献。

（2）知识与能力并重。考生应能在记忆基本史实的基础上，进行综合、归纳、分析、比较，以阐明其相互关系，得出适当的结论。

（3）考生掌握历史知识，还应注意时间与空间（如地理沿革）、抽象概念与形象事物并重。

二、两类试卷的具体比较

（一）两类考试题型分布及分值比较

1. 两校联招

	中国古代史	中国近现代史	世界近现代史	备注
选择题（40分）	12	14	14	
材料解析题（40分）	12	14	14	
简答题（40分）	20	20	20	三题选做两题
论述题（30分）	0	30	30	两题选做一题
所占比例（%）	29.3	35.3	35.3	

2. 全国联招

	中国古代史	中国近现代史	世界近现代史	备注
选择题（60 分）	18	24	18	
材料解析题（30 分）	0	15	15	材料题中国史、世界史各一题，中国史两部分大致轮流出题
问答题（60 分）	30	30	30	三题选做两题
所占比例（%）	32	46	42	

3. 解析

（1）两类考试题型不完全相同，两校联招比全国联招多了一种题型：论述题。

（2）两校联招题量大于全国联招，考题考查的知识点要比全国联招的广泛。

（3）两校联招考题中，主客观题型分值之比约为 11 : 4，客观题型仅占 26.67%；全国联招考题中，主客观题型分值之比约为 3 : 2，客观题型占 40%。两类考试的共同特点是主观题型分值大于客观题型。这也反映了历史学科考试的发展趋势，即越来越重视考查考生的文字表达、综合分析等能力。这就要求考生在复习备考时，切忌死记硬背。考生应在识记基本史实的基础上，有意识地对古今中外的历史进行跨时空的比较、分析和综合。

（4）从考查的知识板块看：

①两校联招：

2009 年考题中，主观题型占 120 分，大部分为政治史（包括政治思想、政治文化演变）的内容，仅选择题中少数题牵涉到中国古代思想文化和对外交往。

由此可知，两校联招历史考试以政治史为主。

②全国联招：

2009 年考题中，主观题型占 90 分，政治史、经济史和思想文化并重；客观题型 60 分亦是如此。中国古代史部分的试题，文化史尤为重要。

因此可以认为，全国联招历史考试侧重考查考生对古今中外文明发展线索的把握，具体而言，主要包括政治史、经济史、文化史、民族关系史及国际关系史等较为广泛的范围。

（二）两类试题所要求的知识层次比较

一般历史试卷对考生的知识要求分为“识记”、“理解”和“运用”等几个层次。下面分题型比较两类考试对考生的不同层次的要求：

1. 选择题

(1) 两校联招：

基本上只要求考生能“识记”一些基础历史知识。如第2题：

公元前十一世纪中，周武王伐纣，建立周朝，定都镐京。镐京位于今天的（　）

A. 洛阳　　B. 西安　　C. 安阳　　D. 开封

正确答案是B。

这里所说的“基础历史知识”主要是指一些重要的历史年代、人名、地名、历史大事、重要制度及著名文献等。

(2) 全国联招：

考生应在“识记”历史事实的基础上，对所学知识能达到“理解”甚至应用的层次要求。如第5题：

导致地方割据势力更加强大的历史事件是（　）

A. 西汉七国之乱　　B. 唐代安史之乱

C. 明代靖难之役　　D. 清代三藩之乱

对这种类型的考题，考生如果仅仅通过死记硬背“识记”选择项中四个历史事件的内容，尚难有效答题。考生应在此基础上，理解上述四个历史事件的起因、经过、结果和影响，然后才能得出正确答案B。总之，全国联招很多选择题的知识层次要求是在“识记”基础上的“应用”。

2. 材料解析题

(1) 两校联招：

材料后的问题项中，有些问题的知识层次要求是“识记”，较为简单；有些问题的知识层次要求是“应用”。

(2) 全国联招：

材料后的问题项中，所有问题的知识层次要求为“理解”和“应用”，即要求考生在分析材料的基础上，进行比较、分析和综合，然后得出结论。

因此，该题型全国联招考试的难度大于两校联招。

3. 问答题

(1) 两校联招：

大体上要求学生对所学知识在“识记”基础上有一定的“理解”。如第25题：

戊戌维新运动的历史意义及失败的原因是什么？

(2) 全国联招：

知识层次要求为“理解”，但较之两校联招的问题难度要大。如第25题：

第一次世界大战后，德国和日本分别出现了法西斯运动。比较德、日法西斯运动的不同，指出德、日法西斯政权造成的危害。

该题不像两校联招问答题那样，仅就单个知识点或某个知识点的单一方面提问，而是将两个（有时是两个以上）知识点串联起来，就该数个知识点的数个方面提问，这就要求考生有更强的跨时空的比较、分析和综合能力。

4. 论述题

该题型为两校联招考试的新增题型，全国联招没有该题型。其知识层次要求是“应用”。该题型不预设固定答案，要求考生自由发表个人见解。考生答题时一定要注意以下几点：观点明确，即要有明确的论点，不能模棱两可；要能正确地引用史实对自己的论点加以论证；要将答案写成一篇短文，短文要通顺、流畅。

总之，该题型考查的是考生的“识记”、“理解”、“应用”以及文字表述等综合能力，其难度是两类考试所有题型中最大的。同时，考生在做该题时，也不要因为难而放弃。因为该题并不要求考生死记硬背，只要平时学有所思，答题时再好好组织思路，就能取得较好的成绩。

三、2010 年两类考试备考复习要点

（一）两校联招

1. 中国古代史

重点章节：秦汉、隋唐、宋、明清。

重点内容：王朝更替、治乱兴衰；专制主义中央集权制度的演变发展；其他重要制度如科举制、三省六部制、均田制、租用调制、两税法、一条鞭法、地丁银制度等；国家的统一和分裂以及多民族国家的巩固；几次重要的民族交往和融合、边疆地区的管理；对重要君主的评价、几次盛世局面的出现；重大历史事件和举措（包括变法）；重要的对外交往如丝绸之路、郑和下西洋等。

2. 中国近现代史

重要线索：中华人民共和国史不作为考试重点。

（1）列强对中国的六次侵略：背景、经过、结果、影响；各国对中国各类权利的侵占、对中国边疆地区的觊觎和侵略。

（2）近现代中国的政治变迁：两次鸦片战争之后清朝政局的变化、戊戌维新、清末新政、清末宪政、辛亥革命、民国政局的变迁、国共两党的分与合。

（3）近现代中国经济的变化：中国资本主义经济的出现、发展。

（4）近现代中国思想文化的发展变化：地主阶级抵抗派、洋务派、维新派、立宪派、革命派、新文化运动、新旧三民主义等。

3. 世界近现代史

重要线索：

（1）资本主义发展史。具体包括政治史、经济史和思想文化史。

政治史：英、法、美三国资产阶级革命，俄国、日本的改革，美国南北战争，德国、意大利的统一，德国、日本的法西斯化，战后盟国对德日的改造等。上述内容均需掌握其背景、经过、结果及影响。就考试而言，最近 3 ~ 5 年已经考过的大题一般不会重复出题。

经济史：三次工业（科技）革命的背景、进程、影响，1929—1933 年世界经济

危机及其影响，美国罗斯福新政，各主要大国（英、法、美、德、日、俄）的经济发展等。

思想文化史：文艺复兴、启蒙运动等。

(2) 国际关系史亦即大国关系史。

①从国别上看，主要包括英、法、美、德、意、日、中等几个大国。

②从国际关系体系看，主要要掌握威斯特伐利亚体系、维也纳体系、凡尔赛—华盛顿体系、雅尔塔体系等四大国际体系中的后面三个体系的形成、发展及其解体的过程，尤其要注意体系中的大国关系、国际条约。

③从时期看，有以下几个重点时期：法国大革命前后；1870 年前后的普法战争；第一次世界大战前各国矛盾及战时各国关系；两次大战之间各国关系的发展变化；“二战”期间各国关系的变化；“二战”后联合国的成立以及冷战的出现等。

(二) 全国联招

总体而言，全国联招考试范围要比两校联招更广，上述两校联招的重点范围同时也是全国联招考试的要点，但非全部，考生还应注意以下几点：

(1) 中国古代史：侧重中国古代的文明成就，如盛世局面、著名君主、重要制度、民族交往和融合、对外友好往来以及哲学、史学、教育、文学等方面的成就。

(2) 中国近现代史：重视中国的政治、经济和思想文化的近代化进程，中华人民共和国史也占有重要的地位。较之两校联招考题更具综合性。

(3) 世界近现代史：除资本主义发展史和国际关系史线索外，有时也兼顾列强殖民争霸史、各殖民地半殖民地人民争取民主自由的历史等。较之两校联招试题更具综合性、分析性和比较性。

地　理

2009 年的试卷和 2008 年的试卷相比，无论是题型、题量、试题的结构，还是所考查的知识点及相关内容，都没有太大的变化。试卷基本体现了考纲所规定的有关原则，较为平稳。综观全卷，考题考查范围的大小、程度的深浅、难易的搭配及题量与题型等都较为合理科学。

一、试卷基本结构分析

表 1　全国联招试题结构对比（总分 150 分）

年份 / 题型	地球与地图		中国地理		世界地理		自然地理		人文地理	
	2009	2008	2009	2008	2009	2008	2009	2008	2009	2008
选择题（共 60 分）	3	6	6	15	36	12	6	12	9	15
填充题（共 20 分）			5		15	11				9
读图、填图题（共 40 分）			20	10	10	30			10	
综合题（共 30 分）		3	15					14	15	13
分值	3	9	46	25	61	53	6	26	34	37
比例（%）	2	6	31	17	41	35	4	17	23	25

表 2　两校联招试题结构对比（总分 150 分）

年份 / 题型	地球与地图		中国地理		世界地理		自然地理		人文地理	
	2009	2008	2009	2008	2009	2008	2009	2008	2009	2008
选择题（共 60 分）	24	12	15	15		6	15	9	6	18
填空题（共 20 分）		8	6	1	12	6	2	4		1
判断改正题（共 10 分）		2	6	2	4			6		
读图填空或连线题（共 40 分）	12	26	12	14	8		8			
读图分析题（共 20 分）	10					10	10	10		
分值	46	48	39	32	24	22	35	29	6	19
比例（%）	31	32	26	21	16	15	23	19	4	13

（一）题型

本次考试试题形式与往年基本一致。

全国联招试卷分为四种类型。选择题均为单项选择题，其中包括读图识图选择题、组合选择题、计算选择题等类型。值得注意的是，2009 年的选择题中有 70% 属于组合选择题，说明全国联招考试对考生综合能力及分析问题、解决问题能力的要求越来越高。非选择题包括填充题，读图、填图题及综合题等类型。主观性试题采用填空和分段指向设问，便于控制误差。

两校联招试卷分为五种类型。选择题均为单项选择题，非选择题包括填空题、判断改正题、读图填空或连线题、读图分析题等类型。

（二）考试内容

全国联招和两校联招的考试内容均包括地球与地图、自然地理、人文地理、中国地理、世界地理五大部分。从表 1 可以看出，全国联招试卷中世界地理部分分值占 41%，中国地理部分分值占 31%；从表 2 可以看出，两校联招试卷中中国地理部分占 26%，世界地理部分占 16%。由此可见，区域地理内容仍居试卷的重要地位。

2009 年两校联招试卷中，地球与地图部分分值所占比例继续保持在 1/3 左右，占选择题的 40% 和读图分析题的 50%，足见两校联招对基础知识的重视。而在 2009 年全国联招试卷中，地球与地图部分分值只占 3 分，自然地理部分分值也只有 6 分，而且都分布于选择题中。

二、试卷知识结构分析

总体来看，全国联招和两校联招的试题基本符合考纲规定，重视基础、重视考查学生的能力。但两者也有不同之处，具体如下：

（一）全国联招

全国联招考查面较广，综合性较强。如选择题的第 7 ~ 9 题是读图判断题，考生必须先判读出图中表示的区域属于中美洲地区，才能判断出该地区所在的两大板块是太平洋板块和美洲板块，并根据该地与北京的经度差计算出地方时的差异，再根据所在纬度位置判断该地区所在的风带；涉及的范围包括地球与地图、自然地理等内容，既有简单的提问，也有需要全面思考才可以作答的问题，编排先易后难，有利于考生答题。

利用气温降水资料判读气候类型是历年全国联招考试的重点，而地中海气候的判读，则是全国联招考试最常见的考点。2009 年也不例外，选择题的第 10 ~ 12 题就要求考生根据某地月降水量和平均气温的年变化，判读该地气候类型（地中海气候）、该地位置、该地森林火险比较高的月份（降水量最少的月份）。相信今后地中海气候的判读仍将出现在全国联招考题中，希望考生对该知识点加以重视。

表 3　全国联招知识点分布情况

<table>
<tr><th>内容</th><th colspan="2">选择题</th><th>填充题</th><th>读图、填图题</th><th>综合题</th></tr>
<tr><td>地球与地图</td><td colspan="2">区时的计算</td><td></td><td></td><td></td></tr>
<tr><td rowspan="2">中国地理</td><td colspan="2">水利枢纽工程</td><td rowspan="2">中国河流</td><td>山东省</td><td rowspan="2">西气东输工程</td></tr>
<tr><td colspan="2">旅游资源</td><td>东北地区</td></tr>
<tr><td rowspan="12">世界地理</td><td rowspan="3">大洲和大洋</td><td>亚丁湾</td><td rowspan="4">南亚海洋和国家</td><td rowspan="8">南非</td><td rowspan="12">环境因素对工业区位选择的影响</td></tr>
<tr><td>红海、阿拉伯海</td></tr>
<tr><td>曼德海峡</td></tr>
<tr><td colspan="2">中美洲气候特点</td></tr>
<tr><td rowspan="3">地中海气候</td><td>判读</td><td rowspan="4">世界石油输出大国</td></tr>
<tr><td>分布</td></tr>
<tr><td>特点</td></tr>
<tr><td rowspan="2">极地考察</td><td>黄河站</td></tr>
<tr><td>昆仑站</td><td rowspan="4">亚洲气候</td><td rowspan="4"></td></tr>
<tr><td colspan="2">中亚</td></tr>
<tr><td colspan="2">西亚</td></tr>
<tr><td colspan="2">东南亚</td></tr>
<tr><td rowspan="2">自然地理</td><td colspan="2">洋流</td><td rowspan="2"></td><td rowspan="2"></td><td></td></tr>
<tr><td colspan="2">地壳运动</td><td></td></tr>
<tr><td rowspan="3">人文地理</td><td rowspan="2">能源</td><td>抽水蓄能水电站</td><td rowspan="3"></td><td rowspan="3">人口</td><td rowspan="3"></td></tr>
<tr><td>核电站</td></tr>
<tr><td colspan="2">人口</td></tr>
</table>

地理作为综合性学科之一，与我们的生活息息相关。这一点在全国联招试题中也得到较好的体现。在 2009 年的全国联招试卷中涉及许多热点内容，如抽水蓄能水电站的建设、我国在两极地区建立的四座科学考察站、2008 年我国被收入《世界遗产目录》的道教名山江西三清山、已成为世界上第十一个人口超过 1 亿的国家墨西哥、我国西气东输工程等。这些热点通过命题者的精心设计，巧妙地将热点内容转化为解题所需的背景知识。考查的虽然是地理的主干知识，目的却在于引导考生对现实社会问题的关注和加强社会责任感，突出引导考生提高知识迁移的能力。

地理学最突出的特征之一就是图表丰富。在 2009 年的全国联招试卷中就出现了区域图、统计图、模式图和地形剖面图，涉及地图判读的题目占一半分值（共73分）。大量的图表增强了试题的直观性和视觉冲击力，有利于加强对考生能力的考查。把图表作为丰富的信息载体，既考查了考生读图用图的能力，同时还考查了考生综合分析问题的能力。

令人遗憾的是综合题的第一小题（我国西气东输二线工程西起新疆霍尔果斯口岸，东抵上海，南达香港，2008年开建，计划于2012年建成，年输天然气300亿立方米。回答下列问题。①为什么该工程西部起点修至边境口岸？②简述该工程的修建对于珠江三角洲的意义），许多考生甚至连“口岸”的意思都不能理解，将“口岸”和“港口”混为一谈，导致该题得分率普遍较低。

（二）两校联招

表4　两校联招知识点分布情况

<table>
<tr><th>内容</th><th colspan="2">选择题</th><th>填空题</th><th>判断改正题</th><th>读图填空或连线题</th><th>读图分析题</th></tr>
<tr><td rowspan="8">地球与地图</td><td colspan="2">地球自转偏向力</td><td rowspan="8"></td><td rowspan="8"></td><td rowspan="8">地形图判读</td><td rowspan="8">地球运动</td></tr>
<tr><td colspan="2">地图判读</td></tr>
<tr><td colspan="2">纬线</td></tr>
<tr><td colspan="2">昼夜长短变化</td></tr>
<tr><td colspan="2">比例尺</td></tr>
<tr><td colspan="2">本初子午线</td></tr>
<tr><td colspan="2">时区</td></tr>
<tr><td colspan="2">昼夜长度</td></tr>
<tr><td rowspan="5">中国地理</td><td rowspan="3">气候</td><td>旱涝灾害成因</td><td>气候分界线</td><td>季风</td><td rowspan="5">地形：主要山脉的分布</td><td rowspan="5"></td></tr>
<tr><td>夏季气温</td><td rowspan="2">河流</td><td rowspan="2">内流河补给</td></tr>
<tr><td>划分温度带根据</td></tr>
<tr><td colspan="2">黄河泥沙来源</td><td rowspan="2">地形</td><td rowspan="2">雨季影响时间</td></tr>
<tr><td colspan="2">水资源分布</td></tr>
<tr><td rowspan="5">世界地理</td><td colspan="2" rowspan="5"></td><td>大洲和大洋</td><td rowspan="2">美国</td><td rowspan="5">欧洲河流、湖泊的特征与形成条件</td><td rowspan="5"></td></tr>
<tr><td>气候类型分布</td></tr>
<tr><td>气候类型分布</td><td rowspan="2">亚马孙河</td></tr>
<tr><td>欧洲河流</td></tr>
<tr><td>美国城市</td><td></td></tr>
</table>

（续上表）

内容	选择题	填空题	判断改正题	读图填空或连线题	读图分析题
自然地理	气候差异成因	地震成因		气候：等温线判读	地形：外力作用形成的地貌
	侵蚀作用形成的地貌				
	地质灾害				
	水循环				
	自然带				
人文地理	美国工业				
	水稻分布				

两校联招试题突出学科主干知识，立足基础，强调运用，考查能力。2009 年的考题也突出了这一特点，与气候相关的考点共 22 分，与地形相关的考点共 39 分，占 40% 左右的分值。在 2009 年两校联招中，再次出现了中国主要山脉分布图的判读，出现了等高线地形图的判读。而地球与地图部分所占比例仍保持在 1/3 左右，说明命题者对基础知识的考查十分重视。中国地理、世界地理、自然地理、人文地理部分考查的主要内容均是地理学的重点主干知识，也是考生必须要掌握的基础知识，有些内容甚至年年都考。

从地理试题考查的形式来看，两校联招试题难度系数较小。只要考生按照考试大纲认真复习，相信一定能考出理想的成绩。

物　理

一、两校联招试卷分析

1. 试卷基本情况

两校联招通过考查考生的理解能力、推理能力、分析综合能力、应用数学处理物理问题的能力、实验能力，在众多考生中把那些基础较好、能力较强、具有学习潜能的考生挑选出来。2009 年两校联招物理试卷整体上与 2008 年保持一定的连续性，表现出很好的稳定性，选择题和填空题难度降低，计算题难度保持一致，无偏题、怪题，试题内容与《两校联招入学考试复习大纲》吻合，试题富于变化，灵活新颖，符合考试制度改革的发展趋势。

2009 年两校联招物理试卷满分是 150 分，分为三部分：单项选择题，计 60 分，占 40%；填空题，计 30 分，占 20%；计算题，计 60 分，占 40%。考试时间为 120 分钟。最后四道计算题为选做题，四题选两题，分别为电磁学、光学和力学题，其中有一道选做题是电磁学实验题。卷面总分数为 174 分，需解答试题的分数为 150 分。

表 1　各部分内容所占分数统计表

	选择题（分）	填空题（分）	计算题（分）	合计（分）	所占比例（%）	考纲中规定的所占比例（%）
力学	16	18	24	58	33	35
电磁学	20	6	36	62	36	35
热学	4	0	12	16	9	10
光学	12	3	12	27	16	10
原子物理学	8	3	0	11	6	10
实验	0	0	12	12	7	未单独列出

注：实验内容已包括在各部分内容中，为了便于统计，又单独列出。

从表 1 可以看出，试卷考查了力学、电磁学、热学、光学、原子物理学和实验内容，基本反映了中学物理的主体面貌，力学和电磁学分数所占比例最大，占 69%，比 2008 年的 63% 有所增加；必做计算题中有一道热学题，热学内容占 9%，与 2008 年一致；光学和原子物理学所占分数减少，占 22%；充分考虑了各地区学生物理实验教学水平的差异，实验题设计为选做题，分数占 7%。

表 2　知识点分布情况统计表

	考查知识点	选择题题号（分数），难易程度	填空题题号（分数），难易程度	计算题题号（分数），难易程度
力学	物体的平衡	1（4 分）易		
	匀变速直线运动，加速度	2（4 分）易		
	单摆的周期公式	3（4 分）易		
	惯性	4（4 分）易		
	质点做匀速圆周运动时的向心力		16（3 分）易	
	波速，波长，频率及三者的关系		17（6 分）易	
	匀速直线运动		18（9 分）易	
	功，动能，动量守恒定律			22（12 分）中
	功率，牛顿第二定律			27（12 分）中
电磁学	库仑定律	11（4 分）易		
	带电粒子在匀强电场中的运动	12（4 分）易		
	电阻的串联和并联	13（4 分）中		25（12 分）中
	洛伦兹力	14（4 分）易		
	变压器原理	15（4 分）易		
	均匀磁场对通电流的直导线的作用力，左手定则		21（6 分）易	
	均匀磁场对通电流的直导线的作用力，法拉第电磁感应定律，楞次定律，电容器			23（12 分）中
	欧姆定律，电阻的串联和并联，描绘小电珠的伏安特性曲线			28（12 分）中
热学	热力学温标	8（4 分）易		
	气体的状态和状态参量，理想气体状态方程			24（12 分）难
光学	透镜成像	5（4 分）易		
	折射率	6（4 分）易		
	光的衍射（定性）	7（4 分）易		
	反射定律		19（3 分）易	
	全反射，临界角			26（12 分）中
原子物理学	氢原子的玻尔模型	9（4 分）中		
	核反应方程，放射性同位素	10（4 分）易		
	半衰期		20（3 分）易	
实验	欧姆定律，电阻的串联和并联，描绘小电珠的伏安特性曲线			28（12 分）中

注：表格中列出了每道试题考查的知识点、分数以及题目难度。

从表1和表2可以看出，两校联招入学考试的试卷结构、考查内容的分布基本稳定。试卷突出了对物理基本概念和基本规律的考查，所考查的知识点基本覆盖了入学考试复习大纲中的全部重要内容，突出了力学、电磁学重点章节的知识，无超纲题，题目新而不怪。客观题与主观题所占分数的比为2：3，这个比例既能保证试卷对知识点有一定的覆盖面，同时也兼顾到对知识技能的考查。

试题注重对非主干内容重要物理知识的考查。与力学、电磁学相比，热学、光学、原子物理学是非主干内容，在试卷中占31%。这些非重点部分的内容注重对物理学思想的考查，如热学的热力学温标、气体的状态和状态参量、理想气体状态方程；光学的透镜成像、光的衍射、反射定律、全反射，临界角；原子物理学中的氢原子的玻尔模型、核反应方程、放射性同位素、半衰期，这些知识与现代物理联系紧密。该部分内容多以较容易的题目出现，侧重对知识的理解，同时也体现出一定的综合度。

试卷中考查实验的内容为12分，占7%，所占比例与2008年持平。实验题设计为选做的计算题，灵活地考查了电阻的串并联、电阻的测量、欧姆定律，加强了对有关实验理论及灵活应用已学实验技能的考查。

2. 典型题目分析

2009年两校联招物理试卷平均分比2008年有大幅提高，出现多个满分，有大约10%的考生分数超过140分，题目难度适中，区分度较大，适于高校选拔新生。试卷中大部分题目为容易和中等难度的题目，个别难题设置为计算题。两校联招考试的目的是考查考生掌握基础知识和考纲要求的五种能力，为高校选拔新生，不在于题目的推陈出新。

1～15题为选择题，大多为容易题和中等难度题，多数题目是定性分析，不需要计算，得分率较高。第13题得分率最低，第1题、第5题、第9题得分率也较低。第1题考查的是共点力作用下物体的平衡，很多考生没留意题目要求的是选错误答案。第5题灵活考查透镜成像，画出成像示意图即可得出答案。第9题考查玻尔模型、氢原子能级，需掌握能级跃迁和发射光子的原理。第13题考查电阻的串并联、电压表和电流表的特点，不考虑电源内阻。理想电压表电阻很大，理想电流表电阻很小。电压表 V_1 测量的是路端电压，读数是6V；电压表 V_2 被短路，读数为0；电流表 A_1 测量的是干路总电流，为3A；电流表 A_2 测量通过电阻 R_2 的电流，示数为1A；电流表 A_3 测量通过电阻 R_1 的电流，示数为2A。

16～21题为填空题，大多为容易题和中等难度题，计算量不大。有些考生数学知识和计算能力差，得分不理想。第16题，依题意列出两种情况的向心力之差为40N。第17题，根据频率的定义及波速、波长、频率的关系公式得出答案。第18题，要进行受力分析，明确题意。第19题，题目灵活，考生在草稿纸上画一个简图，利用平面几何知识即可作答。第20题是求剩余的未衰变样品的质量，不是总质量，衰变后原子核改变了，就不是原来的物质了。第21题得分率低，考查安培力的公式和左手定则，题目中给出导线的横截面半径，这是一个多余的条件，很多考生受到干扰，说明考生对基础知识、基本概念掌握不扎实，对概念和规律的理解不深入。另外，有的考生没分清左、右手定则的适用范围。简单地说，受力用左手（安培力、洛伦兹力），其他用右手。

22 ~ 28 题是计算题，为中等难度题或难题。很多考生因为书写不规范失分，例如缺少公式、单位等。第 22 题难度中等，是个传统题目，考查动能定理和动量守恒定律，是常考的知识点，得分率较高。第 23 题难度中等，但物理思维的深度和运用知识的综合度较高，考查的知识点多，考查了安培力、功能转化、感应电动势、电容、楞次定律（右手定则）。该题入手容易，第 1 小题是常规题，第 2、3 小题有一定的灵活性，要求考生有较好的分析能力和数学运算能力。第 24 题是热学与力学结合的题目，难度较高，有一定创新性，很多考生分辨不出考查的知识点，不知从何入手分析。第 24 题是整份试卷的压轴题，难度高，综合性强，预计 2010 年两校联招试卷中热学题目难度会降低。第 25 题，难度中等，考查电阻的串、并联，根据题意画出等效电路，当 ab 两端接测试电源时，R_1、R_3 串联，cd 两端电压就是 R_3 上分得的电压；当 cd 两端接测试电源，ab 两端短路时，R_1、R_3 并联后与 R_2 串联，电流表 A 测量的是 R_1 支路的电流。第 26 题新颖但难度不大，考查几何光学的全反射和临界角，在考查基础知识的同时还考查了分析推理能力。由几何关系可以得出透光液面的最大直径，如果透光直径变大，则深度变大。第 27 题难度中等，但很多考生不知道公式 $P = FV$，得分率偏低。第 28 题是一道实验题，难度中等，得分率低，说明考生实验技能较弱，平时实验过程中有些学生不认真操作、观察、记录和分析。该题考查了欧姆定律、电阻的串联和并联、伏安特性曲线的测定、电流表和电压表的选取，第 1 小题中因为电流表 A_1 的内阻小，所以该电路不能精确测出其内阻；第 2 小题较容易，但仍失分严重，说明考生没理解实验的基本原理；第 3 小题，由电阻的串、并联关系可得出答案。

3. 解读新考纲

2010 年的两校联招入学考试使用新的考试大纲（2008—2010），试卷满分由原来的 120 分调整为 150 分。现对新、旧考纲的知识点进行对比，希望对考生的复习有所帮助。

表 3　两校联招入学考试物理考试新大纲中增加和删除的主要内容

	增加内容	删除内容
力学	自由落体运动 竖直上抛运动	运动的合成和分解 力矩 超重和失重 力学单位制 波的叠加
热学	热容量，比热容 热力学第一定律 永动机不可能（定性） 能源的利用和环境保护（定性）	

（续上表）

	增加内容	删除内容
电磁学	电阻率与温度的关系 荷质比（e/m）的测定 质谱仪，回旋加速器（定性）	同种电池的串联
光学	光导纤维（定性） 光路的可逆性 激光的特性及应用（定性）	本影和半影 光电管及其应用
原子物理学	放射性污染及防护（定性）	
实验	验证牛顿第二定律 用描迹法画出电场中平面上的等势线 描绘小电珠的伏安特性曲线	验证动量守恒定律 验证机械能守恒定律 测定金属的电阻率

两校联招入学考试新大纲的修订原则是：

（1）保持考查范围和知识点的基本稳定。

（2）删除一些难度较大的内容，以减轻考生压力，如删除运动的合成和分解、力矩等考查点，并调整实验的考查范围。

（3）对一些考查点进行细化，增加了自由落体运动、竖直上抛运动、光路的可逆性等。

（4）鉴于考试改革的发展趋势，对一些内容进行了调整，例如增加了比热容和热力学第一定律。为便于设计题目，保留理想气体状态方程知识点。

（5）增加与日常生活和现代科技发展密切相关的内容，例如质谱仪、回旋加速器、光导纤维、激光的特性及应用。

（6）加强对环境保护意识的培养，增加了能源的利用和环境保护、放射性污染及防护等，只要求定性掌握。

二、全国联招试卷分析

1. 试卷基本情况

全国联招是全国近 200 所著名高校的联合招生，现对 2009 年的全国联招物理试卷分析如下：

表 4　全国联招物理试卷中各部分内容所占分数统计表

	选择题（分）	普通题（分）		合计（分）	所占比例（%）	考纲中规定的所占比例（%）
		必答题	选答题			
力学	24	6	15	45	27	34
电磁学	12	14	45	71	43	34
热学	4	18	0	22	13	12

（续上表）

	选择题（分）	普通题（分）		合计（分）	所占比例（%）	考纲中规定的所占比例（%）
		必答题	选答题			
光学	4	15	0	19	12	10
原子物理学	8	0	0	8	5	10
实验	0	20	0	20	12	未单独列出

2009年全国联招物理试卷满分为150分，总分数是165分（最后四道计算题为选做题，四题选三题）。考试时间为120分钟。试卷结构与历年考题大体一致。试卷分为两部分：单项选择题和普通题。单项选择题共13题，每题4分，计52分，占35%；普通题共98分，占65%。普通题分为必答题和选答题，必答题为53分，占35%；选答题（四题选做三题）满分45分，占30%。客观题与主观题的比约为1∶2，与考试大纲中规定的2∶3有些差距。

由表4可以看出，力学和电磁学为主要考查内容，分数占整份试卷的70%。热学、光学、原子物理学为非主要内容，占30%，这部分题目以中等难度的题目为主，考生应认真复习，提高得分率。2009年全国联招试题中增大了电磁学的比重，提高了热学、光学部分的比重，减少了力学、原子物理学的内容。有些电磁学的题目也考查了力学知识点，例如第18和20题。

实验题按惯例设计成填空题和作图题，一道力学实验题，一道电磁学实验题，为方便统计和便于比较，分数归在力学和电磁学内容中，表4又将实验部分单独列出。

表5　全国联招物理试卷知识点分布情况统计表

	考查知识点	选择题题号（分数）	普通题题号（分数）	
			必答题	选答题
力学	匀变速运动 图示法（$s-v$图和$v-t$图）	1（4）易		
	牛顿第二定律，力	3（4）中		
	弹簧振子，简谐振动 振幅，周期和频率	5（4）易		
	动能，动量守恒定律	6（4）难		
	落体和抛体运动	9（4）难		
	万有引力定律 质点做匀速圆周运动时的向心力 人造地球卫星的运动（限于圆轨道）	13（4）易		
	研究单摆的振动周期（实验）		14（6）中	

（续上表）

	考查知识点	选择题 题号（分数）	普通题 题号（分数）	
			必答题	选答题
力学	胡（虎）克定律 弹簧的势能 机械能守恒定律			21（15）难
电磁学	互感现象，变压器原理	7（4）中		
	点电荷的电场强度，电势差和电势，等势面，电场力做功	8（4）中		
	楞次定律	10（4）中		
	用电压表和电流表测电阻（实验），欧姆定律，电阻的串联和并联		15（14）中	
	带电粒子在匀强电场中的运动 洛伦兹力 匀速圆周运动			18（15）难
	法拉第电磁感应定律 电阻的串联和并联 欧姆定律 均匀磁场对通电流的直导线的作用力 左手定则			19（15）中
	电容器的串联和并联 电容器，电容 平行板电容器的电容与板面积和板间距的关系（不要求推导） 带电粒子在匀强电场中的运动 共点力作用下物体的平衡			20（15）难
热学	分子力	11（4）中		
	理想气体，普通气体恒量，理想气体状态方程（考纲未列出）		17（18）难	
光学	折射率，全反射，临界角	2（4）易		
	透镜成像		16（15）中	
原子物理学	氢原子的玻尔模型 波速、波长、频率及三者的关系	4（4）难		
	质能关系式	12（4）易		
实验	研究单摆的振动周期		14（6）中	
	用电压表和电流表测电阻		15（14）中	

试题中有些综合性题目考查不同章节的几个知识点，按照题目涉及的主要知识点进行分类列表。例如选答题的第18题，既考查电磁学的带电粒子在匀强电场中的运

动、洛伦兹力，又考查了力学中的匀速圆周运动公式等，但以考查洛伦兹力为主，因此将该题目列在电磁学的表格中。又如选答题的第20题，除了考查了电磁学内容，还考查了力学内容，但以考查电容器的相关知识点为主，因此该题目列入电磁学的表格中。

从表5可以看出，试题内容与《全国联招入学考试复习大纲》基本吻合，热学部分有超纲现象，考纲中没列出“理想气体状态方程”，但必答题第17题考查了这个知识点。

2. 典型题目分析

1~13题为单项选择题，以容易题和中等难度题为主。第1题比较简单，掌握了速度、加速度的基本概念，即可作答，得分率较高。第2题考查了全反射和折射率，题目设计比较新颖，难度不大。第3题为考查牛顿第二定律的常规题目，较为简单。第4题考查了氢原子的玻尔模型和能级间跃迁的理论，要对两种可能，即E_3-E_1和E_3-E_2进行验算，运算量比较大，失分严重。第5题考查了简谐振动的原理。第6题难度较高，虽然是考查动量守恒和动能定理的题目，但题目设计有新意，考生得分率低。第7题是考查变压器的常规题目，要求一定的运算能力，但题目难度不高。第8题考查电场力做功，难度较大，首先要判断电荷的正负。

第9题考查平抛运动，需要一定的技巧，得分率低。简要说明如下：

$$\frac{\frac{1}{2}gt^2}{vt}=\tan\alpha$$

设小物块接触斜面时速度与水平方向的夹角为β，

$$\frac{gt}{v}=\tan\beta$$

联立两式，$\tan\beta=2\tan\alpha$

由上可知不同水平速度的小物块接触斜面时，速度方向与斜面夹角相同，是与α相关的常数。

第10题考查楞次定律，新颖之处在于磁场为平行四边形区域，而且两个角是45°。第11题考查了分子力以及分子势能，是比较基础的题目。第12题有明显错误，试题将氚核（$^3_1\mathrm{H}$）的符号写错，这可能会误导考生。该题难度不大，基础扎实的考生能发现这个错误，可向监考老师提出。

第13题也是比较容易的题目，考查万有引力定律、匀速圆周运动和同步卫星知识点，是常规题目。由$G\frac{Mm}{r^2}=m\frac{v^2}{r}$和$v=\frac{2\pi r}{T}$得出$r\propto M^{\frac{1}{3}}T^{\frac{2}{3}}$。

14~17题为必答题，其中第14、15题延续了前几年的惯例，为填空型和作图型的实验题，一道考查力学实验，一道考查电磁学实验。第14题考查单摆测重力加速度的实验，涉及数学的函数知识，难度中等。第15题测量未知电阻的阻值。为提高准确度，电流表的选择是该题的难点，通过估算得出电流近似值。选择电流表的原则是：指针尽可能在表盘中间$\frac{1}{3}$的范围内。

第 16 题是必做计算题，考查透镜成像，难度中等。以狭缝作为物体，两次成像，由透镜成像公式和光路可逆解题。

第 17 题难度较大，因为涉及活塞的重量和活塞的高度，运算难度较大，很多考生理解题意，但无法算出正确答案。

第 18 题考查带电粒子在匀强电场、匀强磁场中的运动，要运用洛伦兹力和匀速圆周运动的公式。该题的难点在于画出粒子的轨迹示意图，并由几何关系得出$OB=l$。

第 19 题有明显错误，原试题中没给出金属棒的长度，应改为“一长为 l 的轻质金属棒……”。阅卷时只要考生定义了金属棒的长度，并得出合理答案，都可得满分。该题目的难点是：运动的金属棒产生感应电动势，作为电源，电源内阻为 r，金属框被分成两部分，并联起来作为外电路。外力与安培力相等，感应电流为最小值时外力最小，此时外电阻取最大值，金属框被分成的两部分电阻相等时总电阻最大。

全国联招差不多每年都有一道考查电容器串联和并联的计算题。第 20 题考查电容器的串联、带电粒子在匀强电场中受力平衡，要求熟练掌握电容器的相关知识点，难度较高，得分率低。

第 21 题作为压轴题，难度很高。本题的突破口是胡克定律，以弹簧上不压重物时上端位置为坐标原点。

三、两校联招与全国联招考查的知识点对比

两校联招和全国联招入学考试复习大纲（物理）的考点基本一致，个别章节有侧重，表 6 列举了两校联招考纲（2008—2010）和全国联招考纲中知识点的差异。

光电效应部分，两校联招考纲将知识点细化，列出“爱因斯坦光电方程”，全国联招考纲应该也包括了这个知识点。实验“描绘小电珠的伏安特性曲线”与“用电压表和电流表测电阻”表述不同，考查内容基本一致。

表 6　两校联招考纲与全国联招考纲的差异比较

	两校联招考纲中知识点	全国联招考纲中知识点
力学		相对速度 斜抛运动
电磁学	质谱仪，回旋加速器（定性） 电能的输送	电容器的串联和并联
热学	理想气体状态方程 永动机不可能（定性） 能源的开发、利用与环境保护（定性）	普通气体恒量

（续上表）

	两校联招考纲中知识点	全国联招考纲中知识点
光学	光导纤维（定性） 爱因斯坦光电方程 激光的特性及应用（定性）	
原子物理学	放射性污染及防护（定性）	
实验	验证力的平行四边形定则 描绘小电珠的伏安特性曲线 练习使用示波器	学习使用变阻器 用电压表和电流表测电阻 电流表改装成电压表 学习使用多用电表

四、复习建议

1. 加强基础知识、基本概念的学习

对基础知识、基本概念、基本方法的考查在两校联招和全国联招的试卷中占很大比重，也是解答综合题的基础。掌握了扎实的基础知识，才能有较强的理解能力，这是形成科学思维的正确途径。例如牛顿定律、匀变速直线运动、圆周运动、动能定理、机械能守恒定律、动量守恒定律、带电粒子在磁场中的运动、法拉第电磁感应定律等都是考查的重点内容。

中学物理知识具有系统性，认真研修考试大纲，把握总复习的范围，建议在教师的指导下将知识结成网，形成知识体系，这样才能比较清楚地了解物理知识的全貌，从全局的高度掌握物理知识，运用物理知识，将知识转化为能力。

推荐使用回忆复习法，按照考纲的要求，将知识点一条一条在脑子里回忆，回忆完了再打开书，看看回忆得怎么样。回忆复习法是进行系统复习的有效方法。

精选习题很重要，训练知识点和方法要有的放矢，难度要针对自己的实际情况，建议以中等难度的题目为主，避免出现偏离考纲、脱离教材、拼命抠难题，避免陷入茫茫无边的题海中。考生如果把容易的基本题、多数的中等难度题、较容易的计算题答对了，就可以得到理想的分数。

2. 强化实验能力和素养的提高

物理学是一门实验科学，因而联招考试把对考生实验能力的考查放在重要位置。物理实验是多数考生的薄弱环节。实验是一种全面的综合能力，包括实际操作技能、处理实际问题的本领、准确的测量、数据分析、严密的推理和清晰的表达，实验能力的提高对于学生的终生发展大有益处。实验题的设计多是以规定的学生实验为背景加以适当的变化，目的是考查学生对实验原理的理解和灵活运用的水平。因此，复习时应重点掌握考纲规定实验中实验仪器的使用方法、实验原理和实验操作步骤，这是完成实验的基本要求，也是灵活设计实验的基础。

3. 培养利用数学知识解决物理问题的能力

运用数学知识解决物理问题的能力是重点考查的能力之一，要求考生根据具体问题列出物理量之间的关系式，进行推导、运算和求解，根据结果得出物理结论，绝大部分考生该能力有待加强。有些考生能列出解题所需要的方程，但无法推导出所求物理量的表达式或解出最后结果。复习时要加强数学推导和运算能力，加强实验数据处理方法、有效数字表达的训练，加强数形结合、运用图像解题的能力。

严格规范答题，用科学术语准确表达物理概念、物理过程和物理规律，减少无谓的失分。很多考生因为不写公式、直接代入数据计算、缺少单位、文字表达不准确而失分。计算题要有必要的文字说明，公式的写法要规范，尤其对于不同研究对象或状态应有不同的脚标，要注重情景分析，矢量式要注意正负号的意义，物理量是矢量的要注意方向。

4. 重视分析综合能力的训练

难度较高的题目通常设计一些新的情境，这是课本和教学参考书中很难看到的，通常是多个基本的物理模型综合而成。因此，复习时要加强对物理状态、过程、情境的分析，培养综合分析问题的能力和创新能力。

物理的综合题考查频率较高的内容是：牛顿运动定律与圆周运动和万有引力定律综合；动量守恒、能量转化与直线运动或平抛运动综合；带电粒子在匀强磁场中的运动问题与运动学考点结合；带电粒子在电场中的加速和偏转；电磁感应现象与电路计算综合，等等。

5. 关注最新科技进展和社会热点

物理知识与现代科技和日常生活密切相关，应用物理知识可以解决生活中的很多实际问题。生活中的现象和热点问题常常是考查能力的创新性题目。例如，光导纤维可以考查光学全反射、临界角等知识点。神舟七号宇宙飞船、嫦娥一号月球探测器可以与圆周运动、动量守恒、万有引力等结合，设计成综合题，这类题目新颖、巧妙，有一定难度和区分度。

五、2010 年试题预测

1. 2010 年两校联招试题预测

2010 年两校联招物理试题结构、考查知识点的分布、试题难度将与 2009 年的试题接近。必做计算题有可能是力学、电磁学、光学各一题。热学题目的难度可能会降低，压轴难题有可能考查力学知识点。实验题可能会考查力学实验。

2. 2010 年全国联招试题预测

2010 年全国联招物理试题将保持一贯风格，难度较高、计算量大、综合性强。试题结构和知识点分布与 2009 年试题接近。可能会有一道电容器串联、并联的题目。

化 学

全国联招和两校联招考试是专门为境外生设置的，招生对象是港澳台侨等学生。由于各地的基础教育不同，考试要求也各不相同，为了利于境外生参加内地高校联合招生考试，使考生能够有针对性地进行复习应考，我们对2008和2009两年的全国联招和两校联招考试试题在试卷结构、考点分布、试题特点等做了比较和分析，并提出了复习建议，希望能对考生有一定的启示和帮助。

一、全国联招试卷分析

1. 试卷结构

题型＼年度	2008	2009
选择题	18题，每题3分，共54分，占36.0%	18题，每题3分，共54分，占36.0%
填空题	2题，共28分，占18.6%	2题，共24分，占16.0%
解答题	2题，共27分，占18.0%	2题，共34分，占22.6%
解答题	1题，共21分，占14.0%	1题，共18分，占12.0%
计算题	2题选1题，共10分，占6.7%	2题选1题，共10分，占6.7%
计算题	2题选1题，共10分，占6.7%	2题选1题，共10分，占6.7%
总分	150分	150分

2. 考查内容及考点分布

内容＼年度	2008年试题所占分数及百分比	2009年试题所占分数及百分比
原子结构、元素周期律	24分、16.0%	24分、16.0%
化学反应与能量变化、化学反应速率、化学平衡、水的电离、离子平衡	25分、16.7%	24分、16.0%
电化学、氧化还原反应	15分、10.0%	24分、16.0%
元素化合物（离子性质和检验）	48分、32.0%	49分、32.7%
有机化学	30分、20.0%	27分、18.0%
化学实验（与实验相关知识）	55分、36.7%	61分、40.7%
化学计算（与计算相关知识）	61分、40.7%	53分、35.3%

3. 试题特点

2008 年和 2009 年的全国联招试题严格遵守考试大纲的要求，体现了考试大纲的权威性和可信性。试卷结构和考点分布基本保持不变，试题难度也相当。试题考查的知识面较广，没有出现“繁、难、偏”的试题，既保持试题的灵活性和基础性，又有较好的区分度，并不失试题应有的选拔和甄别功能。近年来，全国联招试题更注重考查学生对化学概念和理论的分析、判断、理解能力，灵活运用所学知识解决实际问题的能力，增加了有关化学实验和化学计算等方面的考查力度。命题中有关原子结构、元素的判断、化合物的性质、化学式的确定、离子的性质、氧化还原反应、有机化学等知识点都与化学实验和化学计算联系在一起。例如，2008 年试题中的第 19 题就是把氧化还原反应方程式的配平与化学计算联系起来，涉及的知识点包括气体摩尔体积、溶质的质量分数、物质的量浓度等以及它们之间的关系。近两年的全国联招试卷中与化学实验和化学计算相关的知识占全卷分值的 76% 左右。

二、两校联招试卷分析

1. 试卷结构

题型 \ 年度	2008	2009
选择题	20 题，每题 3 分，共 60 分，占 40.0%	20 题，每题 3 分，共 60 分，占 40.0%
填空题	6 题，共 26 分，占 17.3%	5 题，共 22 分，占 14.7%
问答题	4 题，共 34 分，占 22.7%	4 题，共 38 分，占 25.3%
计算题	3 题选 2 题，共 30 分，占 20.0%	3 题选 2 题，共 30 分，占 20.0%
总分	150 分	150 分

2. 考查内容及考点分布

内容 \ 年度	2008 年试题所占分数及百分比	2009 年试题所占分数及百分比
原子结构、元素周期律	20 分、13.3%	23 分、15.3%
化学反应与能量变化、化学反应速率、化学平衡、水的电离、离子平衡	24 分、16.0%	17 分、11.3%
电化学、氧化还原反应	6 分、4.0%	10 分、6.7%
元素化合物（离子性质和检验）	39 分、26.0%	34 分、22.7%
有机化学	31 分、20.7%	34 分、22.7%
化学实验（与实验相关知识）	43 分、28.7%	30 分、20.0%
化学计算（与计算相关知识）	41 分、27.3%	36 分、24.0%

3. 试题特点

2008 年和 2009 年两校联招化学试卷的分数由原来的 120 分增加到 150 分，难度略有增加，题型、题量和考点分布基本不变，保持原有的选择题、填空题、问答题和计算题等题型。从考查的内容来看，与基本概念和基础理论知识相关的考点占 60%左右。涉及的内容有：物质的分类、化学量、溶液的组成和溶液浓度、原子组成和结构、分子结构与化学键、元素周期表和元素周期律、氧化还原反应的概念、化学反应速率和化学平衡原理及应用、化学反应与能量变化、离子反应和离子方程式等。有关化学实验和化学计算方面的考点 2008 年占 56%、2009 年占 44%。计算题涉及的内容有化学反应热、气体摩尔体积、物质的量及物质的量浓度、混合物中各种物质的质量分数、中和反应、溶液的 pH 值等。在问答题中设计了综合运用元素化合物、元素周期律、氧化还原反应、化学反应与能量变化等知识解决实验问题的命题，全面考查了学生对化学知识的掌握、理解和应用等能力。

三、复习建议

从近两年的对外联招考试化学试题来看，都比较注重对基础知识和基本技能的考查，化学实验和化学计算相关知识的考点有所增加。针对境外考生的特点以及试题的变化，对复习应考提出以下几点建议：

1. 加深对基本概念和基础理论知识的理解和掌握

近几年来，全国联招和两校联招试题都增大了对基本概念和基础理论知识的考查。我们在阅卷中发现，部分考生对试题本身不能完全理解，遇到多个知识点相联系的题目就不知所措，无从下笔。例如，2009 年全国联招试题的第 16 题，虽说只是一道选择题，但涉及的知识点有酸碱中和反应、一元酸与多元酸跟碱的反应的量的关系、强酸和弱酸、盐类水解、溶液的 pH 值等化学概念和理论，由于考生对本题目的理解不够全面，造成本题的错误率非常高。再如 2009 年两校联招试题选择题中的第 1 题，考查的是最基本的概念——物质的分类、物质的组成和物质的变化等，多数考生混淆了一些基本概念如混合物与化合物、原子与分子、物理变化与化学变化、金属与非金属等，本来是比较简单的题目，结果得分率却很低。所以，建议在复习应考时要加强对化学基本概念和基础理论知识的学习，并加深理解和灵活掌握。要明确概念的类别和概念之间的关系，明确概念的本质属性和概念所确定的对象范围。掌握化学基础理论知识以及各种概念和理论之间的相互联系，并能灵活运用所学知识解答化学现象、物质的性质、化学计算、化学实验等问题。

2. 化学基础理论和物质的性质与化学实验结合起来复习

化学是一门以实验为基础的学科，化学实验是学习化学的基础。化学试题的设计大多数与实验有关。例如，2008 年和 2009 年的全国联招试题的第 21 题、两校联招试题的第三题的第 2 小题，考查的内容都是关于元素、化合物、离子等性质方面的知识，命题的形式是通过化学实验、化学现象和实验操作过程等推断元素和化合物的种类、化合物的性质以及离子的性质等。考生解答这类题目时，往往是思路比较混乱，不能准确掌握实验现象、实验过程和实验结果，常常得到错误结论。再如 2009 年全国联招试题的第 15 题，考查学生对化学知识的积累、对化学现象的观察、对物质性质的理解等。由于考生平时疏于观察，也不善于总结，结果本题的得分率最低。所以在今后的复习应考中，要加强对化学实验知识的学习，特别要注意观察生活中和实验中的化学现象，在实验过程中要特别注意每一个步骤的细节，要把化学实验与化学反应原理、元素化合物、有机化学等知识联系在一起。运用已学的知识，掌握化学变化规律，能对化学现象提出科学合理的解释，不断提高观察能力、思维能力和解决化学问题的能力。

3. 加强计算能力和计算技巧的训练

近年来，全国联招和两校联招试题中的计算题难度变化不大，但涉及计算的命题有所增加，全国联招试题中有关化学计算的命题占试卷总分的 35% ~40%。从评阅试卷中发现，大多数考生的计算能力有限，遇到计算问题不能进行深入思考，往往放弃解答计算题。存在的主要问题有理解题目有偏差、死记硬背公式、张冠李戴、混淆化学量的单位、化学方程式不配平、计算失误等。在今后的复习应考中，要加强对化学概念、原理、计算公式等知识的理解和掌握，加强解题的灵活性、严谨性、规范性的训练，在准确、熟练、合理地进行物质的量、气体摩尔体积、固体物质的溶解度、溶质的质量分数、物质的量浓度、化学反应热、化学反应速率、化学平衡浓度等相关的计算方面多下工夫。

生　物

两校联招生物试题是为了考查学生在基础学习和专题复习过程中对生物学基础知识、基本技能的掌握情况，选拔优秀学生进入暨南大学、华侨大学进一步深造。2009 年两校联招考试体现了考试大纲中“以能力测试为主，考查学生基本知识、基本技能的掌握程度，以及运用这些知识分析和解决实际问题的能力”的指导思想，整套试题中没有偏题、怪题，有利于考生正常发挥。研究生物学两校联招的命题特点与备考策略对指导现阶段生物学教学的复习，指导学生提高备考针对性具有重要意义。

一、试题保持稳定

2009 年两校联招生物试题在试卷结构、题型、设问和试题编排形式方面趋于稳定。全卷分为三道大题，第一道大题为选择题，共 30 个小题，每小题 2 分，共 60 分；第二道大题为判断题，共 10 个小题，每小题 2 分，共 20 分；第三道大题为综合简答题，共 8 个小题，共 70 分。总分为 150 分。考试时间为 120 分钟，闭卷独立完成。

二、试题覆盖章节及分值

两校联招生物试题全部考查的是考试说明中的主干知识，命题围绕着生物学科的主干知识、核心知识做文章。每道题都有一定的综合性，但又不超出考试说明所规定的考试范围和考试要求，引导中学教学回归教材。试题中知识点的分布、所占分数和比重如表 1 所示：

表 1　2009 年两校联招生物试题覆盖章节及分值、比重

相关章节	选择题	判断题	综合简答题	分值	比重（%）
人体生理	第 25、26、27、28、29 题	第 10 题	第 5、7 题	27	18
细胞学	第 1、2、3、4、5、7、8、9、13、14、15 题	第 1、5、8 题	第 1、8 题	58	38.7
细胞代谢	第 10、12 题	第 6、7 题		8	5.3
微生物	第 6、11、30 题	第 2 题		8	5.3
遗传和变异	第 16、17、18、19、20、21、22、23、24 题	第 3、4 题	第 2、3 题	32	21.3
生物与环境		第 9 题	第 4、6 题	17	11.4
合计	30 题	10 题	8 题	150	

三、命题特点

1. 对内容进行有效的取舍

从试题在各章节中所占的比重可以看出，试题以考查学科主干知识为主，其中以细胞学、遗传和变异、人体生理、生物与环境所占比重较大。由于细胞学、遗传和变异、生物与环境、人体生理是生物学的重要内容，因此这些章节比重较大是符合大纲要求的。与2007年和2008年两校联招生物试题比较，2009年的试题又作了适当调整。与2007年两校联招生物试题比较，2008年试题作了适当调整，取消了“协调与反应”、“生殖和发育”、“植物类群”的内容，增加了“起源进化”、“生物分类”的内容。个别章节的分值比重也作了调整，如增加了“人体生理”、“细胞学”、“遗传和变异”、“微生物”、“生物与环境”等重点章节的比重，降低了“细胞代谢”、“植物体结构”章节的比重。在此基础上，2009年试题又取消了“起源进化”、“生物分类”、“植物类群”、“植物体结构”、“动物学”的内容，使得出题的范围、内容更加靠近预科部编写的《暨南大学、华侨大学联合招收港澳台、海外华侨、华人及其他外籍学生考试复习丛书·生物》，具体如表2所示。

表2　2007年、2008年和2009年两校联招生物试题各相关章节分值及比重

相关章节	2007年		2008年		2009年	
	分值	比重（%）	分值	比重（%）	分值	比重（%）
人体生理	12	10	26	17.3	27	18
细胞学	24.5	20.42	36	24	58	38.7
遗传和变异	19.5	16.25	30	20	32	21.3
细胞代谢	15	12.5	9	6	8	5.3
微生物	3	2.5	9	6	8	5.3
协调与反应	1.5	1.25	0	0	0	0
生殖和发育	3	2.5	0	0	0	0
起源进化	0	0	4	2.7	0	0
生物与环境	9.5	7.92	25	16.7	17	11.4
生物分类	0	0	4	2.7	0	0
植物类群	7.5	6.25	0	0	0	0
植物体结构	21.5	17.91	2	1.3	0	0
动物学	3	2.5	5	3.3	0	0

2. 充分体现考试大纲的能力要求

具体包括以下几方面：

（1）能应用学过的知识和专业术语，正确阐述基本的生物学现象、概念、方法和原理。

如简答题第 8 题，要求用给定的专业术语完成细胞结构图的填写。

（2）重视能力和素质考查，命题由“以知识立意”为主转向“以能力立意”为主。

如简答题第 3 题，要求学生用给定的数据，通过所学的生态学知识，分析回答提出的问题，既考查了学生的知识基础，也考查了学生的分析问题能力、数据整理能力和综合归纳能力、对未来的发展趋势作预测的能力。

（3）正确理解、分析生物学中以图表、图解等表达的内容和意义，并能用图表等多种表达形式准确地描述生物学现象。理解生物体的结构和功能、部分与整体及生物与环境的关系。

如简答题第 1、第 5、第 6 和第 7 题。

从以上的特点可以看出，2009 年两校联招生物试卷仍然坚持了注重基础知识，强调考查灵活运用所学知识的能力，说明中学教学应该让学生牢固掌握基础知识，在此基础上培养学生对基础知识灵活运用的能力。

四、备考策略

根据 2009 年两校联招生物试题的特点以及多年的高考复习教学经验，提出以下 2010 年两校联招生物科备考策略：

1. 紧扣教材，夯实基础

夯实基础是提高综合能力的前提，没有扎实深厚的基础知识，解题效率、综合能力就不可能提高。从 2009 年两校联招生物试题来看，考试内容紧扣教材，注重基础，没有超纲题、偏题、怪题，没超出现行教材，基础性强，试题面貌比较熟悉，难度降低。因此，从试题命题导向给出的信息看，第一轮复习必须以教材为本，不脱离教材，在极为关键的第一轮复习中，步步夯实教材基础知识是关键，不迷信课本以外的东西，不搞题海战术，不追求学科间的综合。

2. 对基础知识的复习要做到多层次多角度的理解和把握

在第一轮复习时对每一个知识点，教师必须有目的地引导学生深入理解，多角度多层次地发问和引导思考分析，然后进行典型题目的练习，通过典型题目来训练和巩固，加深记忆。只有这样才能培养学生对基础知识灵活运用并能成功迁移的能力。

3. 避免简单重复式的复习，构建新的复习体系

复习中要坚决避免简单重复式的复习，复习过程中要努力进行创新，对不同的内容可以有不同的创新方式：知识编排顺序的创新；内容的创新，有些内容应该适当地加深拓宽；教学方法的创新，等等。

4. 把构建完整知识体系的思想贯穿于整个复习过程中

多层次多角度地理解和把握基础知识点，构建知识体系，是贯穿整个复习过程的主线。对知识体系的构建要通过师生共同努力，做到网络化、立体开放化和学生自身化。教师以每节考点知识为起点或平台，联系穿插相关章节的内容，使知识结构合理化，让学生在消化记忆中构建知识框架，这种通过教师的引导，由个人融会各章节内容而完成的知识网络，便于迅速准确地提取信息、处理信息，科学地解决问题。

5. 严格把关、精选习题

现在的各种复习资料大同小异，其内容编排顺序以及习题基本相同，而且各种复习资料为了突出其与众不同之处，编一些所谓的原创新题，试题严重超纲、超教材，甚至有知识性错误，学生做题时难度很大，对于这样的习题应大胆删除。

6. 重视实验与探究能力的培养

基础实验的复习要到位。基础实验的复习一方面要求理解所学实验、实习的内容，包括实验目的、原理、方法和操作步骤，掌握相关的操作技能；另一方面要能将这些实验、实习涉及的方法和技能进行综合的运用。

加强实验的基本思想、方法以及实验题的解题技能、技巧的形成训练，要掌握实验与探究的基本方法以及解答实验类试题的基本技能。